SAINT MARY'S COLLEGE OF CALIFORNIA
COLLEGIATE SEMINAR PROGRAM
COLLEGIATE SEMINAR 001

CRITICAL STRATEGIES
AND
GREAT QUESTIONS

SECOND EDITION

XanEdu
Change the course.

ISBN-13: 978-1-58390-089-5

Cover Image: © Can Stock Photo Inc./LeonART

Acknowledgments:

pp. 5–10: First appeared in *The Wind's Twelve Quarters*. Copyright © 1973,
2001 by Ursula K. Le Guin. Reprinted by permission of the author's agents,
Virginia Kidd Agency, Inc.
pp. 11–20: From *The Common Reader* by Virginia Woolf. Copyright © 1925
by Random House, Ltd. Reprinted by permission of the publisher.
pp. 27–35: From *Seneca in Ten Volumes: V Ad Lucilium Epitulae Morales*
(Volume 2), translated by Richard M. Gummere. Copyright © 1970 by
Harvard University Press.
pp. 36–41: From *The Papers of Thomas Jefferson, 1760–1776*, edited by Julian
P. Boyd. Copyright © 1950. Published by Princeton University Press.
pp. 46–60: Reprinted by arrangement with The Heirs of the Estate of Martin
Luther King Jr., c/o Writers House as agent for the proprietor, New York, NY.
Copyright © 1963 by Dr. Martin Luther King Jr. Copyright renewed 1991
by Coretta Scott King.
pp. 61–95: From *Don Quixote* by Miguel Cervantes, translated by Edith
Grossman. Translation copyright © 2003 by Edith Grossman; introduction
copyright © by Harold Bloom. Used by permission of HarperCollins
Publishers, Inc.

Change the course.

530 Great Road
Acton, MA 01720
800-562-2147

Contents

Collegiate Seminar Learning Outcomes

Critical Thinking

Critical thinking within Seminar is grounded on the processes of analysis, synthesis and evaluation necessary to read with understanding. Through careful reading, listening, and reflection, which lead to a solid understanding of the texts, critical thinking allows students to make perceptive insights and connections between texts, Seminars and ultimately their life experiences. Critical thinking within Seminar also includes skills that allow for sound judgments to be made when multiple, competing viewpoints are possible. Seminar is a place where reading critically is transformed and integrated into a habit of mind, providing students with the tools to question the authority of the text and the foundations of their own assumptions. In short, critical thinking allows students to recognize, formulate and pursue meaningful questions, which are not only factual but also interpretive and evaluative, about the ideas of others as well as their own.

Critical Thinking Learning Outcomes

As a result of their participation in the Collegiate Seminar Program, students will grow in their ability to:

1. Distinguish the multiple senses of a text (literal and beyond the literal).
2. Identify and understand assumptions, theses, and arguments that exist in the work of authors.
3. Evaluate and synthesize evidence in order to draw conclusions consistent with the text. Seek and identify confirming and opposing evidence relevant to original and existing theses.
4. Ask meaningful questions and originate plausible theses.
5. Critique and question the authority of texts, and explore the implications of those texts.

Written and Oral Communication

A mind is not truly liberated until it can effectively communicate what it knows. Thus the Collegiate Seminar Program seeks to develop strong written and oral communication skills in its students. Students will develop skills that demonstrate an understanding of the power of language to shape thought and experience. They will learn to write and speak logically, with clarity, and with originality, and grow in their intellectual curiosity through the process of writing.

Written and Oral Communication Learning Outcomes

As a result of their participation in the Collegiate Seminar Program, students will grow in their ability to:

1. Recognize and compose readable prose, as characterized by clear and careful organization, coherent paragraphs and well-constructed sentences that employ the conventions of Standard Written English and appropriate diction.
2. Recognize and formulate effective written and oral communication, giving appropriate consideration to audience, context, format, and textual evidence.
3. Analyze arguments so as to construct ones that are well supported (with appropriate use of textual evidence), are well reasoned, and are controlled by a thesis or exploratory question.
4. Use discussion and the process of writing to enhance intellectual discovery and unravel complexities of thought.

Shared Inquiry

Shared inquiry is the act of reasoning together about common texts, questions, and problems. It is a goal of Collegiate Seminar to advance students' abilities to develop and pursue meaningful questions in collaboration with others, even in the context of confusion, paradox, and/or disagreement. Through the habits of shared inquiry students will carefully consider and understand the perspectives and reasoned opinions of others, reconsider their own opinions, and develop rhetorical skills.

Shared Inquiry Learning Outcomes

As a result of their participation in the Collegiate Seminar Program, students will grow in their ability to:

1. Advance probing questions about a common text or other objects of study.
2. Pursue new and enriched understandings of the texts through sustained collaborative inquiry.
3. Reevaluate initial hypotheses in light of evidence and collaborative discussion with the goal of making considered judgments.
4. Engage in reflective listening and inclusive, respectful conversation.

Honor Code and Seminar

The Student Honor Council (of academic 2004–2005) has requested that all Seminar sections discuss the proper use of other persons' opinions in Seminar classes. The Governing Board of Collegiate Seminar proposes the following list of good practices:

Authentic engagement in seminar classes requires that—

1. Students read only the assigned texts in preparation;

2. Students give their own thoughts about the assigned readings;

3. Students do not introduce opinions of experts into the conversation;

4. Student essays present the student's own thoughts on the agreed-upon topic;

5. Instructors advise whether and how essays should respond to, use, or cite opinions which other students have voiced in class.

(CSGB, 5/19/04)

Collegiate Seminar Guidelines for Grading Oral Participation

The following criteria shall be considered in evaluating seminar students:

- Good listening and close attention to the discussion.
- Frequency of contribution to discussion.
- Quality of contributions in terms of forwarding the conversation.
- Clear evidence of reflection upon the reading.
- Ability, with respect to the reading, to describe, propose insights, analyze, see alternatives, compare, and evaluate.
- Ability to counter questions and/or challenge other discussants (including the seminar leader) respectfully.
- Seriousness of engagement, degree of interest in the ideas under discussion, and spontaneity.
- Sense of responsibility for the group's understanding of the text and for the progress of the conversation.

In regard to these criteria—

A student who:

1) Is rarely if ever absent from class and is likely to inform the instructor in advance.
2) Is always excellently prepared and demonstrates her/his preparation by consistently offering text-related contributions throughout the discussion.
3) Is self-motivated, entering the discussion with pertinent and useful contributions as appropriate.
4) Is engaged and active in pursuing questions and in testing opinions.
5) Regularly forwards the discussion by drawing comparisons, analyzing problems and questions, offering opinions on interpretations, and responding critically and respectfully to the contributions of others.

6) Listens with active interest to the comments of others; questions others in an effort to understand not only what they are saying but also the reasons and implications of what they are saying.

7) Takes responsibility for the "health and well-being" of the seminar.

might receive an "A" grade.

A student who:

1) Is rarely, if ever, absent from class and is likely to inform the instructor in advance.

2) Is nearly always well prepared and demonstrates her/his preparation by often offering text-related contributions to the discussion.

3) Is often self-motivated, entering the discussion with pertinent and useful contributions as appropriate.

4) Is sometimes engaged and active, sometimes more passive, in pursuing questions and in testing opinions.

5) Sometimes forwards the conversation, sometimes takes a less active role, supporting or questioning the more positive contributions of others.

6) Listens with active interest to the comments of others.

7) Does not obstruct or retard the "health and well being" of the seminar.

might receive a "B" grade.

A student who:

1) Is seldom absent from class.

2) Is generally prepared and demonstrates her/his preparation by offering text-related contributions at some point in the discussion.

3) Regularly contributes to discussion but takes a follower's rather than a leader's role in forwarding the conversation.

4) Listens respectfully to the comments of others.

5) Does not obstruct or retard the "health and well-being" of the seminar.

might receive a "C" grade.

A student who:

1) May be absent from class more than three or four times per semester.

2) May be unprepared for discussion or fail to demonstrate preparation by pertinent text-related contributions to the discussion.

3) Often does not contribute, even as a follower, in the seminar discussion.

4) May fail to listen to others; may engage in disruptive "side conversations."

5) May obstruct or retard the "health and well-being" of the seminar.

might receive a "D" grade.

A student who:

1) May be often absent from seminar.

2) Is unprepared for the majority of classes.

3) Rarely, if ever, contributes to the discussion.

4) Does not listen to others or follow the course of the discussion; may engage in disruptive behavior.

5) May obstruct or retard the seminar.

might receive an "F" grade.

Saint Mary's College Writing Standards
Collegiate Seminar Program
Seminar 10/02

	The C essay is competent, exhibiting no serious or frequent deficiencies.	*The B essay is strong in most areas.*
Purpose	The C essay addresses the topic and offers a thesis. The thesis, however, may not explore the topic with sufficient complexity or take on a significant intellectual challenge.	The B essay exhibits intellectual engagement. It is narrowly focused, with a clear sense of purpose and audience. It explores the topic in some depth and with some complexity.
Organization and Development	The C essay offers support for its thesis; however, this support may not be evaluated or analyzed thoughtfully, or may tend toward plot summary. The C essay has an introduction, body, and conclusion, generally unified paragraphs, and transitions between paragraphs. However, it may proceed formulaically or mechanically. The conclusion may not move much beyond the initial thesis.	The B essay proceeds logically and offers appropriate support for its thesis. It is a generally unified essay, with a clear introduction, coherent paragraphs, and effective transitions. Its conclusion does not merely restate the argument, but attempts to draw together preceding insights in a new way.
Language	The C essay employs readable prose, but the sentences may be simple and lack variety.	In the B essay, sentences are sufficiently varied. Language is generally concise and appropriate.
Mechanics	The C essay employs generally correct formatting, grammar, syntax, spelling, and documentation as needed. Errors, however, may be serious enough to detract from the effectiveness of the essay.	The B essay employs generally correct formatting, grammar, syntax, spelling, and documentation as needed. Errors, when they appear, do not detract from the overall effectiveness of the essay.

The F essay is seriously deficient. It may exhibit a poor grasp of the assignment or a lack of familiarity with assigned texts. It may be deficient in one or more of the following areas: purpose, organization and development, language, and mechanics. It may lack a clear thesis or fail to support its thesis.

	The A essay excels in all areas.	*The D essay* is deficient in one or more areas.
	The A essay has a clearly defined, intellectually challenging focus and a strong sense of purpose and audience. It exhibits depth and complexity in its analysis and originality in its thought.	The D essay may lack a clear thesis, or the thesis may be weak or overly general.
	The A essay is distinguished by sound logic. It offers sufficient and appropriate support for the thesis in the form of concrete, specific, and relevant evidence. It is a unified essay that proceeds coherently with an effective introduction, well-developed and unified paragraphs, graceful transitions, and a conclusion that, rather than summarizing previous points, explores the implications of the preceding analysis.	The D essay may fail to provide adequate support for its thesis in the form of textual analysis or other evidence; it may substitute repetition for development or make inaccurate claims. It may lack a clear structure and paragraphs may lack coherence. Transitions may be awkward or nonexistent.
	In the A essay, sentences are skillfully crafted and effectively varied; langauge is fresh, precise, and economical. It maintains a consistent and appropriate tone.	The D essay often lacks variety in sentence structure and suffers from inappropriate diction.
	The A essay is almost entirely free of errors in formatting, grammar, syntax, spelling, and documentation as needed.	A D essay is often characterized by grammatical errors such as but not limited to: fragments, comma splices, agreement errors, or inappropriate shifts in tense, voice, mood, or person. It may also be rife with spelling errors and improperly formatted.

Other common features of failing essays are: faulty logic, ineffective organization, incoherent paragraphs, incorrect diction, and so many syntactic and grammatical errors that the essay becomes unreadable.

Kinds of Questions

Questions of Fact

To a question of fact there will be only one answer which can be supported using evidence from the text; this answer may, however, take some effort to discover.

Example: In "The Analogy of the Cave", why do philosophers (those with "beatific vision") appear foolish in the everyday world (such as in the law courts)?

Questions of Interpretation

Your purpose is to make sense of the text. You might ask what conclusions we can draw about the author's meaning, purpose, or basic assumptions. Or you might question the relationship of two statements which seem to be in contradiction. To questions of interpretation, attentive readers can give differing answers, each of which can be supported using evidence from the text.

Example: According to Socrates, the prisoners of "The Analogy of the Cave" are "like us." How does the reading support this view?

Questions of Evaluation

Judge what is presented in the reading. Is what is written true? False? Neither true nor false? Likely? Unlikely? Wrong? Right? Fair? Unfair? Insightful? Obvious? Of course, these categories of judgment (and others like them) are often themselves the very subject of the readings.

Example: Is "The Analogy of the Cave" a good and useful image of human existence? (And what do I mean by "good" or by "useful" or by "image"?)

from the *Republic*
"Allegory of the Cave"

Plato

(In this reading the first person narrator is Socrates. The one to whom he is speaking is Glaucon.)

And now, I said, let me show in a figure how far our nature is enlightened or unenlightened: Behold! human beings living in an underground den, which has a mouth open toward the light and reaching all along the den; here they have been from their childhood, and have their legs and necks chained so that
5 they cannot move, and can only see before them, being prevented by the chains from turning round their heads. Above and behind them a fire is blazing at a distance, and between the fire and the prisoners there is a raised way; and you will see, if you look, a low wall built along the way, like the screen which marionette players have in front of them, over which they show the puppets.
10   I see.

And do you see, I said, men passing along the wall carrying all sorts of vessels, and statues and figures of animals made of wood and stone and various materials, which appear over the wall? Some of them are talking, others silent.

You have shown me a strange image, and they are strange prisoners.
15   Like ourselves, I replied; and they see only their own shadows, or the shadows of one another, which the fire throws on the opposite wall of the cave?

True, he said; how could they see anything but the shadows if they were never allowed to move their heads?

And of the objects which are being carried in like manner they would
20 only see the shadows?

Yes, he said.

And if they were able to converse with one another, would they not suppose that they were naming what was actually before them?

Very true.
25   And suppose further that the prison had an echo which came from the other side, would they not be sure to fancy when one of the passers-by spoke that the voice which they heard came from the passing shadow?

1

No question, he replied.

To them, I said, the truth would be literally nothing but the shadows of the images.

³⁰ That is certain.

And now look again, and see what will naturally follow if the prisoners are released and disabused of their error. At first, when any of them is liberated and compelled suddenly to stand up and turn his neck round and walk and look toward the light, he will suffer sharp pains; the glare will distress him, and ³⁵ he will be unable to see the realities of which in his former state he had seen the shadows; and then conceive someone saying to him, that what he saw before was an illusion, but that now, when he is approaching nearer to being and his eye is turned toward more real existence, he has a clearer vision—what will be his reply? And you may further imagine that his instructor is pointing ⁴⁰ to the objects as they pass and requiring him to name them—will he not be perplexed? Will he not fancy that the shadows which he formerly saw are truer than the objects which are now shown to him?

Far truer.

And if he is compelled to look straight at the light, will he not have a pain ⁴⁵ in his eyes which will make him turn away to take refuge in the objects of vision which he can see, and which he will conceive to be in reality clearer than the things which are now being shown to him?

True, he said.

And suppose once more, that he is reluctantly dragged up a steep and ⁵⁰ rugged ascent, and held fast until he is forced into the presence of the sun himself, is he not likely to be pained and irritated? When he approaches the light his eyes will be dazzled, and he will not be able to see anything at all of what are now called realities.

Not all in a moment, he said.

⁵⁵ He will require to grow accustomed to the sight of the upper world. And first he will see the shadows best, next the reflections of men and other objects in the water, and then the objects themselves; then he will gaze upon the light of the moon and the stars and the spangled heaven; and he will see the sky and the stars by night better than the sun or the light of the sun by day?

⁶⁰ Certainly.

Last of all he will be able to see the sun, and not mere reflections of him in the water, but he will see him in his own proper place, and not in another; and he will contemplate him as he is.

Certainly.

⁶⁵ He will then proceed to argue that this is he who gives the season and the years, and is the guardian of all that is in the visible world, and in a certain way

the cause of all things which he and his fellows have been accustomed to behold?

Clearly, he said, he would first see the sun and then reason about him.

70 And when he remembered his old habitation, and the wisdom of the den and his fellow-prisoners, do you not suppose that he would felicitate himself on the change, and pity them?

Certainly, he would.

And if they were in the habit of conferring honors among themselves on 75 those who were quickest to observe the passing shadows and to remark which of them went before, and which followed after, and which were together; and who were therefore best able to draw conclusions as to the future, do you think that he would care for such honors and glories, or envy the possessors of them? Would he not say with Homer,

80 "Better to be the poor servant of a poor master,"

and to endure anything, rather than think as they do and live after their manner?

Yes, he said, I think that he would rather suffer anything than entertain these false notions and live in this miserable manner.

Imagine once more, I said, such a one coming suddenly out of the sun to 85 be replaced in his old situation; would he not be certain to have his eyes full of darkness?

To be sure, he said.

And if there were a contest, and he had to compete in measuring the shadows with the prisoners who had never moved out of the den, while his 90 sight was still weak, and before his eyes had become steady (and the time which would be needed to acquire this new habit of sight might be very considerable), would he not be ridiculous? Men would say of him that up he went and down he came without his eyes; and that it was better not even to think of ascending; and if anyone tried to loose another and lead him up to the light, 95 let them only catch the offender, and they would put him to death.

No question, he said.

This entire allegory, I said, you may now append, dear Glaucon, to the previous argument; the prison-house is the world of sight, the light of the fire is the sun, and you will not misapprehend me if you interpret the journey upward to 100 be the ascent of the soul into the intellectual world according to my poor belief, which, at your desire, I have expressed—whether rightly or wrongly, God knows. But, whether true or false, my opinion is that in the world of knowledge the idea of good appears last of all, and is seen only with an effort; and, when seen, is also inferred to be the universal author of all things beautiful and right, parent of light 105 and of the lord of light in this visible world, and the immediate source of reason and truth in the intellectual; and that this is the power upon which he who would act rationally either in public or private life must have his eye fixed.

I agree, he said, as far as I am able to understand you.

Moreover, I said, you must not wonder that those who attain to this beatific vision are unwilling to descend to human affairs; for their souls are ever hastening into the upper world where they desire to dwell; which desire of theirs is very natural, if our allegory may be trusted.

Yes, very natural.

And is there anything surprising in one who passes from divine contemplations to the evil state of man, misbehaving himself in a ridiculous manner; if, while his eyes are blinking and before he has become accustomed to the surrounding darkness, he is compelled to fight in courts of law, or in other places, about the images or the shadows of images of justice, and is endeavoring to meet the conceptions of those who have never yet seen absolute justice?

Anything but surprising, he replied.

Anyone who has common sense will remember that the bewilderments of the eyes are of two kinds, and arise from two causes, either from coming out of the light or from going into the light, which is true of the mind's eye, quite as much as of the bodily eye; and he who remembers this when he sees anyone whose vision is perplexed and weak, will not be too ready to laugh; he will first ask whether that soul of man has come out of the brighter life, and is unable to see because unaccustomed to the dark, or having turned from darkness to the day is dazzled by excess of light. And he will count the one happy in his condition and state of being, and he will pity the other; or, if he have a mind to laugh at the soul which comes from below into the light, there will be more reason in this than in the laugh which greets him who returns from above out of the light into the den.

That, he said, is a very just distinction.

But then, if I am right, certain professors of education must be wrong when they say that they can put a knowledge into the soul which was not there before, like sight into blind eyes.

They undoubtedly say this, he replied.

Whereas, our argument shows that the power and capacity of learning exists in the soul already; and that just as the eye was unable to turn from darkness to light without the whole body, so too the instrument of knowledge can only by the movement of the whole soul be turned from the world of becoming into that of being, and learn by degrees to endure the sight of being, and of the brightest and best of being, or, in other words, of the good.

Very true.

The Ones Who Walk Away from Omelas
(Variations on a Theme by William James)

Ursula K. Le Guin

With a clamor of bells that set the swallows soaring, the Festival of Summer came to the City of Omelas, bright-towered by the sea. The rigging of the boats in harbor sparkled with flags. In the streets between houses and red roofs and painted walls, between old moss-grown gardens and under avenues of trees, past great parks and public buildings, processions moved. Some were decrous: old people in long stiff robes of mauve and grey, grave master workmen, quiet, merry women carrying their babies and chatting as they walked. In other streets the music beat faster, a shimmering of gong and tambourine, and the people went dancing, the procession was a dance. Children dodged in and out, their high calls rising like the swallows' crossing flights over the music and the singing. All the processions wound towards the north side of the city, where on the great water-meadow called the Green Fields boys and girls, naked in the bright air, with mud-stained feet and ankles and long, lithe arms, exercised their restive horses before the race. The horses wore no gear at all but a halter without bit. Their manes were braided with streamers of silver, gold, and green. They flared their nostrils and pranced and boasted to one another; they were vastly excited, the horse being the only animal who has adopted our ceremonies as his own. Far off to the north and west the mountains stood up half encircling Omelas on her bay. The air of morning was so clear that the snow still crowning the Eighteen Peaks burned with white-gold fire across the miles of sunlit air, under the dark blue of the sky. There was just enough wind to make the banners that marked the racecourse snap and flutter now and then. In the silence of the broad green meadows one could hear the music winding through the city streets, farther and nearer and ever approaching, a cheerful faint sweetness of the air that from time to time trembled and gathered together and broke out into the great joyous clanging of the bells.

Joyous! How is one to tell about joy? How describe the citizens of Omelas?

5

They were not simple folk, you see, though they were happy. But we do not say the words of cheer much any more. All smiles have become archaic. Given a description such as this one tends to make certain assumptions. Given a description such as this one tends to look next for the King, mounted on a splendid stallion and surrounded by his noble knights, or perhaps in a golden litter borne by great-muscled slaves. But there was no king. They did not use swords, or keep slaves. They were not barbarians. I do not know the rules and laws of their society, but I suspect that they were singularly few. As they did without monarchy and slavery, so they also got on without the stock exchange, the advertisement, the secret police, and the bomb. Yet I repeat that these were not simple folk, not dulcet shepherds, noble savages, bland utopians. They were not less complex than us. The trouble is that we have a bad habit, encouraged by pedants and sophisticates, of considering happiness as something rather stupid. Only pain is intellectual, only evil interesting. This is the treason of the artist: a refusal to admit the banality of evil and the terrible boredom of pain. If you can't lick 'em, join 'em. If it hurts, repeat it. But to praise despair is to condemn delight, to embrace violence is to lose hold of everything else. We have almost lost hold; we can no longer describe a happy man, nor make any celebration of joy. How can I tell you about the people of Omelas? They were not naïve and happy children—though their children were, in fact, happy. They were mature, intelligent, passionate adults whose lives were not wretched. O miracle! but I wish I could describe it better. I wish I could convince you. Omelas sounds in my words like a city in a fairy tale, long ago and far away, once upon a time. Perhaps it would be best if you imagined it as your own fancy bids, assuming it will rise to the occasion, for certainly I cannot suit you all. For instance, how about technology? I think that there would be no cars or helicopters in and above the streets; this follows from the fact that the people of Omelas are happy people. Happiness is based on a just discrimination of what is necessary, what is neither necessary nor destructive, and what is destructive. In the middle category, however—that of the unnecessary but undestructive, that of comfort, luxury, exuberance, etc.—they could perfectly well have central heating, subway trains, washing machines, and all kinds of marvelous devices not yet invented here, floating light-sources, fuelless power, a cure for the common cold. Or they could have none of that; it doesn't matter. As you like it. I incline to think that people from towns up and down the coast have been coming to Omelas during the last days before the Festival on very fast little trains and double-decked trams, and that the train station of Omelas is actually the handsomest building in town, though plainer than the magnificent Farmers' Market. But even granted trains, I fear that Omelas so far strikes some of you as goody-goody. Smiles, bells, parades, horses, bleh. If so, please add an orgy. If an orgy would help, don't hesitate. Let us not, however, have temples from which issue beautiful nude priests and priestesses already half in ecstasy and ready to copulate with any man or woman, lover or stranger, who desires union with the deep godhead of the blood, although that was my first idea. But really it would be better not to have any temples in Omelas—at least, not manned temples. Religion yes, clergy no. Surely the beautiful nudes can just wander about, offering themselves like divine soufflés to the hunger of the needy and the rapture of the flesh. Let them join the processions. Let tambourines be struck above the copulations, and the glory of desire be proclaimed upon the gongs, and (a not unimportant point) let the offspring of these delightful rituals be beloved and looked after by all. One thing I know there is none of in Omelas is guilt. But what else should there be? I thought at first there were no drugs, but that is puritanical. For those who like it, the faint insistent sweetness of *drooz* may perfume the ways of the city, *drooz* which first brings a great lightness and brilliance to the mind and limbs, and then after some hours a dreamy languor, and wonderful visions at last of the very arcana and inmost secrets of the Universe, as well as exciting the pleasure of sex beyond belief; and it is not habit-forming. For more modest tastes I think there ought to be beer. What else, what else belongs in the joyous city? The sense of victory, surely, the celebration of courage. But as we did without clergy, let us do without soldiers. The joy built upon successful slaughter is not the right kind of joy; it will not do; it is fearful and it is trivial. A boundless and generous contentment, a magnanimous triumph felt not against some outer enemy but in communion with the finest and fairest in the souls of all men everywhere and the splendor of the world's summer: this is what swells the hearts of the people of Omelas, and the victory they celebrate is that of life. I really don't think many of them need to take *drooz*.

Most of the processions have reached the Green Fields by now. A marvelous smell of cooking goes forth from the red and blue tents of the provisioners. The faces of small children are amiably sticky; in the benign gray beard of a man a couple of crumbs of rich pastry are entangled. The youths and girls have mounted their horses and are beginning to group around the starting line of the course. An old woman, small, fat, and laughing, is passing out flowers from a basket, and tall young men wear her flowers in their shining hair. A child of nine or ten sits at the edge of the crowd, alone, playing on a wooden flute. People pause to listen, and they smile, but they do not speak to him, for he never ceases playing and never sees them, his dark eyes wholly rapt in the sweet, thin magic of the tune.

He finishes, and slowly lowers his hands holding the wooden flute.

As if that little private silence were the signal, all at once a trumpet sounds from the pavilion near the starting line: imperious, melancholy, piercing. The horses rear on their slender legs, and some of them neigh in answer. Sober-faced, the young riders stroke the horses' necks and soothe them, whispering, "Quiet, quiet, there my beauty, my hope. . . ." They begin to form in rank along the starting line. The crowds along the racecourse are like a field of grass and flowers in the wind. The Festival of Summer has begun.

Do you believe? Do you accept the festival, the city, the joy? No? Then let me describe one more thing.

In a basement under one of the beautiful public buildings of Omelas, or perhaps in the cellar of one of its spacious private homes, there is a room. It has one locked door, and no window. A little light seeps in dustily between cracks in the boards, secondhand from a cobwebbed window somewhere across the cellar. In one corner of the little room a couple of mops, with stiff, clotted, foul-smelling heads, stand near a rusty bucket. The floor is dirt, a little damp to the touch, as cellar dirt usually is. The room is about three paces long and two wide: a mere broom closet or disused tool room. In the room a child is sitting. It could be a boy or a girl. It looks about six, but actually is nearly ten. It is feeble-minded. Perhaps it was born defective, or perhaps it has become imbecile through fear, malnutrition, and neglect. It picks its nose and occasionally fumbles vaguely with its toes or genitals, as it sits hunched in the corner farthest from the bucket and the two mops. It is afraid of the mops. It finds them horrible. It shuts its eyes, but it knows the mops are still standing there; and the door is locked; and nobody will come. The door is always locked; and nobody ever comes, except that sometimes—the child has no understanding of time or interval—sometimes the door rattles terribly and opens, and a person, or several people, are there. One of them may come in and kick the child to make it stand up. The others never come close, but peer in at it with frightened, disgusted eyes. The food bowl and the water jug are hastily filled, the door is locked, the eyes disappear. The people at the door never say anything, but the child, who has not always lived in the tool room, and can remember sunlight and its mother's voice, sometimes speaks. "I will be good," it says. "Please let me out. I will be good!" They never answer. The child used to scream for help at night, and cry a good deal, but now it only makes a kind of whining "eh-haa, eh-haa" and it speaks less and less often. It is so thin there are no calves to its legs; its belly protrudes; it lives on a half-bowl of corn meal and grease a day. It is naked. Its buttocks and thighs are a mass of festered sores, as it sits in its own excrement continually.

They all know it is there, all the people of Omelas. Some of them have come to see it, others are content merely to know it is there. They all know that it has to be there. Some of them understand why, and some do not, but they all understand that their happiness, the beauty of their city, the tenderness of their friendships, the health of their children, the wisdom of their scholars, the skill of their makers, even the abundance of their harvest and the kindly weathers of their skies, depend wholly on this child's abominable misery.

This is usually explained to children when they are between eight and twelve, whenever they seem capable of understanding; and most of those who come to see the child are young people, though often enough an adult comes, or comes back, to see the child. No matter how well the matter has been explained to them, these young spectators are always shocked and sickened at the sight. They feel disgust, which they had thought themselves superior to. They feel anger, outrage, impotence, despite all the explanations. They would like to do something for the child. But there is nothing they can do. If the child were brought up into the sunlight out of that vile place, if it were cleaned and fed and comforted, that would be a good thing, indeed; but if it were done, in that day and hour all the prosperity and beauty and delight of Omelas would wither and be destroyed. Those are the terms. To exchange all the goodness and grace of every life in Omelas for that single, small improvement: to throw away the happiness of thousands for the chance of the happiness of one: that would be to let guilt within the walls indeed.

The terms are strict and absolute; there may not even be a kind word spoken to the child.

Often the young people go home in tears, or in a tearless rage, when they have seen the child and faced this terrible paradox. They may brood over it for weeks or years. But as time goes on they begin to realize that even if the child could be released, it would not get much good of its freedom: a little vague pleasure of warmth and food, no doubt, but little more. It is too degraded and imbecile to know any real joy. It has been afraid too long ever to be free of fear. Its habits are too uncouth for it to respond to humane treatment. Indeed, after so long it would probably be wretched without walls about it to protect it, and darkness for its eyes, and its own excrement to sit in. Their tears at the bitter injustice dry when they begin to perceive the terrible justice of reality, and to accept it. Yet it is their tears and anger, the trying of their generosity and the acceptance of their helplessness, which are perhaps the true source of the splendor of their lives. Theirs is no vapid, irresponsible happiness. They know that they, like the child, are not free. They know compassion. It is the existence of the child, and their knowledge of its existence, that makes possible the nobility of their architecture, the poignancy of their music, the profundity of their science. It is because of the child that they are so gentle with children. They know that if the wretched one were not there snivelling in the dark, the other one, the flute-player, could make no joyful music as the young riders line up in their beauty for the race in the sunlight of the first morning of summer.

Now do you believe in them? Are they not more credible? But there is one more thing to tell, and this is quite incredible.

At times one of the adolescent girls or boys who go to see the child does not go home to weep or rage, does not, in fact, go home at all. Sometimes also a man or woman much older falls silent for a day or two, and then leaves home. These people go out into the street, and walk down the street alone. They keep walking, and walk straight out of the city of Omelas, through the beautiful gates. They keep walking across the farmlands of Omelas. Each one goes alone, youth or girl, man or woman. Night falls; the traveler must pass down village streets, between the houses with yellow-lit windows, and on out into the darkness of the fields. Each alone, they go west or north, towards the mountains. They go on. They leave Omelas, they walk ahead into the darkness, and they do not come back. The place they go towards is a place even less imaginable to most of us than the city of happiness. I cannot describe it at all. It is possible that it does not exist. But they seem to know where they are going, the ones who walk away from Omelas.

How Should One Read a Book?[1]

Virginia Woolf

In the first place, I want to emphasize the note of interrogation at the end of my title. Even if I could answer the question for myself, the answer would apply only to me and not to you. The only advice, indeed, that one person can give another about reading is to take no advice, to follow your own instincts, to use your own reason, to come to your own conclusions. If this is agreed between us, then I feel at liberty to put forward a few ideas and suggestions because you will not allow them to fetter that independence which is the most important quality that a reader can possess. After all, what laws can be laid down about books? The battle of Waterloo was certainly fought on a certain day; but is *Hamlet* a better play than *Lear*? Nobody can say. Each must decide that question for himself. To admit authorities, however heavily furred and gowned, into our libraries and let them tell us how to read, what to read, what value to place upon what we read, is to destroy the spirit of freedom which is the breath of those sanctuaries. Everywhere else we may be bound by laws and conventions—there we have none.

But to enjoy freedom, if the platitude is pardonable, we have of course to control ourselves. We must not squander our powers, helplessly and ignorantly, squirting half the house in order to water a single rose-bush; we must train them, exactly and powerfully, here on the very spot. This, it may be, is one of the first difficulties that faces us in a library. What is "the very spot?" There may well seem to be nothing but a conglomeration and huddle of confusion. Poems and novels, histories and memories, dictionaries and bluebooks; books written in all languages by men and women of all tempers, races, and ages jostle each other on the shelf. And outside the donkey brays, the women gossip at the pump, the colts gallop across the fields. Where are we to begin? How are we to bring order into this multitudinous chaos and so get the deepest and widest pleasure from what we read?

It is simple enough to say that since books have classes—fiction, biography, poetry—we should separate them and take from each what it is right that each should give us. Yet few people ask from books what books can give us. Most commonly we come to books with blurred and divided minds, asking of

11

fiction that it shall be true, of poetry that it shall be false, of biography that it shall be flattering, of history that it shall enforce our own prejudices. If we could banish all such preconceptions when we read, that would be an admirable beginning. Do not dictate to your author; try to become him. Be his fellow-worker and accomplice. If you hang back, and reserve and criticise at first, you are preventing yourself from getting the fullest possible value from what you read. But if you open your mind as widely as possible, then signs and hints of almost imperceptible fineness, from the twist and turn of the first sentences, will bring you into the presence of a human being unlike any other. Steep yourself in this, acquaint yourself with this, and soon you will find that your author is giving you, or attempting to give you, something far more definite. The thirty-two chapters of a novel—if we consider how to read a novel first—are an attempt to make something as formed and controlled as a building: but words are more impalpable than bricks; reading is a longer and more complicated process than seeing. Perhaps the quickest way to understand the elements of what a novelist is doing is not to read, but to write; to make your own experiment with the dangers and difficulties of words. Recall, then, some event that has left a distinct impression on you— how at the corner of the street, perhaps, you passed two people talking. A tree shook; an electric light danced; the tone of the talk was comic, but also tragic; a whole vision, an entire conception, seemed contained in that moment.

But when you attempt to reconstruct it in words, you will find that it breaks into a thousand conflicting impressions. Some must be subdued; others emphasized; in the process you will lose, probably, all grasp upon the emotion itself. Then turn from your blurred and littered pages to the opening pages of some great novelist—Defoe, Jane Austen, Hardy. Now you will be better able to appreciate their mastery. It is not merely that we are in the presence of a different person—Defoe, Jane Austen, or Thomas Hardy—but that we are living in a different world. Here, in *Robinson Crusoe*, we are trudging a plain high road; one thing happens after another; the fact and the order of the fact is enough. But if the open air and adventure mean everything to Defoe they mean nothing to Jane Austen. Hers is the drawing-room, and people talking, and by the many mirrors of their talk revealing their characters. And if, when we have accustomed ourselves to the drawing-room and its reflections, we turn to Hardy, we are once more spun round. The moors are round us and the stars are above our heads. The other side of the mind is now exposed—the dark side that comes uppermost in solitude, not the light side that shows in company. Our relations are not towards people, but towards Nature and destiny. Yet different as these worlds are, each is consistent with itself. The maker of each is careful to observe the laws of his own perspective, and however great a strain they may put upon us they will never confuse us, as lesser writers so frequently do, by introducing two different kinds of reality into the same book. Thus to go from one great novelist to another—from Jane Austen to Hardy, from Peacock to Trollope, from Scott to Meredith—is to be wrenched and uprooted; to be thrown this way and then that. To read a novel is a difficult and complex art. You must be capable not only of great fineness of perception, but of great boldness of imagination if you are going to make use of all that the novelist—the great artist—gives you.

But a glance at the heterogeneous company on the shelf will show you that writers are very seldom "great artists;" far more often a book makes no claim to be a work of art at all. These biographies and autobiographies, for example, lives of great men, of men long dead and forgotten, that stand cheek by jowl with the novels and poems, are we to refuse to read them because they are not "art?" Or shall we read them, but read them in a different way, with a different aim? Shall we read them in the first place to satisfy that curiosity which possesses us sometimes when in the evening we linger in front of a house where the lights are lit and the blinds not yet drawn, and each floor of the house shows us a different section of human life in being? Then we are consumed with curiosity about the lives of these people—the servants gossiping, the gentlemen dining, the girl dressing for a party, the old woman at the window with her knitting. Who are they, what are they, what are their names, their occupations, their thoughts, and adventures?

Biographies and memoirs answer such questions, light up innumerable such houses; they show us people going about their daily affairs, toiling, failing, succeeding, eating, hating, loving, until they die. And sometimes as we watch, the house fades and the iron railings vanish and we are out at sea; we are hunting, sailing, fighting; we are among savages and soldiers; we are taking part in great campaigns. Or if we like to stay here in England, in London, still the scene changes; the street narrows; the house becomes small, cramped, diamond-paned, and malodorous. We see a poet, Donne, driven from such a house because the walls were so thin that when the children cried their voices cut through them. We can follow him, through the paths that lie in the pages of books, to Twickenham; to Lady Bedford's Park, a famous meeting-ground for nobles and poets; and then turn our steps to Wilton, the great house under the downs, and hear Sidney read the *Arcadia* to his sister; and ramble among the very marshes and see the very herons that figure in that famous romance; and then again travel north with that other Lady Pembroke, Anne Clifford, to her wild moors, or plunge into the city and control our merriment at the sight of

Gabriel Harvey in his black velvet suit arguing about poetry with Spenser. Nothing is more fascinating than to grope and stumble in the alternate darkness and splendor of Elizabethan London. But there is no staying there. The Temples and the Swifts, the Harleys and the St. Johns beckon us on; hour upon hour can be spent disentangling their quarrels and deciphering their characters; and when we tire of them we can stroll on, past a lady in black wearing diamonds, to Samuel Johnson and Goldsmith and Garrick; or cross the channel, if we like, and meet Voltaire and Diderot, Madame du Deffand; and so back to England and Twickenham—how certain places repeat themselves and certain names!—where Lady Bedford had her Park once and Pope lived later, to Walpole's home at Strawberry Hill. But Walpole introduces us to such a swarm of new acquaintances, there are so many houses to visit and bells to ring that we may well hesitate for a moment, on the Miss Berrys' doorstep, for example, when behold, up comes Thackeray; he is the friend of the woman whom Walpole loved; so that merely by going from friend to friend, from garden to garden, from house to house, we have passed from one end of English literature to another and wake to find ourselves here again in the present, if we can so differentiate this moment from all that have gone before. This, then, is one of the ways in which we can read these lives and letters; we can make them light up the many windows of the past; we can watch the famous dead in their familiar habits and fancy sometimes that we are very close and can surprise their secrets, and sometimes we may pull out a play or a poem that they have written and see whether it reads differently in the presence of the author. But this again rouses other questions. How far, we must ask ourselves, is a book influenced by its writer's life—how far is it safe to let the man interpret the writer? How far shall we resist or give way to the sympathies and antipathies that the man himself rouses in us—so sensitive are words, so receptive of the character of the author? These are questions that press upon us when we read lives and letters, and we must answer them for ourselves, for nothing can be more fatal than to be guided by the preferences of others in a matter so personal.

But also we can read such books with another aim, not to throw light on literature, not to become familiar with famous people, but to refresh and exercise our own creative powers. Is there not an open window on the right hand of the bookcase? How delightful to stop reading and look out! How stimulating the scene is, in its unconsciousness, its irrelevance, its perpetual movement—the colts galloping round the field, the woman filling her pail at the well, the donkey throwing back his head and emitting his long, acrid moan. The greater part of any library is nothing but the record of such fleeting moments in the lives of men, women, and donkeys. Every literature, as it grows old, has its rubbish-heap, its record of vanished moments and forgotten lives told in faltering and feeble accents that have perished. But if you give yourself up to the delight of rubbish-reading you will be surprised, indeed you will be overcome, by the relics of human life that have been cast out to moulder. It may be one letter—but what a vision it gives! It may be a few sentences—but what vistas they suggest! Sometimes a whole story will come together with such beautiful humour and pathos and completeness that it seems as if a great novelist had been at work, yet it is only an old actor, Tate Wilkinson, remembering the strange story of Captain Jones; it is only a young subaltern serving under Arthur Wellesley and falling in love with a pretty girl at Lisbon; it is only Maria Allen letting fall her sewing in the empty drawing-room and sighing how she wishes she had taken Dr Burney's good advice and had never eloped with her Rishy. None of this has any value; it is negligible in the extreme; yet how absorbing it is now and again to go through the rubbish-heaps and find rings and scissors and broken noses buried in the huge past and try to piece them together while the colt gallops round the field, the woman fills her pail at the well, and the donkey brays.

But we tire of rubbish-reading in the long run. We tire of searching for what is needed to complete the half-truth which is all that the Wilkinsons, the Bunburys and the Maria Allens are able to offer us. They had not the artist's power of mastering and eliminating; they could not tell the whole truth even about their own lives; they have disfigured the story that might have been so shapely. Facts are all that they can offer us, and facts are a very inferior form of fiction. Thus the desire grows upon us to have done with half-statements and approximations; to cease from searching out the minute shades of human character, to enjoy the greater abstractness, the purer truth of fiction. Thus we create the mood, intense and generalised, unaware of detail, but stressed by some regular, recurrent beat, whose natural expression is poetry; and that is the time to read poetry . . . when we are almost able to write it.

> Western wind, when wilt thou blow?
> The small rain down can rain.
> Christ, if my love were in my arms,
> And I in my bed again!

The impact of poetry is so hard and direct that for the moment there is no other sensation except that of the poem itself. What profound depths we visit then—how sudden and complete is our immersion! There is nothing here to catch hold of; nothing to stay us in our flight. The illusion of fiction is gradual; its effects are prepared; but who when they read these four lines stops to ask who wrote them, or conjures up the thought of Donne's house or Sidney's secretary; or enmeshes them in the intricacy of the past and the succession of generations? The poet is always our contemporary. Our being for the moment is centred and constricted, as in any violent shock of personal emotion. Afterwards, it is true, the sensation begins to spread in wider rings through our minds; remoter senses are reached; these begin to sound and to comment and we are aware of echoes and reflections. The intensity of poetry covers an immense range of emotion. We have only to compare the force and directness of

> I shall fall like a tree, and find my grave,
> Only remembering that I grieve,

with the wavering modulation of

> Minutes are numbered by the fall of sands,
> As by an hour glass; the span of time
> Doth waste us to our graves, and we look on it;
> An age of pleasure, revelled out, comes home
> At last, and ends in sorrow; but the life,
> Weary of riot, numbers every sand,
> Wailing in sighs, until the last drop down,
> So to conclude calamity in rest

or place the meditative calm of

> whether we be young or old,
> Our destiny, our being's heart and home,
> Is with infinitude, and only there;
> With hope it is, hope that can never die,
> Effort, and expectation, and desire,
> And effort evermore about to be,

beside the complete and inexhaustible loveliness of

> The moving Moon went up the sky,
> And nowhere did abide:
> Softly she was going up,

And a star or two beside—

or the splendid fantasy of

And the woodland haunter
Shall not cease to saunter
When, far down some glade,
Of the great world's burning,
One soft flame upturning
Seems to his discerning,
Crocus in the shade,

to bethink us of the varied art of the poet; his power to make us at once actors
and spectators; his power to run his hand into characters as if it were a glove,
and be Falstaff or Lear; his power to condense, to widen, to state, once and for
ever.

"We have only to compare"—with those words the cat is out of the bag,
and the true complexity of reading is admitted. The first process, to receive
impressions with the utmost understanding, is only half the process of reading; it must be completed, if we are to get the whole pleasure from a book, by
another. We must pass judgment upon these multitudinous impressions; we
must make of these fleeting shapes one that is hard and lasting. But not directly. Wait for the dust of reading to settle; for the conflict and the questioning to
die down; walk, talk, pull the dead petals from a rose, or fall asleep. Then suddenly without our willing it, for it is thus that Nature undertakes these transi-
tions, the book will return, but differently. It will float to the top of the mind
as a whole. And the book as a whole is different from the book received cur-
rently in separate phrases. Details now fit themselves into their places. We see
the shape from start to finish; it is a barn, a pig-sty, or a cathedral. Now then
we can compare book with book as we compare building with building. But
this act of comparison means that our attitude has changed; we are no longer
the friends of the writer, but his judges; and just as we cannot be too sympa-
thetic as friends, so as judges we cannot be too severe. Are they not criminals,
books that have wasted our time and sympathy; are they not the most insid-
ious enemies of society, corrupters, defilers, the writers of false books, faked
books, books that fill the air with decay and disease? Let us then be severe in
our judgments; let us compare each book with the greatest of its kind. There
they hang in the mind the shapes of the books we have read solidified by the
judgments we have passed on them—*Robinson Crusoe, Emma, The Return of*

the Native. Compare the novels with these—even the latest and least of novels has a right to be judged with the best. And so with poetry when the intoxication of rhythm has died down and the splendor of words has faded, a visionary shape will return to us and this must be compared with *Lear*, with *Phèdre*, with *The Prelude*; or if not with these, with whatever is the best or seems to us to be the best in its own kind. And we may be sure that the newness of new poetry and fiction is its most superficial quality and that we have only to alter slightly, not to recast, the standards by which we have judged the old.

It would be foolish, then, to pretend that the second part of reading, to judge, to compare, is as simple as the first—to open the mind wide to the fast flocking of innumerable impressions. To continue reading without the book before you, to hold one shadow-shape against another, to have read widely enough and with enough understanding to make such comparisons alive and illuminating—that is difficult; it is still more difficult to press further and to say, "Not only is the book of this sort, but it is of this value; here it fails; here it succeeds; this is bad; that is good." To carry out this part of a reader's duty needs such imagination, insight, and learning that it is hard to conceive any one mind sufficiently endowed; impossible for the most self-confident to find more than the seeds of such powers in himself. Would it not be wiser, then, to remit this part of reading and to allow the critics, the gowned and furred authorities of the library, to decide the question of the book's absolute value for us? Yet how impossible! We may stress the value of sympathy; we may try to sink our own identity as we read. But we know that we cannot sympathize wholly or immerse ourselves wholly; there is always a demon in us who whispers, "I hate, I love," and we cannot silence him. Indeed, it is precisely because we hate and we love that our relation with the poets and novelists is so intimate that we find the presence of another person intolerable. And even if the results are abhorrent and our judgments are wrong, still our taste, the nerve of sensation that sends shocks through us, is our chief illuminant; we learn through feeling; we cannot suppress our own idiosyncrasy without impoverishing it. But as time goes on perhaps we can train our taste; perhaps we can make it submit to some control. When it has fed greedily and lavishly upon books of all sorts—poetry, fiction, history, biography—and has stopped reading and looked for long spaces upon the variety, the incongruity of the living world, we shall find that it is changing a little; it is not so greedy, it is more reflective. It will begin to bring us not merely judgments on particular books, but it will tell us that there is a quality common to certain books. Listen, it will say, what shall we call *this*? And it will read us perhaps *Lear* and then perhaps the *Agamemnon* in order to bring out that common quality. Thus, with our taste to guide us, we shall venture beyond the particular book in search of qualities that group books together; we shall give them names and thus frame a rule that brings order into our perceptions. We shall gain a further and a rarer pleasure from that discrimination. But as a rule only lives when it is perpetually broken by contact with the books themselves—nothing is easier and more stultifying than to make rules which exists out of touch with facts, in a vacuum—now at last, in order to steady ourselves in this difficult attempt, it may be well to turn to the very rare writers who are able to enlighten us upon literature as an art. Coleridge and Dryden and Johnson, in their considered criticism, the poets and novelists themselves in their unconsidered sayings, are often surprisingly relevant; they light up and solidify the vague ideas that have been tumbling in the misty depths of our minds. But they are only able to help us if we come to them laden with questions and suggestions won honestly in the course of our own reading. They can do nothing for us if we herd ourselves under their authority and lie down like sheep in the shade of a hedge. We can only understand their ruling when it comes in conflict with our own and vanquishes it.

If this is so, if to read a book as it should be read calls for the rarest qualities of imagination, insight, and judgment, and you may perhaps conclude that literature is a very complex art and that it is unlikely that we shall be able, even after a lifetime of reading, to make any valuable contribution to its criticism. We must remain readers; we shall not put on the further glory that belongs to those rare beings who are also critics. But still we have our responsibilities as readers and even our importance. The standards we raise and the judgments we pass steal into the air and become part of the atmosphere which writers breathe as they work. An influence is created which tells upon them even if it never finds its way into print. And that influence, if it were well instructed, vigorous and individual and sincere, might be of great value now when criticism is necessarily in abeyance; when books pass in review like the procession of animals in a shooting gallery, and the critic has only one second in which to load and aim and shoot and may well be pardoned if he mistakes rabbits for tigers, eagles for barndoor fowls, or misses altogether and wastes his shot upon some peaceful cow grazing in a further field. If behind the erratic gunfire of the press the author felt that there was another kind of criticism, the opinion of people reading for the love of reading, slowly and unprofessionally, and judging with great sympathy and yet with great severity, might this not improve the quality of his work? And if by our means books were to become stronger, richer, and more varied, that would be an end worth reaching.

Yet who reads to bring about an end, however desirable? Are there not some pursuits that we practise because they are good in themselves, and some pleasures that are final? And is not this among them? I have sometimes dreamt, at least, that when the Day of judgment dawns and the great conquerors and lawyers and statesmen come to receive their rewards—their crowns, their laurels, their names carved indelibly upon imperishable marble—the Almighty will turn to Peter and will say, not without a certain envy when he sees us coming with our books under our arms, "Look, these need no reward. We have nothing to give them here. They have loved reading."

Note

[1] A paper read at a school.

Manners to Be Observed by
Teachers and Students

Al-Ghazālī

Manners to be observed by teachers and students. These manners comprise ten duties.

(1) The first duty of a student is to keep himself free from impure habit and evil matters. Effort to acquire knowledge is the worship of mind. It purifies secret faults and takes to God. Prayer is observed by outward organs and as outward purity is not gained except by outward organs, so worship by mind, the fountain head of acquisition of knowledge, cannot be attained without the removal of bad habits and evil attributes. The Prophet[1] said: Religion is founded on cleanliness. So outward and inward purities are necessary. God says: The polytheists are impure. . . . It is understood from this that purity and impurity are not merely external as the polytheists also keep their dresses clean and bodies clean, but as their mind is impure, so they are generally impure. The inward purity is of greatest importance. The Prophet therefore said: Angels do not enter a house wherein there are dogs. Human mind is a house, the abode of angels, the place of their movements. The blameworthy evils like anger, lust, rancour, envy, pride, conceit and the like are dogs. When dogs reside in a heart, where is the place for the angels? God takes the secrets of knowledge to the hearts through the angels. They do not take it except to the pure souls. Hazrat Ibn Masud[2] said: Knowledge is not acquired through much learning. It is a light cast in heart. A certain sage said: Knowledge is God-fear. As God said: The learned among the people fear God most.

(2) The second duty of a student is to reduce his worldly affairs and keep aloof from kith and kin as acquisition of knowledge is not possible in these environments. For this reason, a certain sage said: God has not gifted two minds to a man. For this reason, a certain sage said: Knowledge will not give you its full share till you surrender your entire mind to it.

(3) The third duty of a student is not to take pride or exalt himself over the teacher but rather entrust to him the conduct of all his affairs and submit to his advices as a patient submits to his physician. The Prophet said: It is the habit of a believer not to flatter anyone except when he seeks knowledge.

Therefore a student should not take pride over his teacher. Knowledge cannot be acquired except through modesty and humility. God said: Herein there is warning for one who has got a heart or sets up ear while he himself being a witness. . . . The meaning of having a heart is to be fit for receiving knowledge and one who is prepared and capable of understanding knowledge. Whatever the teacher should recommend to the student, the latter should follow it putting aside his own opinion. . . .

(4) The fourth duty of a student is that he should first pay no attention to the difference, whether about worldly sciences or sciences of the hereafter, as it may perplex his mind and he may lose enthusiasm. He should adopt first what the teacher says and should not argue about the different mazhabs[3] or sects.

(5) The fifth duty is that a student should not miss any branch of knowledge. He should try to become perfect in them as all branches of learning help one another and some branches are allied with others. If a man does not get a thing, it becomes his enemy. God says: When they do not find guidance they say, it is an age-long lie. . . . A poet said: A sweet thing is bitter in the mouth of a patient as sweet water is tasteless to a sick man. Good knowledge is acquired according to one's genius. It leads man to God or helps him in that way. Each branch of knowledge has got its fixed place. He who guards it, is like a guard who patrols the frontiers in jihad.[4] Each has got a rank in it and each has got a reward in the hereafter according to his rank. The only condition required is that the object of acquisition of knowledge should be to please God.

(6) The sixth duty of a student is that he should not take up all branches of knowledge at a time, but should take up the most important one at first as life is not sufficient for all branches of knowledge. A little learning if acquired with enthusiasm perfects the knowledge of the hereafter or the sciences of the worldly usages and the sciences of revelation. The object of the science of worldly usages is to acquire spiritual knowledge. The goal of the spiritual knowledge is to know God. Our object by this knowledge is not that belief which is handed down from generations to generations. Our object for this knowledge is to acquire light arising out of certain faith which God casts in soul. Such light was acquired by Hazrat Abu Bakr.[5] The Prophet said about Abu Bakr: If the faith of the people of the world is weighed with the faith of Abu Bakr, his faith would be heavy. In short, the highest and the noblest of all science, is to know God. This science is like a sea of which the depth cannot be ascertained. In this science, the highest rank is that of the Prophets, then of the friends of God and finally that of those who follow them. It has been narrated that the portraits of two ancient wise men were seen on the wall of a mosque. One of them held a piece of paper in which it was written: If you purify everything, don't understand that you have even purified one thing till

you know God and know that He is the cause of all Causes and the Creator of everything. In the hand of the second man, there was a scroll in which it was written: I removed thirst before by drinking water and then I have come to know God. But when I have come to know God, my thirst was quenched without any water.

(7) The seventh duty of a student is that he should not take up a new branch of learning till he has learnt fully the previous branch of learning, because it is requisite for the acquisition of knowledge. One branch of knowledge is a guide to another branch. God says: Whoso has been given the Quran recites it with due recitation. . . . In other words, he does not take up one learning till he masters the previous one. Hazrat Ali[6] said: Don't conceal truth from men, rather know the truth, then you will be the masters of truths.

(8) The eighth duty of a student is to know the causes for which noble sciences are known. It can be known from two things, nobility of its fruit and the authenticity of its principles. Take for example the science of religion as medicine. The fruit of the science of religion is to gain an eternal life and the fruit of the other is to gain a temporary life. From these points of view, the science of religion is more noble as its result is more noble. Take up mathematics and astrology; the former is nobler because the former is more authentic in its foundations. From this, it is clear that the science of the knowledge of God, of His angels, of His books and of His prophets is the noblest and also the branches of knowledge which help it.

(9) The ninth duty of a student is to purify mind and action with virtues, to gain proximity to God and His angels and to live in the company of those who live near Him. His aims should not be to gain worldly matters, to acquire riches and properties, to argue with the illiterate and to show pride and haughtiness. He whose object is to gain nearness of God should seek such learning as helps towards that goal, namely the knowledge of the hereafter and the learnings which are auxiliary to it. God said: God will raise herewith in rank who are believers and to whom knowledge have been given. . . . God said: They have got stages, some lower, some higher. The highest rank is that of the Prophets, then of the friends of God and then of the learned who are firm in knowledge and then of the pious who follow them.

(10) The tenth duty of a student is that he should keep attention to the primary object of knowledge. It is not in your power to enjoy bliss of this world and that of the next world together. This world is a temporary abode. Body is a conveyance and the actions run towards the goal. The goal is God and nothing else. All bliss and happiness lie in Him. So give more importance to the sciences which take to that ultimate goal. . . .

Second Subject—Duties of a Teacher

Whoever takes up the profession of teaching should observe the following duties:—

Patun

(1) He will show kindness and sympathy to the students and treat them as his own children. The Prophet said: I am to you like a father to his son. His object should be to protect the student from the fire of Hell. As parents save their children from the fire of this world, so a teacher should save his students or disciples from the fire of Hell. The duties of a teacher are more than those of parents. A father is the immediate cause of this transient life, but a teacher is the cause of immortal life. It is because of the spiritual teacher that the hereafter is much remembered. By teacher, I mean the teacher of the sciences of the hereafter or the sciences of the world with the object of the hereafter. A teacher ruins himself and also his students if he teaches for the sake of the world. For this reason, the people of the hereafter are journeying towards the next world and to God and remain absent from the world. The months and years of this world are so many stations of their journey. There is no miserliness in the fortunes of the next world and so there is no envy among them. They turn to the verse: The believers are brethren. . . .

(2) The second duty of a teacher is to follow the usages and ways of the Prophet. In other words, he should not seek remuneration for teaching but nearness to God. . . . God instructs us to say: I don't want any remuneration for this from you. . . . Wealth and property are the servants of body which is the vehicle of soul of which the essence is knowledge and for which there is honour of soul. He who searches for wealth in lieu of knowledge is like one who has got his face besmeared with impurities but wants to cleanse his body. In that case, the master is made a servant and the servant a master.

(3) The third duty of a teacher is that he should not withhold from his students any advice. After he finishes the outward sciences, he should teach them the inward sciences. He should tell them that the object of education is to gain nearness of God, not power or riches and that God created ambition as a means of perpetuating knowledge which is essential for these sciences.

(4) The fourth duty of a teacher is to dissuade his students from evil ways with care and caution, with sympathy and not with rebuke and harshness, because in that case it destroys the veil of awe and encourages disobedience. The Holy Prophet is the guide of all teachers. He said: If men had been forbidden to make porridge of camel's dung, they would have done it saying that they would not have been forbidden to do it unless there has been some good in it.

(5) The fifth duty of a teacher is that he shall not belittle the value of other sciences before his students. He who teaches grammar naturally thinks of the science of jurisprudence[7] as bad and he who teaches jurisprudence discourages the science of traditions and so on. Such evils are blameworthy. In fact the teacher of one learning should prepare his students for study of other learnings and then he should observe the rules of gradual progress from one stage to another.

(6) The sixth duty that a teacher should do is to teach his students up to the power of their understanding. The students should not be taught such things as are beyond the capacity of their understanding. In this matter, he should follow the Prophet, who said: We prophets form one class. We have been commanded to give every man his rightful place and to speak to men according to their intellect. The Prophet said: When a man speaks such a word to a people who cannot grasp it with their intellect, it becomes a danger to some persons. Hazrat Ali said, pointing to his breast: There is much knowledge in it, but then there should be some people to understand it. The hearts of pious men are graves of secret matter. From this, it is understood that whatever the teacher knows should not all be communicated to the students at the same time. Jesus Christ said: Don't hang pearls around the neck of a swine. Wisdom is better than pearls. He who knows it as bad is worse than swine. Once a learned man was questioned about something but he gave no reply. The questioner said: Have you not heard what the Prophet said?—He who conceals any useful knowledge will on the Resurrection Day be bridled with a bridle of fire. The learned man said: You may place the bridle of fire and go.

If I don't disclose it to one who understands it, then put the bridle of fire upon me. God said: Don't give to the fools your property. . . . There is warning in this verse that it is better to safeguard knowledge from those who might be corrupted by it. To give a thing to one who is not fit for it and not to give a thing to one who is fit for it are equally oppression. A certain poet therefore said:

> Should I cast pearls before the illiterate shepherds?
> They will not understand, nor know their worth.

If God by His knowledge sends one with knowledge, I will give my goods to him, and gain his love. He wastes his learning who gives it to one unworthy. He commits sin who withholds it from one worthy.

(7) The seventh duty of a teacher is that he should teach his backward students only such things as are clear and suited to their limited understanding. Every man thinks that his wisdom is perfect and the greatest fool is he who

rests satisfied with the knowledge that his intellect is perfect. In short, the door of debates should not be opened before the common men.

(8) The eighth duty of a teacher is that he should himself do what he teaches and should not give a lie to his teaching. Knowledge can be grasped by internal eye and actions by external eye. Many people have got external eyes but very few have got internal eyes. So if the actions of a teacher are contrary to what he preaches, it does not help towards guidance, but it is like poison. A teacher is like a stamp to clay and a student is like clay. If the stamp has no character, there is no impression on clay. Or he is like a cane and the student is like the shadow of the cane. How can the shadow of the cane be straight when the cane itself is crooked? God said: Do you enjoin good to the people and forget it for yourselves. . . ? Hazrat Ali said: Two men have broken my back, the learned man who ruins himself and the fool who adopts asceticism. The learned man misleads the people through his sins and the fool through his evil actions.

Notes

[1] The Prophet: Mohammed.

[2] Hazrat Ibn Masud: "Hazrat" is a Persian title of respect used in the Sufi tradition to designate great teachers or leaders. Abdullah ibn Mas'ud was an early convert to Islam and a companion of Mohammed.

[3] Mazhabs: the major schools of thought about Islamic law. The four current mazhabs within Sunni Islam have been consolidated from many more that existed in al-Ghazālī's time.

[4] Jihad: This Islamic concept is much misunderstood in contemporary political discourse. In traditional Islamic law, *jihad*, or "holy war," can refer to the personal struggle to acquire knowledge and live the tenets of Islam. It can also refer to a defensive war necessary to preserve Islam itself. It cannot, in classical Islamic thought, refer to a war of conquest, a war to punish enemies of Islam, or a war designed to bring about religious conversion. *yes it can*

[5] Hazrat Abu Bakr: A close associate of Mohammed who succeeded him as leader of the Muslim community in Mecca, Abu Bakr is generally considered the first caliph, or non-prophetic Islamic leader.

[6] Hazrat Ali: Mohammed's son-in-law and the fourth caliph.

[7] Jurisprudence: the study of law or of legal philosophy.

LXXXVIII.
On Liberal and Vocational Studies

Lucius Annaeus Seneca

You have been wishing to know my views with regard to liberal studies. My answer is this: I respect no study, and deem no study good, which results in money-making. Such studies are profit-bringing occupations, useful only in so far as they give the mind a preparation and do not engage it permanently. One should linger upon them only so long as the mind can occupy itself with nothing greater; they are our apprenticeship, not our real work. Hence you see why "liberal studies" are so called; it is because they are studies worthy of a free-born gentleman. But there is only one really liberal study,—that which gives a man his liberty. It is the study of wisdom, and that is lofty, brave, and great-souled. All other studies are puny and puerile. You surely do not believe that there is good in any of the subjects whose teachers are, as you see, men of the most ignoble and base stamp? We ought not to be learning such things; we should have done with learning them.

Certain persons have made up their minds that the point at issue with regard to the liberal studies is whether they make men good; but they do not even profess or aim at a knowledge of this particular subject. The scholar busies himself with investigations into language, and if it be his desire to go farther afield, he works on history, or, if he would extend his range to the farthest limits, on poetry. But which of these paves the way to virtue? Pronouncing syllables, investigating words, memorizing plays, or making rules for the scansion of poetry,— what is there in all this that rids one of fear, roots out desire, or bridles the passions? The question is: do such men teach virtue, or not? If they do not teach it, then neither do they transmit it. If they do teach it, they are philosophers. Would you like to know how it happens that they have not taken the chair for the purpose of teaching virtue? See how unlike their subjects are; and yet their subjects would resemble each other if they taught the same thing. It may be, perhaps, that they make you believe that Homer was a philosopher, although they disprove this by the very arguments through which they seek to prove it. For sometimes they make of him a Stoic, who approves nothing but virtue, avoids pleasures, and refuses to relinquish honour even at the price of immortality; sometimes they make him an Epicurean, praising the condition of a state in repose, which passes its days in feasting and song; sometimes a Peripatetic, classifying goodness in three ways; sometimes an Academic, holding that all things are uncertain. It is clear, however, that no one of these doctrines is to be fathered upon Homer, just because they are all there; for they are irreconcilable with one another. We may admit to these men, indeed, that Homer was a philosopher; yet surely he became a wise man before he had any knowledge of poetry. So let us learn the particular things that made Homer wise.

It is no more to the point, of course, for me to investigate whether Homer or Hesiod was the older poet, than to know why Hecuba, although younger than Helen, showed her years so lamentably. What, in your opinion, I say, would be the point in trying to determine the respective ages of Achilles and Patroclus? Do you raise the question, "Through what regions did Ulysses stray?" instead of trying to prevent ourselves from going astray at all times? We have no leisure to hear lectures on the question whether he was sea-tost between Italy and Sicily, or outside our known world (indeed, so long a wandering could not possibly have taken place within its narrow bounds); We ourselves encounter storms of the spirit, which toss us daily, and our depravity drives us into all the ills which troubled Ulysses. For us there is never lacking the beauty to tempt our eyes, or the enemy to assail us; on this side are savage monsters that delight in human blood, on that side the treacherous allurements of the ear, and yonder is shipwreck and all the varied category of misfortunes. Show me rather, by the example of Ulysses, how I am to love my country, my wife, my father, and how, even after suffering shipwreck, I am to sail toward these ends, honourable as they are. Why try to discover whether Penelope was a pattern of purity or whether she had the laugh on her contemporaries? Or whether she suspected that the man in her presence was Ulysses, before she knew it was he? Teach me rather what purity is, and how great a good we have in it, and whether it is situated in the body or in the soul. Now I will transfer my attention to the musician. You, sir, are teaching me how the treble and the bass are in accord with one another, and how, though the strings produce different notes, the result is a harmony; rather bring my soul into harmony with itself, and let not my purposes be out of tune. You are showing me what the doleful keys are; show me rather how, in the midst of adversity, I may keep from uttering a doleful note. The mathematician teaches me how to lay out the dimensions of my estates; but I should rather be taught how to lay out what is enough for a man to own. He teaches me to count, and adapts my fingers to avarice; but I should prefer him to teach me that there is no point in such calculations, and that one is none the happier for tiring out the bookkeepers with his possessions——or rather, how useless property is to any man who would find it the greatest misfortune if he should be required to reckon out, by his own wits, the amount of his holdings. What good is there for me in knowing how to parcel out a piece of land, if I know not how to share it with my brother? What good is there in working out to a nicety the dimensions of an acre, and in detecting the error if a piece has so much as escaped my measuring-rod, if I am embittered when an ill-tempered neighbour merely scrapes off a bit of my land? The mathematician teaches me how I may lose none of my boundaries; I, however, seek to learn how to lose them all with a light heart. "But," comes the reply, "I am being driven from the farm which my father and grandfather owned !" Well? Who owned the land before your grandfather? Can you explain what people (I will not say what person) held it originally? You did not enter upon it as a master, but merely as a tenant. And whose tenant are you? If your claim is successful, you are tenant of the heir. The lawyers say that public property cannot be acquired privately by possession; what you hold and call your own is public property— indeed, it belongs to mankind at large. O what marvellous skill! You know how to measure the circle; you find the square of any shape which is set before you; you compute the distances between the stars; there is nothing which does not come within the scope of your calculations. But if you are a real master of your profession, measure me the mind of man! Tell me how great it is, or how puny ! You know what a straight line is; but how does it benefit you if you do not know what is straight in this life of ours?

I come next to the person who boasts his knowledge of the heavenly bodies, who knows

> Whither the chilling star of Saturn hides.
> And through what orbit Mercury doth stray.

Of what benefit will it be to know this? That I shall be disturbed because Saturn and Mars are in opposition, or when Mercury sets at eventide in plain view of Saturn, rather than learn that those stars, wherever they are, are propitious, and that they are not subject to change? They are driven along by an unending round of destiny, on a course from which they cannot swerve. They return at stated seasons; they either set in motion, or mark the intervals of the whole world's work. But if they are responsible for whatever happens, how will it help you to know the secrets of the immutable? Or if they merely give indications, what good is there in foreseeing what you cannot escape? Whether you know these things or not, they will take place.

emetic: [the power, vomiting]
having the power to produce vomiting.

30 ◆ **Critical Strategies and Great Questions**

> Behold the fleeting sun,
> The stars that follow in his train, and thou
> Shalt never find the morrow play thee false,
> Or be misled by nights without a cloud.

It has, however, been sufficiently and fully ordained that I shall be safe from anything that may mislead me. "What," you say, "does the 'morrow never play me false'? Whatever happens without my knowledge plays me false." I, for my part, do not know what is to be, but I do know what may come to be. I shall have no misgivings in this matter; I await the future in its entirety; and if there is any abatement in its severity, I make the most of it. If the morrow treats me kindly, it is a sort of deception; but it does not deceive me even at that. For just as I know that all things can happen, so I know, too, that they will not happen in every case. I am ready for favourable events in every case, but I am prepared for evil.

In this discussion you must bear with me if I do not follow the regular course. For I do not consent to admit painting into the list of liberal arts, any more than sculpture, marble-working, and other helps toward luxury. I also debar from the liberal studies wrestling and all knowledge that is compounded of oil and mud; otherwise, I should be compelled to admit perfumers also, and cooks, and all others who lend their wits to the service of our pleasures. For what "liberal" element is there in these ravenous takers of emetics, whose bodies are fed to fatness while their minds are thin and dull? Or do we really believe that the training which they give is "liberal" for the young men of Rome, who used to be taught by our ancestors to stand straight, and hurl a spear, to wield a pike, to guide a horse, and to handle weapons? Our ancestors used to teach their children nothing that could be learned while lying down. But neither the new system nor the old teaches or nourishes virtue. For what good does it do us to guide a horse and control his speed with the curb, and then find that our own passions, utterly uncurbed, bolt with us? Or to beat many opponents in wrestling or boxing, and then to find that we ourselves are beaten by anger?

"What then," you say, "do the liberal studies contribute nothing to our welfare?" Very much in other respects, but nothing at all as regards virtue. For even these arts of which I have spoken, though admittedly of a low grade—depending as they do upon handiwork—contribute greatly toward the equipment of life, but nevertheless have nothing to do with virtue. And if you inquire, "Why, then, do we educate our children in the liberal studies?" it is not because they can bestow virtue, but because they prepare the soul for the reception of virtue. Just as that "primary course," as the ancients called it, in grammar, which gave boys their elementary training, does not teach them the liberal arts, but prepares the ground for their early acquisition of these arts, so the liberal arts do not conduct the soul all the way to virtue, but merely set it going in that direction.

Posidonius divides the arts into four classes: first we have those which are common and low, then those which serve for amusement, then those which refer to the education of boys, and, finally, the liberal arts. The common sort belong to workmen and are mere hand-work; they are concerned with equipping life; there is in them no pretence to beauty or honour. The arts of amusement are those which aim to please the eye and the ear. To this class you may assign the stage-machinists, who invent scaffolding that goes aloft of its own accord, or floors that rise silently into the air, and many other surprising devices, as when objects that fit together then fall apart, or objects which are separate then join together automatically, or objects which stand erect then gradually collapse. The eye of the inexperienced is struck with amazement by these things; for such persons marvel at everything that takes place without warning, because they do not know the causes. The arts which belong to the education of hoys, and are somewhat similar to the liberal arts, are those which the Greeks call the "cycle of studies," but which we Romans call the "liberal." However, those alone are really liberal —or rather, to give them a truer name, "free"—whose concern is virtue.

"But," one will say, "just as there is a part of philosophy which has to do with nature, and a part which has to do with ethics, and a part which has to do with reasoning, so this group of liberal arts also claims for itself a place in philosophy. When one approaches questions that deal with nature, a decision is reached by means of a word from the mathematician. Therefore mathematics is a department of that branch which it aids." But many things aid us and yet are not parts of ourselves. Nay, if they were, they would not aid us. Food is an aid to the body, but is not a part of it. We get some help from the service which mathematics renders; and mathematics is as indispensable to philosophy as the carpenter is to the mathematician. But carpentering is not a part of mathematics, nor is mathematics a part of philosophy. Moreover, each has its own limits; for the wise man investigates and learns the causes of natural phenomena, while the mathematician follows up and computes their numbers and their measurements." The wise man knows the laws by which the heavenly bodies persist, what powers belong to them, and what attributes; the astronomer merely notes their comings and goings, the rules which govern their settings and their risings, and the occasional periods during which they seem to stand still, although as a matter of fact no heavenly body can stand still. The wise man will know what causes the reflection in a mirror; but the mathematician can merely tell you how far the body should be from the reflection, and what shape of mirror will produce a given reflection. The philosopher will demonstrate that the sun is a large body, while the astronomer will compute just how large, progressing in knowledge by his method of trial and experiment; but in order to progress, he must summon to his aid certain principles. No art, however, is sufficient unto itself, if the foundation upon which it rests depends upon mere favour. Now philosophy asks no favours from any other source; it builds everything on its own soil; but the science of numbers is, so to speak, a structure built on another man's land—it builds on alien soil. It accepts first principles, and by their favour arrives at further conclusions. If it could march unassisted to the truth, if it were able to understand the nature of the universe, I should say that it would offer much assistance to our minds; for the mind grows by contact with things heavenly, and draws into itself something from on high. There is but one thing that brings the soul to perfection—the unalterable knowledge of good and evil. But there is no other art which investigates good and evil.

I should like to pass in review the several virtues. Bravery is a scorner of things which inspire fear; it looks down upon, challenges, and crushes the powers of terror and all that would drive our freedom under the yoke. But do "liberal studies" strengthen this virtue? Loyalty is the holiest good in the human heart; it is forced into betrayal by no constraint, and it is bribed by no rewards. Loyalty cries: "Burn me, slay me, kill me! I shall not betray my trust; and the more urgently torture shall seek to find my secret, the deeper in my heart will I bury it!" Can the "liberal arts" produce such a spirit within us? Temperance controls our desires; some it hates and routs, others it regulates and restores to a healthy measure, nor does it ever approach our desires for their own sake. Temperance knows that the best measure of the appetites is not what you want to take, but what you ought to take. Kindliness forbids you to be over-bearing towards your associates, and it forbids you to be grasping. In words and in deeds and in feelings it shows itself gentle and courteous to all men. It counts no evil as another's solely. And the reason why it loves its own good is chiefly because it will some day be the good of another. Do "liberal studies" teach a man such character as this? No; no more than they teach simplicity, moderation and self-restraint, thrift and economy, and that kindliness which spares a neighbour's life as if it were one's own and knows that it is not for man to make wasteful use of his fellow-man.

"But," one says, "since you declare that virtue cannot be attained without the 'liberal studies,' how is it that you deny that they offer any assistance to virtue?" Because you cannot attain virtue without food, either; and yet food has nothing to do with virtue. Wood does not offer assistance to a ship, although a ship cannot be built except of wood. There is no reason, I say, why you should think that anything is made by the assistance of that without which it cannot be made. We might even make the statement that it is possible to attain wisdom without the "liberal studies"; for although virtue is a thing that must be learned, yet it is not learned by means of these studies.

What reason have I, however, for supposing that one who is ignorant of letters will never be a wise man, since wisdom is not to be found in letters? Wisdom communicates facts and not words; and it may be true that the memory is more to be depended upon when it has no support outside itself. Wisdom is a large and spacious thing. It needs plenty of free room. One must learn about things divine and human, the past and the future, the ephemeral and the eternal; and one must learn about Time. See how many questions arise concerning time alone: in the first place, whether it is anything in and by itself; in the second place, whether anything exists prior to time and without time; and again, did time begin along with the universe, or, because there was something even before the universe began, did time also exist then? There are countless questions concerning the soul alone: whence it comes, what is its nature, when it begins to exist, and how long it exists; whether it passes from one place to another and changes its habitation, being transferred successively from one animal shape to another, or whether it is a slave but once, roaming the universe after it is set free; whether it is corporeal or not; what will become of it when it ceases to use us as its medium; how it will employ its freedom when it has escaped from this present prison; whether it will forget all its past, and at that moment begin to know itself when, released from the body, it has withdrawn to the skies. Thus, whatever phase of things human and divine you have apprehended, you will be wearied by the vast number of things to be answered and things to be learned. And in order that these manifold and mighty subjects may have free entertainment in your soul, you must remove therefrom all superfluous things. Virtue will not surrender herself to these narrow bounds of ours; a great subject needs wide space in which to move. Let all other things be driven out, and let the breast be emptied to receive virtue.

"But it is a pleasure to be acquainted with many arts." Therefore let us keep only as much of them as is essential. Do you regard that man as blameworthy who puts superfluous things on the same footing with useful things, and in his house makes a lavish display of costly objects, but do not deem him blameworthy who has allowed himself to become engrossed with the useless furniture of learning? This desire to know more than is sufficient is a sort of intemperance. Why? Because this unseemly pursuit of the liberal arts makes men troublesome, wordy, tactless, self-satisfied bores, who fail to learn the essentials just because they have learned the non-essentials. Didymus the scholar wrote four thousand books. I should feel pity for him if he had only read the same number of superfluous volumes. In these books he investigates Homer's birthplace, who was really the mother of Aeneas, whether Anacreon was more of a rake or more of a drunkard, whether Sappho was a bad lot, and other problems the answers to which, if found, were forthwith to be forgotten. Come now, do not tell me that life is long! Nay, when you come to consider our own countrymen also, I can show you many works which ought to be cut down with the axe.

It is at the cost of a vast outlay of time and of vast discomfort to the ears of others that we win such praise as this: "What a learned man you are!" Let us be content with this recommendation, less citified though it be: "What a good man you are!" Do I mean this? Well, would you have me unroll the annals of the world's history and try to find out who first wrote poetry? Or, in the absence of written records, shall I make an estimate of the number of years which lie between Orpheus and Homer? Or shall I make a study of the absurd writings of Aristarchus, wherein he branded the text of other men's verses, and wear my life away upon syllables? Shall I then wallow in the geometrician's dust? Have I so far forgotten that useful saw "Save your time"? Must I know these things? And what may I choose not to know?

Apion, the scholar; who drew crowds to his lectures all over Greece in the days of Gaius Caesar and was acclaimed a Homerid by every state, used to maintain that Homer, when he had finished his two poems, the *Iliad* and the *Odyssey*, added a preliminary poem to his work, wherein he embraced the whole Trojan war. The argument which Apion adduced to prove this statement was that Homer had purposely inserted in the opening line two letters which contained a key to the number of his books. A man who wishes to know many things must know such things as these, and must take no thought of all the time which one loses by ill-health, public duties, private duties, daily duties, and sleep. Apply the measure to the years of your life; they have no room for all these things.

I have been speaking so far of liberal studies; but think how much superfluous and unpractical matter the philosophers contain! Of their own accord they also have descended to establishing nice divisions of syllables, to determining the true meaning of conjunctions and prepositions; they have been envious of the scholars, envious of the mathematicians. They have taken over into their own art all the superfluities of these other arts; the result is that they know more about careful speaking than about careful living. Let me tell you what evils are due to over-nice exactness, and what an enemy it is of truth! Protagoras declares that one can take either side on any question and debate it with equal success—even on this very question, whether every subject can be debated from either point of view. Nausiphanes holds that in things which seem to exist, there is no difference between existence and non-existence. Parmenides maintains that nothing exists of all this which seems to exist, except the universe alone. Zeno of Elea removed all the difficulties by removing one; for he declares that nothing exists. The Pyrrhonean, Megarian, Eretrian, and Academic schools are all engaged in practically the same task; they have introduced a new knowledge, non-knowledge. You may sweep all these theories in with the superfluous troops of "liberal" studies; the one class of men give me a knowledge that will be of no use to me, the other class do away with any hope of attaining knowledge. It is better, of course, to know useless things than to know nothing. One set of philosophers offers no light by which I may direct my gaze toward the truth; the other digs out my very eyes and leaves me blind. If I cleave to Protagoras, there is nothing in the scheme of nature that is not doubtful; if I hold with Nausiphanes, I am sure only of this—that everything is unsure; if with Parmenides, there is nothing except the One; if with Zeno, there is not even the One.

What are we, then? What becomes of all these things that surround us, support us, sustain us? The whole universe is then a vain or deceptive shadow. I cannot readily say whether I am more vexed at those who would have it that we know nothing, or with those who would not leave us even this privilege. Farewell.

Pusillanimous [Lat pusillus - small, mean, weak + animus soul, mind]
Of a person lacking in courage or strength of purpose;
faint-hearted, craven, cowardly.

from *The Papers of Thomas Jefferson*

Editor, Julian P. Boyd

to reprobate [L. pat p of reprobare to reject, condemn]
1. theol. of God: to reject or cast off (a person) spec. to predestine a person
to damn
2. to reject or refuse; to put away, set aside

July 2.   Congress proceeded the same day to consider the declaration of Independence, which had been reported & laid on the table the Friday preceding, and on Monday referred to a commee. of the whole. the pusillanimous idea that we had friends in England worth keeping terms with, still haunted the minds of many. for this reason those passages which conveyed censures on the people of England were struck out, lest they should give them offence. the clause too, reprobating the enslaving the inhabitants of Africa, was struck out in complaisance to South Carolina & Georgia, who had never attempted to restrain the importation of slaves, and who on the contrary still wished to continue it. our Northern brethren also I believe felt a little tender *(on that)* under these censures; for tho' their people have very few slaves themselves yet they had been pretty considerable carriers of them to others. the debates hav-

July 3. 4. ing taken up the greater parts of the 2d. 3d. & 4th. days of July were, in the evening of the last closed. the declaration was reported by the commee., agreed to by the house, and signed by every member present except Mr. Dickinson. As the sentiments of men are known not only by what they receive, but what they reject also, I will state the form of the declaration as originally reported *(is here subjoined)*. The parts *(omitted and)* struck out by Congress *(are)* shall be distinguished by a black line drawn under them; & those inserted *(are)* by them shall be placed in the margin or in a concurrent column(s).

     A Declaration by the representatives of the United States of America, in General Congress assembled

     When in the course of human events it becomes necessary for one people to dissolve the political bands which have connected them with another, and to assume among the powers of the earth the separate & equal station to which the laws of nature and of nature's god entitle them, a decent respect to the opinions of mankind requires that they should declare the causes which impel them to the separation.

usurpation > usurpatio [L. usurpare – to ...] usurp = to intrude
forcibly, illegally, or without just cause
— unwarranted encroachment

from *The Papers of Thomas Jefferson* ◆ 37

We hold the truths to be self evident: that all men are created equal; that they are endowed by their creator with ∧ inherent and ∧certain inalienable rights; that among these are life, liberty & the pursuit of happiness: that to secure these rights, governments are instituted among men, deriving their just powers from the consent of the governed; that whenever any form of government becomes destructive of these ends, it is the right of the people to alter or to abolish it, & to institute new government, laying its foundation on such principles, & organising it's powers in such form, as to them shall seem most likely to effect their safety & happiness. prudence indeed will dictate that governments long established should not be changed for light & transient causes; and accordingly all experience hath shewn that mankind are more disposed to suffer while evils are sufferable than to right themselves by abolishing the forms to which they are accustomed. but when a long train of abuses & usurpations [begun at a distinguished period and] pursuing invariably the same object, evinces a design to reduce them under absolute despotism it is their right, it is their duty to throw off such government, & to provide new guards for their future security. such has been the patient sufferance of these colonies; & such is now the necessity which constrains them to ∧ [expunge] their former systems of government. the ∧alter history of the present king of Great Britain is a history of ∧ [unremit- ∧repeated ting] injuries & usurpations, [among which appears no solitary fact to contradict the uniform tenor of the rest but all have] ∧ in direct object ∧all having the establishment of an absolute tyranny over these states. to prove this let facts be submitted to a candid world [for the truth of which we pledge a faith yet unsullied by falsehood.]

he has refused his assent to laws the most wholsome & necessary for the public good.

he has forbidden his governors to pass laws of immediate & pressing importance, unless suspended in their operation till his assent should be obtained; & when so suspended, he has utterly neglected to attend to them.

he has refused to pass other laws for the accomodation of large districts of people, unless those people would relinquish the right of representation in the legislature, a right inestimable to them, & formidable to tyrants only.

he has called together legislative bodies at places unusual, uncomfortable, and distant from the depository of their public records, for the sole purpose of fatiguing them into compliance with his measures.

inestimable:
[L. inaestimabilis
in + aestimabilis
estimable =
capable of being
estimated,
valued,
appraised]
So: incapable of
being estimated;
cannot be reckoned
up or computed;
for great profound
to be estimated

evince: [L. e + vincere to conquer] to overcome, subdue,
prevail over.

candid: [L. candere to be white, glisten]
1 White. 2 Splendid, illustrious; b. pure, clean; stainless; 3 Free from bias; fair, impartial
4. free from malice; not desirous to find faults; gentle, courteous.

he has dissolved representative houses repeatedly [& continually] for opposing with manly firmness his invasions on the rights of the people.

he has refused for a long time after such dissolutions to cause others to be elected, whereby the legislative powers, incapable of annihilation, have returned to the people at large for their exercise, the state remaining in the mean time exposed to all the dangers of invasion from without & convulsions within.

he has endeavored to prevent the population of these states, for that purpose obstructing the laws for naturalization of foreigners, refusing to pass others to encourage their migrations hither, & raising the conditions of new appropriations of lands.

∧obstructed   he has ∧ [suffered] the administration of justice [totally to cease
∧by in some of these states] ∧ refusing his assent to laws for establishing judiciary powers.

he has made [our] judges dependant on his will alone, for the tenure of their offices, & the amount & paiment of their salaries.

he has erected a multitude of new offices [by a self assumed power] and sent hither swarms of new officers to harrass our people and eat out their substance.

he has kept among us in times of peace standing armies [and ships of war] without the consent of our legislatures.

he has affected to render the military independant of, & superior to the civil power.

he has combined with others to subject us to a jurisdiction foreign to our constitutions & unacknoleged by our laws, giving his assent to their acts of pretended legislation for quartering large bodies of armed troops among us; for protecting them by a mock-trial from punishment for any murders which they should commit on the inhabitants of these states; for cutting off our trade with all parts of the world; for imposing
∧in many taxes on us without our consent; for depriving us ∧ of the benefits of
cases trial by jury; for transporting us beyond seas to be tried for pretended offences; for abolishing the free system of English laws in a neighboring province, establishing therein an arbitrary government, and enlarging it's boundaries, so as to render it at once an example and fit instrument
∧colonies for introducing the same absolute rule into these ∧ [states]; for taking away our charters, abolishing our most valuable laws, and altering fundamentally the forms of our governments; for suspending our own

abdicate [L. abdicare resign, withdraw] to proclaim or declare to be no longer
one's own; cast off

Perfidy: [L. perfidia per + fides faithless, treachery] deceitfulness, untrustworthiness, breach
of faith or promise

legislatures, & declaring themselves invested with power to legislate for
us in all cases whatsoever.

he has abdicated government here ∧ [withdrawing his governors ∧by declaring
and declaring us out of his allegiance & protection] us out of his
protection &
waging war
against us

he has plundered our seas, ravaged our coasts, burnt our towns, &
destroyed the lives of our people.

he is at this time transporting large armies of foreign mercenaries
to compleat the works of death, desolation & tyranny already begun
with circumstances of cruelty and perfidy ∧ unworthy the head of a civ- ∧scarcely par-
ilized nation. alleled in the
most barbarous

he has constrained our fellow citizens taken captive on the high ages, & totally
seas to bear arms against their country, to become the executioners of
their friends & brethren, or to fall themselves by their hands.

he has ∧ endeavored to bring on the inhabitants of our frontiers ∧excited
the merciless Indian savages, whose known rule of warfare is an undis- domestic
tinguished destruction of all ages, sexes, & conditions [of existence.] insurrections
amongst us

[he has incited treasonable insurrections of our fellow-citizens with & has
the allurements of forfeiture & confiscation of our property.

he has waged cruel war against human nature itself, violating it's
most sacred rights of life and liberty in the persons of a distant people
who never offended, him captivating & carrying them into slavery in
another hemisphere or to incur miserable death in their transportation opprobrium
thither. this piratical warfare, the opprobrium of infidel powers is, the [L. opprobrium :
warfare of the Christian king of Great Britain. determined to keep open cause of reproach
a market where Men should be bought & sold, he has prostituted his shame, disgrace]
negative for suppressing every legislative attempt to prohibit or to 1. occasion, object a
restrain this execrable commerce. and that this assemblage of horrors cause of reproach,
might want no fact of distinguished die. he is now exciting those very criticism; shame;
people to rise in arms among us, and to purchase that liberty of which or disgrace;
he has deprived them: by murdering the people on whom he also Shameful or
obtruded them, thus paying off former crimes committed against the disgraceful
Liberties of one people, with crimes which he urges them to commit conduct.
against the lives of another.]

In every stage of these oppressions we have petitioned for redress
in the most humble terms: our repeated petitions have been answered
only by repeated injuries, a prince whose character is thus marked by
every act which may define a tyrant is unfit to be the ruler of a ∧ peo- ∧free
ple [who mean to be free. future ages will scarcely believe that the har-
diness of one man adventured, within the short compass of twelve years

execrable [L. execrabilis ; execrari execrate to pronounce a curse upon; declare accursed]
1. Expressing or invoking a curse; hence of an imprecation
2 a person a thing deserving to be execrated or cursed

imprecation [L. imprecari imprecate to pray for; invoke] action of imprecating & invoking
evil, calamity, or divine vengeance

only, to lay a foundation so broad & so undisguised for tyranny over a people fostered & fixed in principles of freedom.]

Nor have we been wanting in attentions to our British brethren. we have warned them from time to time of attempts by their legislature to extend ∧ [a] jurisdiction over ∧ [these our states.] we have reminded them of the circumstances of our emigration & settlement here, [no one of which could warrant so strange a pretension: that these were effected at the expence of our own blood & treasure, unassisted by the wealth or the strength of Great Britain: that in constituting indeed our several forms of government, we had adopted one common king, thereby laying a foundation for perpetual league & amity with them: but that submission to their parliament was no part of our constitution, nor ever in idea, if history may be credited; and,] we ∧ appealed to their native justice and magnanimity ∧ [as well as to] the ties of our common kindred to disavow these usurpations which ∧ [were likely to] interrupt our connection and correspondence. they too have been deaf to the voice of justice & of consanguinity, [and when occasions have been given them by the regular course of their laws, of removing from their councils the disturbers of our harmony, they have, by their free election, re-established them in power, at this very time too they are permitting their chief magistrate to send over not only souldiers of our common blood, but Scotch & foreign mercenaries to invade & destroy us. these facts have given the last stab to agonizing affection, and manly spirit bids us to renounce for ever these unfeeling brethren. we must endeavor to forget our former love for them, and to hold them as we hold the rest of mankind enemies in war, in peace friends. we might have been a free and a great people together; but a communication of grandeur & of freedom it seems is below their dignity. be it so, since they will have it. the road to happiness & to glory is open to us too. we will tread it apart from them, and] ∧ acquiesce in the necessity which denounces our [eternal] separation ∧!

Margin notes (left):
∧ an unwarrantable
∧ us
∧ have
∧ and we have conjured them by
∧ would inevitably
∧ we must therefore
∧ and hold them as we hold the rest of mankind, enemies in war, in peace friends.

We therefore the representatives of the United states of America in General Congress assembled do in the name, & by the authority of the good people of these [states reject & renounce all allegiance & subjection to the kings of Great Britain & all others who may hereafter claim by, through or

We therefore the representatives of the United states of America in General Congress assembled, appealing to the supreme judge of the world for the rectitude of our intentions, do in the name, & by the authority of the good people of these colonies, solemnly publish & declare that these United colonies

<u>under them: we utterly dissolve all political connection which may heretofore have subsisted between us & the people or parliament of Great Britain: & finally we do assert & declare these colonies to be free & independant states,</u>] & that as free & independant states, they have full power to levy war, conclude peace, contract alliances, establish commerce, & to do all other acts & things which independant states may of right do. and for the support of this declaration we mutually pledge to each other our lives, our fortunes & our sacred honour.

are & of right ought to be free & independant states; that they are absolved from all allegiance to the British crown, and that all political connection between them & the state of Great Britain is, & ought to be, totally dissolved; & that as free & independant states they have full power to levy war, conclude peace, contract alliances, establish commerce & to do all other acts & things which independant states may of right do.

and for the support of this declaration, with a firm reliance on the protection of divine providence we mutually pledge to each other our lives, our fortunes & our sacred honour.

[Editor's note: The original and revised versions of the final two paragraphs are placed side by side for comparison.]

The Declaration of Independence

In Congress, July 4, 1776
The Unanimous Declaration of the Thirteen
United States of America

When in the course of human events, it becomes necessary for one people to dissolve the political bands which have connected them with another, and to assume among the powers of the earth, the separate and equal station to which the Laws of Nature and of Nature's God entitle them, a decent respect to the opinions of mankind requires that they should declare the causes which impel them to the separation.

We hold these truths to be self-evident, that all men are created equal, that they are endowed by their Creator with certain unalienable rights, that among these are life, liberty and the pursuit of happiness. That to secure these rights, governments are instituted among men, deriving their just powers from the consent of the governed. That whenever any form of government becomes destructive of these ends, it is the right of the people to alter or to abolish it, and to institute new government, laying its foundation on such principles and organizing its powers in such form, as to them shall seem most likely to effect their safety and happiness. Prudence, indeed, will dictate that governments long established should not be changed for light and transient causes; and accordingly all experience hath shown, that mankind are more disposed to suffer, while evils are sufferable, than to right themselves by abolishing the forms to which they are accustomed. But when a long train of abuses and usurpations, pursuing invariably the same object evinces a design to reduce them under absolute despotism, it is their right, it is their duty, to throw off such government, and to provide new guards for their future security. Such has been the patient sufferance of these Colonies; and such is now the necessity which constrains them to alter their former systems of government. The history of the present King of Great Britain is a history of repeated injuries and usurpations, all having in direct object the establishment of an absolute tyranny over these States. To prove this, let facts be submitted to a candid world.

He has refused his assent to laws, the most wholesome and necessary for the public good.

He has forbidden his Governors to pass laws of immediate and pressing importance, unless suspended in their operation till his assent should be obtained; and when so suspended, he has utterly neglected to attend to them.

He has refused to pass other laws for the accommodation of large districts of people, unless those people would relinquish the right of representation in the Legislature, a right inestimable to them and formidable to tyrants only.

He has called together legislative bodies at places unusual, uncomfortable, and distant from the depository of their public records, for the sole purpose of fatiguing them into compliance with his measures.

He has dissolved representative houses repeatedly, for opposing with manly firmness his invasions on the rights of the people.

He has refused for a long time, after such dissolutions, to cause others to be elected; whereby the legislative powers, incapable of annihilation, have returned to the people at large for their exercise; the State remaining in the meantime exposed to all the dangers of invasion from without and convulsions within.

He has endeavored to prevent the population of these states; for that purpose obstructing the laws of naturalization of foreigners; refusing to pass others to encourage their migration hither, and raising the conditions of new appropriations of lands.

He has obstructed the administration of justice, by refusing his assent to laws for establishing judiciary powers.

He has made judges dependent on his will alone, for the tenure of their offices, and the amount and payment of their salaries.

He has erected a multitude of new offices, and sent hither swarms of officers to harass our people, and eat out their substance.

He has kept among us, in times of peace, standing armies without the consent of our legislatures.

He has affected to render the military independent of and superior to the civil power.

He has combined with others to subject us to a jurisdiction foreign to our constitution, and unacknowledged by our laws; giving his assent to their acts of pretended legislation:

For quartering large bodies of armed troops among us:

For protecting them, by a mock trial, from punishment for any murders which they should commit on the inhabitants of these States:

For cutting off our trade with all parts of the world:

For imposing taxes on us without our consent:

For depriving us in many cases, of the benefits of trial by jury:

For transporting us beyond seas to be tried for pretended offenses:

For abolishing the free system of English laws in a neighboring Province, establishing therein an arbitrary government, and enlarging its boundaries so as to render it at once an example and fit instrument for introducing the same absolute rule into these Colonies:

For taking away our Charters, abolishing our most valuable laws, and altering fundamentally the forms of our governments:

For suspending our own Legislatures, and declaring themselves invested with power to legislate for us in all cases whatsoever.

He has abdicated government here, by declaring us out of his protection and waging war against us.

He has plundered our seas, ravaged our coasts, burnt our towns, and destroyed the lives of our people.

He is at this time transporting large armies of foreign mercenaries to complete the works of death, desolation and tyranny, already begun with circumstances of cruelty and perfidy scarcely paralleled in the most barbarous ages, and totally unworthy the head of a civilized nation.

He has constrained our fellow citizens taken captive on the high seas to bear arms against their country, to become the executioners of their friends and brethren, or to fall themselves by their hands.

He has excited domestic insurrections amongst us, and has endeavored to bring on the inhabitants of our frontiers, the merciless Indian savages, whose known rule of warfare is an undistinguished destruction of all ages, sexes, and conditions.

In every stage of these oppressions we have petitioned for redress in the most humble terms: our repeated petitions have been answered only by repeated injury. A prince whose character is thus marked by every act which may define a tyrant is unfit to be the ruler of a free people.

Nor have we been wanting in attention to our British brethren. We have warned them from time to time of attempts by their legislature to extend an unwarrantable jurisdiction over us. We have reminded them of the circumstances of our emigration and settlement here. We have appealed to their native justice and magnanimity, and we have conjured them by the ties of our common kindred to disavow these usurpations, which would inevitably interrupt our connections and correspondence. They too have been deaf to the voice of justice and of consanguinity. We must, therefore, acquiesce in the necessity, which denounces our separation, and hold them, as we hold the rest of mankind, enemies in war, in peace friends.

WE THEREFORE, the Representatives of the UNITED STATES OF AMERICA, in General Congress assembled, appealing to the Supreme Judge of the world for the rectitude of our intentions, do, in the name, and by the authority of the good people of these Colonies, solemnly publish and declare. That these United Colonies are, and of right ought to be FREE and INDEPENDENT STATES; that they are absolved from all allegiance to the British Crown, and that all political connection between them and the State of Great Britain is, and ought to be totally dissolved; and that as Free and Independent States they have full power to levy war, conclude peace, contract alliances, establish commerce, and to do all other acts and things which Independent States may of right do. And for the support of this Declaration, with a firm reliance on the protection of Divine Providence, we mutually pledge to each other our lives, our fortunes, and our sacred honor.

Letter from Birmingham Jail

Martin Luther King, Jr.
Birmingham City Jail, April 16, 1963

Bishop C. C. J. Carpenter
Bishop Joseph A. Durick
Rabbi Milton L. Grafman
Bishop Paul Hardin
Bishop Nolan B. Harmon
The Rev. George M. Murray
The Rev. Edward V. Ramage
The Rev. Earl Stallings

My Dear Fellow Clergymen:

While confined here in the Birmingham City Jail, I came across your recent statement calling our present activities "unwise and untimely." Seldom, if ever, do I pause to answer criticism of my work and ideas. If I sought to answer all the criticisms that cross my desk, my secretaries would be engaged in little else in the course of the day and I would have no time for constructive work. But since I feel that you are men of genuine good will and your criticisms are sincerely set forth, I would like to answer your statement in what I hope will be patient and reasonable terms.

I think I should give the reason for my being in Birmingham, since you have been influenced by the argument of "outsiders coming in." I have the honor of serving as president of the Southern Christian Leadership Conference, an organization operating in every Southern state, with headquarters in Atlanta, Georgia. We have some eighty-five affiliate organizations all across the South—one being the Alabama Christian Movement for Human Rights. Whenever necessary and possible we share staff, educational, and financial resources with our affiliates. Several months ago our local affiliate here in Birmingham invited us to be on call to engage in a nonviolent direct action program if such were deemed necessary. We readily consented and when the hour came we lived up to our promises. So I am here, along with several members of my staff, because we were invited here. I am here because

46

I have basic organizational ties here. Beyond this, I am in Birmingham because injustice is here. Just as the eighth century prophets left their little villages and carried their "thus saith the Lord" far beyond the boundaries of their home town, and just as the Apostle Paul left his little village of Tarsus and carried the gospel of Jesus Christ to practically every hamlet and city of the Graeco-Roman world, I too am compelled to carry the gospel of freedom beyond my particular home town. Like Paul, I must constantly respond to the Macedonian call for aid.

Moreover, I am cognizant of the interrelatedness of all communities and states. I cannot sit idly by in Atlanta and not be concerned about what happens in Birmingham. Injustice anywhere is a threat to justice everywhere. We are caught in an inescapable network of mutuality tied in a single garment of destiny. Whatever affects one directly affects all indirectly. Never again can we afford to live with the narrow, provincial "outside agitator" idea. Anyone who lives inside the United States can never be considered an outsider anywhere in this country.

You deplore the demonstrations that are presently taking place in Birmingham. But I am sorry that your statement did not express a similar concern for the conditions that brought the demonstrations into being. I am sure that each of you would want to go beyond the superficial social analyst who looks merely at effects, and does not grapple with underlying causes. I would not hesitate to say that it is unfortunate that so-called demonstrations are taking place in Birmingham at this time, but I would say in more emphatic terms that it is even more unfortunate that the white power structure of this city left the Negro community with no other alternative.

In any nonviolent campaign there are four basic steps: (1) collection of the facts to determine whether injustices are alive; (2) negotiation; (3) self-purification; and (4) direct action. We have gone through all of these steps in Birmingham. There can be no gainsaying of the fact that racial injustice engulfs this community. Birmingham is probably the most thoroughly segregated city in the United States. Its ugly record of police brutality is known in every section of this country. Its unjust treatment of Negroes in the courts is a notorious reality. There have been more unsolved bombings of Negro homes and churches in Birmingham than any city in this nation. These are the hard, brutal, and unbelievable facts. On the basis of these conditions Negro leaders sought to negotiate with the city fathers. But the political leaders consistently refused to engage in good faith negotiation.

Then came the opportunity last September to talk with some of the leaders of the economic community. In these negotiating sessions certain promises were made by the merchants—such as the promise to remove the humiliating racial signs from the stores. On the basis of these promises Rev. Shuttlesworth and the leaders of the Alabama Christian Movement for Human Rights agreed to call a moratorium on any type of demonstrations. As the weeks and months unfolded we realized that we were the victims of a broken promise. The signs remained. As in so many experiences of the past we were confronted with blasted hopes, and the dark shadow of a deep disappointment settled upon us. So we had no alternative except that of preparing for direct action, whereby we would present our very bodies as a means of laying our case before the conscience of the local and national community. We were not unmindful of the difficulties involved. So we decided to go through a process of self-purification. We started having workshops on nonviolence and repeatedly asked ourselves the questions, "Are you able to accept blows without retaliating?" "Are you able to endure the ordeals of jail?"

We decided to set our direct action program around the Easter season, realizing that with the exception of Christmas, this was the largest shopping period of the year. Knowing that a strong economic withdrawal program would be the by-product of direct action, we felt that this was the best time to bring pressure on the merchants for the needed changes. Then it occurred to us that the March election was ahead, and so we speedily decided to postpone action until after election day. When we discovered that Mr. Connor was in the run-off, we decided again to postpone so that the demonstrations could not be used to cloud the issues. At this time we agreed to begin our nonviolent witness the day after the run-off.

This reveals that we did not move irresponsibly into direct action. We too wanted to see Mr. Connor defeated; so we went through postponement after postponement to aid in this community need. After this we felt that direct action could be delayed no longer.

You may well ask: "Why direct action? Why sit-ins, marches, etc.? Isn't negotiation a better path?" You are exactly right in your call for negotiation. Indeed, this is the purpose of direct action. Nonviolent direct action seeks to create such a crisis and establish such creative tension that a community that has constantly refused to negotiate is forced to confront the issue. It seeks so to dramatize the issue that it can no longer be ignored. I just referred to the creation of tension as a part of the work of the nonviolent resister. This may sound rather shocking. But I must confess that I am not afraid of the word tension. I have earnestly worked and preached against violent tension, but there is a type of constructive nonviolent tension that is necessary for growth. Just as Socrates felt that it was necessary to create a tension in the mind so that individuals could rise from the bondage of myths and half-truths to the unfettered realm of creative analysis and objective appraisal, we must see the need of having nonviolent gadflies to create the kind of tension in society that will help men to rise from the dark depths of prejudice and racism to the majestic heights of understanding and brotherhood. So the purpose of the direct action is to create a situation so crisis-packed that it will inevitably open the door to negotiation. We, therefore, concur with you in your call for negotiation. Too long has our beloved Southland been bogged down in the tragic attempt to live in monologue rather than dialogue.

One of the basic points in your statement is that our acts are untimely. Some have asked, "Why didn't you give the new administration time to act?" The only answer that I can give to this inquiry is that the new administration must be prodded about as much as the outgoing one before it acts. We will be sadly mistaken if we feel that the election of Mr. Boutwell will bring the millennium to Birmingham. While Mr. Boutwell is much more articulate and gentle than Mr. Connor, they are both segregationists dedicated to the task of maintaining the status quo. The hope I see in Mr. Boutwell is that he will be reasonable enough to see the futility of massive resistance to desegregation. But he will not see this without pressure from the devotees of civil rights. My friends, I must say to you that we have not made a single gain in civil rights without determined legal and nonviolent pressure. History is the long and tragic story of the fact that privileged groups seldom give up their privileges voluntarily. Individuals may see the moral light and voluntarily give up their unjust posture; but as Reinhold Niebuhr has reminded us, groups are more immoral than individuals.

We know through painful experience that freedom is never voluntarily given by the oppressor; it must be demanded by the oppressed. Frankly, I have never yet engaged in a direct action movement that was "well timed," according to the timetable of those who have not suffered unduly from the disease of segregation. For years now I have heard the word "Wait!" It rings in the ear of every Negro with a piercing familiarity. This "wait" has almost always meant "never." It has been a tranquilizing thalidomide, relieving the emotional stress for a moment, only to give birth to an ill-formed infant of frustration. We must come to see with the distinguished jurist of yesterday that "justice too long delayed is justice denied." We have waited for more than three hundred and forty years for our constitutional and God-given rights. The nations of Asia and Africa are moving with jet-like speed toward the goal of political independence, and we still creep at horse and buggy pace toward the gaining of a cup of coffee at a lunch counter.

I guess it is easy for those who have never felt the stinging darts of segregation to say wait. But when you have seen vicious mobs lynch your mothers and fathers at will and drown your sisters and brothers at whim; when you have seen hate filled policemen curse, kick, brutalize, and even kill your black brothers and sisters with impunity; when you see the vast majority of your twenty million Negro brothers smothering in an air-tight cage of poverty in the midst of an affluent society; when you suddenly find your tongue twisted and your speech stammering as you seek to explain to your six-year-old daughter why she can't go to the public amusement park that has just been advertised on television, and see tears welling up in her eyes when she is told that Funtown is closed to colored children, and see the depressing clouds of inferiority begin to form in her little mental sky, and see her begin to distort her little personality by unconsciously developing a bitterness toward white people; when you have to concoct an answer for a five-year-old son asking in agonizing pathos: "Daddy, why do white people treat colored people so mean?"; when you take a cross country drive and find it necessary to sleep night after night in the uncomfortable corners of your automobile because no motel will accept you; when you are humiliated day in and day out by nagging signs reading "white" and "colored"; when your first name becomes "nigger" and your middle name becomes "boy" (however old you are) and your last name becomes "John," and when your wife and mother are never given the respected title "Mrs."; when you are harried by day and haunted by night by the fact that you are a Negro, living constantly at tip-toe stance never quite knowing what to expect next, and plagued with inner fears and outer resentments; when you are forever fighting a degenerating sense of "nobodiness"—then you will understand why we find it difficult to wait. There comes a time when the cup of endurance runs over, and men are no longer willing to be plunged into an abyss of injustice where they experience the bleakness of corroding despair. I hope, sirs, you can understand our legitimate and unavoidable impatience.

You express a great deal of anxiety over our willingness to break laws. This is certainly a legitimate concern. Since we so diligently urge people to obey the Supreme Court's decision of 1954 outlawing segregation in the public schools, it is rather strange and paradoxical to find us consciously breaking laws. One may well ask: "How can you advocate breaking some laws and obeying others?" The answer is found in the fact that there are two types of laws. There are *just* and there are *unjust* laws. I would be the first to advocate obeying just laws. One has not only a legal but moral responsibiity to obey just laws. Conversely, one has a moral responsibility to disobey unjust laws. I would agree with Saint Augustine that "An unjust law is no law at all."

Now what is the difference between the two? How does one determine when a law is just or unjust? A just law is a man-made code that squares with the moral law or the law of God. An unjust law is a code that is out of harmony with the moral law. To put it in the terms of Saint Thomas Aquinas, an unjust law is a human law that is not rooted in eternal and natural law. Any law that uplifts human personality is just. Any law that degrades human personality is unjust. All segregation statutes are unjust because segregation distorts the soul and damages the personality. It gives the segregator a false sense of superiority and the segregated a false sense of inferiority. To use the words of Martin Buber, the Jewish philosopher, segregation substitutes an "I-it" relationship for an "I-thou" relationship, and ends up relegating persons to the status of things. So segregation is not only politically, economically, and sociologically unsound, but it is morally wrong and sinful. Paul Tillich has said that sin is separation. Isn't segregation an existential expression of man's tragic separation, an expression of his awful estrangement, his terrible sinfulness? So I can urge men to obey the 1954 decision of the Supreme Court because it is morally right, and I can urge them to disobey segregation ordinances because they are morally wrong.

Let us turn to a more concrete example of just and unjust laws. An unjust law is a code that a majority inflicts on a minority that is not binding on itself. This is *difference* made legal. On the other hand a just law is a code that a majority compels a minority to follow that it is willing to follow itself. This is *sameness* made legal.

Let me give another explanation. An unjust law is a code inflicted upon a minority which that minority had no part in enacting or creating because they did not have the unhampered right to vote. Who can say that the legislature of Alabama which set up the segregation laws was democratically elected? Throughout the state of Alabama all types of conniving methods are used to prevent Negroes from becoming registered voters and there are some counties without a single Negro registered to vote despite the fact that the Negro constitutes a majority of the population. Can any law set up in such a state be considered democratically structured?

These are just a few examples of unjust and just laws. There are some instances when a law is just on its face and unjust in its application. For instance, I was arrested Friday on a charge of parading without a permit. Now there is nothing wrong with an ordinance which requires a permit for a parade, but when the ordinance is used to preserve segregation and to deny citizens the

First Amendment privilege of peaceful assembly and peaceful protest, then it becomes unjust.

I hope you can see the distinction I am trying to point out. In no sense do I advocate evading or defying the law as the rabid segregationist would do. This would lead to anarchy. One who breaks an unjust law must do it *openly, lovingly,* (not hatefully as the white mothers did in New Orleans when they were seen on television screaming "nigger, nigger, nigger") and with a willingness to accept the penalty. I submit that an individual who breaks a law that conscience tells him is unjust, and willingly accepts the penalty by staying in jail to arouse the conscience of the community over its injustice, is in reality expressing the very highest respect for law.

Of course, there is nothing new about this kind of civil disobedience. It was seen sublimely in the refusal of Shadrach, Meshach, and Abednego to obey the laws of Nebuchadnezzar because a higher moral law was involved. It was practiced superbly by the early Christians who were willing to face hungry lions and the excruciating pain of chopping blocks, before submitting to certain unjust laws of the Roman Empire. To a degree academic freedom is a reality today because Socrates practiced civil disobedience.

We can never forget that everything Hitler did in Germany was "legal" and everything the Hungarian freedom fighters did in Hungary was "illegal." It was "illegal" to aid and comfort a Jew in Hitler's Germany. But I am sure that if I had lived in Germany during that time, I would have aided and comforted my Jewish brothers even though it was illegal. If I lived in a communist country today where certain principles dear to the Christian faith are suppressed, I believe I would openly advocate disobeying those antireligious laws.

I must make two honest confessions to you, my Christian and Jewish brothers. First I must confess that over the last few years I have been gravely disappointed with the white moderate. I have almost reached the regrettable conclusion that the Negros' great stumbling blocks in the stride toward freedom is not the White Citizens' "Councillor" or the Ku Klux Klanner, but the white moderate who is more devoted to "order" than to justice; who prefers a negative peace which is the absence of tension to a positive peace which is the presence of justice; who constantly says "I agree with you in the goal you seek, but I can't agree with your methods of direct action"; who paternalistically feels that he can set the timetable for another man's freedom; who lives by the myth of time and who constantly advises the Negro to wait until a "more convenient season." Shallow understanding from people of good will is more frustrating than absolute misunderstanding from people of ill will. Lukewarm acceptance is much more bewildering than outright rejection.

I had hoped that the white moderate would understand that law and order exist for the purpose of establishing justice, and that when they fail to do this they become dangerously structured dams that block the flow of social progress. I had hoped that the white moderate would understand that the present tension in the South is merely a necessary phase of the transition from an obnoxious negative peace, where the Negro passively accepted his unjust plight, to a substance-filled positive peace, where all men will respect the dignity and worth of human personality. Actually, we who engage in nonviolent direct action are not the creators of tension. We merely bring to the surface the hidden tension that is already alive. We bring it out in the open where it can be seen and dealt with. Like a boil that can never be cured as long as it is covered up but must be opened with all its pus-flowing ugliness to the natural medicines of air and light, injustice must likewise be exposed, with all of the tension its exposing creates, to the light of human conscience and the air of national opinion before it can be cured.

In your statement you asserted that our actions, even though peaceful, must be condemned because they precipitate violence. But can this assertion be logically made? Isn't this like condemning the robbed man because his possession of money precipitated the evil act of robbery? Isn't this like condemning Socrates because his unswerving commitment to truth and his philosophical delvings precipitated the misguided popular mind to make him drink the hemlock? Isn't this like condemning Jesus because His unique God consciousness and never-ceasing devotion to His will precipitated the evil act of crucifixion? We must come to see, as the federal courts have consistently affirmed, that it is immoral to urge an individual to withdraw his efforts to gain his basic constitutional rights because the quest precipitates violence. Society must protect the robbed and punish the robber.

I had also hoped that the white moderate would reject the myth of time. I received a letter this morning from a white brother in Texas which said: "All Christians know that the colored people will receive equal rights eventually, but it is possible that you are in too great of a religious hurry. It has taken Christianity almost 2000 years to accomplish what it has. The teachings of Christ take time to come to earth." All that is said here grows out of a tragic misconception of time. It is the the strangely irrational notion that there is something in the very flow of time that will inevitably cure all ills. Actually time is neutral. It can be used either destructively or constructively. I am coming to feel that the people of ill will have used time much more effectively than the people of good will. We will have to repent in this generation not merely for the vitriolic words and actions of the bad people, but for the appalling silence of the

vitriolic

good people. We must come to see that human progress never rolls in on wheels of inevitability. It comes through the tireless efforts and persistent work of men willing to be co-workers with God, and without this hard work time itself becomes an ally of the forces of social stagnation.

We must use time creatively, and forever realize that the time is always ripe to do right. Now is the time to make real the promise of democracy, and transform our pending national elegy into a creative psalm of brotherhood. Now is the time to lift our national policy from the quicksand of racial injustice to the solid rock of human dignity.

You spoke of our activity in Birmingham as extreme. At first I was rather disappointed that fellow clergymen would see my nonviolent efforts as those of the extremist. I started thinking about the fact that I stand in the middle of two opposing forces in the Negro community. One is a force of complacency made up of Negroes who, as a result of long years of oppression, have been so completely drained of self-respect and a sense of "somebodiness" that they have adjusted to segregation, and of a few Negroes in the middle class who, because of a degree of academic and economic security, and because at points they profit by segregation, have unconsciously become insensitive to the problems of the masses. The other force is one of bitterness and hatred and comes perilously close to advocating violence. It is expressed in the various black nationalist groups that are springing up over the nation, the largest and best known being Elijah Muhammad's Muslim movement. This movement is nourished by the contemporary frustration over the continued existence of racial discrimination. It is made up of people who have lost faith in America, who have absolutely repudiated Christianity, and who have concluded that the white man is an incurable "devil." I have tried to stand between these two forces saying that we need not follow the "do-nothingism" of the complacent or the hatred and despair of the black nationalist. There is the more excellent way of love and nonviolent protest. I'm grateful to God that, through the Negro church, the dimension of nonviolence entered our struggle. If this philosophy had not emerged I am convinced that by now many streets of the South would be flowing with floods of blood. And I am further convinced that if our white brothers dismiss us as "rabble rousers" and "outside agitators"—those of us who are working through the channels of nonviolent direct action—and refuse to support our nonviolent efforts, millions of Negroes, out of frustration and despair, will seek solace and security in black nationalist ideologies, a development that will lead inevitably to a frightening racial nightmare.

Oppressed people cannot remain oppressed forever. The urge for freedom will eventually come. This is what happened to the American Negro.

Something within has reminded him of his birthright of freedom; something without has reminded him that he can gain it. Consciously and unconsciously, he has been swept in by what the Germans call the *Zeitgeist*, and with his black brothers of Africa, and his brown and yellow brothers of Asia, South America, and the Caribbean, he is moving with a sense of cosmic urgency toward the promised land of racial justice. Recognizing this vital urge that has engulfed the Negro community, one should readily understand public demonstrations. The Negro has many pent-up resentments and latent frustrations. He has to get them out. So let him march sometime; let him have his prayer pilgrimages to the city hall; understand why he must have sit-ins and freedom rides. If his repressed emotions do not come out in these nonviolent ways, they will come out in ominous expressions of violence. This is not a threat; it is a fact of history. So I have not said to my people, "Get rid of your discontent." But I have tried to say that this normal and healthy discontent can be channeled through the creative outlet of nonviolent direct action. Now this approach is being dismissed as extremist. I must admit that I was initially disappointed in being so categorized.

But as I continued to think about the matter I gradually gained a bit of satisfaction from being considered an extremist. Was not Jesus an extremist in love? "Love your enemies, bless them that curse you, pray for them that despitefully use you." Was not Amos an extremist for justice—"Let justice roll down like waters and righteousness like a mighty stream." Was not Paul an extremist for the gospel of Jesus Christ—"I bear in my body the marks of the Lord Jesus." Was not Martin Luther an extremist—"Here I stand; I can do none other so help me God." Was not John Bunyan an extremist—"I will stay in jail to the end of my days before I make a butchery of my conscience." Was not Abraham Lincoln an extremist—"This nation cannot survive half slave and half free." Was not Thomas Jefferson an extremist—"We hold these truths to be self-evident, that all men are created equal." So the question is not whether we will be extremist but what kind of extremist will we be. Will we be extremists for hate or will we be extremists for love? Will we be extremists for the preservation of injustice—or will we be extremists for the cause of justice? In that dramatic scene on Calvary's hill, three men were crucified. We must never forget that all three were crucified for the same crime—the crime of extremism. Two were extremists for immorality, and thus fell below their environment. The other, Jesus Christ, was an extremist for love, truth, and goodness, and thereby rose above His environment. So, after all, maybe the South, the nation and the world are in dire need of creative extremists.

I had hoped that the white moderate would see this. Maybe I was too optimistic. Maybe I expected too much. I guess I should have realized that few members of a race that has oppressed another race can understand or appreciate the deep groans and passionate yearnings of those that have been oppressed, and still fewer have the vision to see that injustice must be rooted out by strong, persistent, and determined action. I am thankful, however, that some of our white brothers have grasped the meaning of this social revolution and committed themselves to it. They are still all too small in quantity, but they are big in quality. Some like Ralph McGill, Lillian Smith, Harry Golden, and James Dabbs have written about our struggle in eloquent, prophetic, and understanding terms. Others have marched with us down nameless streets of the South. They have languished in filthy roach-infested jails, suffering the abuse and brutality of angry policemen who see them as "dirty nigger lovers." They, unlike so many of their moderate brothers and sisters, have recognized the urgency of the moment and sensed the need for powerful "action" anti-dotes to combat the disease of segregation.

Let me rush on to mention my other disappointment. I have been so greatly disappointed with the white Church and its leadership. Of course there are some notable exceptions. I am not unmindful of the fact that each of you has taken some significant stands on this issue. I commend you, Rev. Stallings, for your Christian stand on this past Sunday, in welcoming Negroes to your worship service on a nonsegregated basis. I commend the Catholic leaders of this state for integrating Spring Hill College several years ago.

But despite these notable exceptions I must honestly reiterate that I have been disappointed with the Church. I do not say that as one of those negative critics who can always find something wrong with the Church. I say it as a minister of the gospel, who loves the Church; who was nurtured in its bosom; who has been sustained by its spiritual blessings and who will remain true to it as long as the cord of life shall lengthen.

I had the strange feeling when I was suddenly catapulted into the leader-ship of the bus protest in Montgomery several years ago that we would have the support of the white Church. I felt that the white ministers, priests, and rabbis of the South would be some of our strongest allies. Instead, some have been outright opponents, refusing to understand the freedom movement and misrepresenting its leaders; all too many others have been more cautious than courageous and have remained silent behind the anesthetizing security of the stained glass windows.

In spite of my shattered dreams of the past, I came to Birmingham with the hope that the white religious leadership of this community would see the justice of our cause and, with deep moral concern, serve as the channel through which our just grievances would get to the power structure. I had hoped that each of you would understand. But again I have been disappointed.

I have heard numerous religious leaders of the South call upon their worshippers to comply with a desegregation decision because it is the law, but I have longed to hear white ministers say follow this decree because integration is morally right and the Negro is your brother. In the midst of blatant injustices inflicted upon the Negro, I have watched white churches stand on the sideline and merely mouth pious irrelevancies and sanctimonious trivialities. In the midst of a mighty struggle to rid our nation of racial and economic injustice, I have heard so many ministers say, "Those are social issues with which the Gospel has no real concern," and I have watched so many churches commit themselves to a completely otherworldly religion which made a strange distinction between body and soul, the sacred and the secular.

So here we are moving toward the exit of the twentieth century with a religious community largely adjusted to the status quo, standing as a tail light behind other community agencies rather than a headlight leading men to higher levels of justice.

I have traveled the length and breadth of Alabama, Mississippi, and all the other Southern states. On sweltering summer days and crisp autumn mornings I have looked at her beautiful churches with their lofty spires pointing heavenward. I have beheld the impressive outlay of her massive religious education buildings. Over and over again I have found myself asking: "Who worships here? Who is their God? Where were their voices when the lips of Governor Barnett dripped with words of interposition and nullification? Where were they when Governor Wallace gave the clarion call for defiance and hatred? Where were their voices of support when tired, bruised, and weary Negro men and women decided to rise from the dark dungeons of complacency to the bright hills of creative protest?"

Yes, these questions are still in my mind. In deep disappointment, I have wept over the laxity of the Church. But be assured that my tears have been tears of love. There can be no deep disappointment where there is not deep love. Yes, I love the Church; I love her sacred walls. How could I do otherwise? I am in the rather unique position of being the son, the grandson and the great-grandson of preachers. Yes, I see the Church as the body of Christ. But, oh! How we have blemished and scarred that body through social neglect and fear of being nonconformists.

There was a time when the Church was very powerful. It was during that period when the early Christians rejoiced when they were deemed worthy to suffer for what they believed. In those days the Church was not merely a thermometer that recorded the ideas and principles of popular opinion; it was a thermostat that transformed the mores of society. Wherever the early Christians entered a town the power structure got disturbed and immediately sought to convict them for being "disturbers of the peace" and "outside agitators." But they went on with the conviction that they were a "colony of heaven" and had to obey God rather than man. They were small in number but big in commitment. They were too God-intoxicated to be "astronomically intimidated." They brought an end to such ancient evils as infanticide and gladiatorial contest.

Things are different now. The contemporary Church is often a weak, ineffectual voice with an uncertain sound. It is so often the archsupporter of the status quo. Far from being disturbed by the presence of the Church, the power structure of the average community is consoled by the Church's silent and often vocal sanction of things as they are.

But the judgment of God is upon the Church as never before. If the Church of today does not recapture the sacrificial spirit of the early Church, it will lose its authentic ring, forfeit the loyalty of millions, and be dismissed as an irrelevant social club with no meaning for the twentieth century. I am meeting young people every day whose disappointment with the Church has risen to outright disgust.

Maybe again I have been too optimistic. Is organized religion too inextricably bound to status quo to save our nation and the world? Maybe I must turn my faith to the inner spiritual Church, the church within the Church, as the true *ecclesia* and the hope of the world. But again I am thankful to God that some noble souls from the ranks of organized religion have broken loose from the paralyzing chains of conformity and joined us as active partners in the struggle for freedom. They have left their secure congregations and walked the streets of Albany, Georgia, with us. They have gone through the highways of the South on tortuous rides for freedom. Yes, they have gone to jail with us. Some have been kicked out of their churches, and lost support of their bishops and fellow ministers. But they have gone with the faith that right defeated is stronger than evil triumphant. These men have been the leaven in the lump of the race. Their witness has been the spiritual salt that has preserved the true meaning of the Gospel in these troubled times. They have carved a tunnel of hope though the dark mountain of disappointment.

I hope the Church as a whole will meet the challenge of this decisive hour. But even if the Church does not come to the aid of justice, I have no despair about the future. I have no fear about the outcome of our struggle in

Birmingham, even if our motives are presently misunderstood. We will reach the goal of freedom in Birmingham and all over the nation, because the goal of America is freedom. Abused and scorned though we may be, our destiny is tied up with the destiny of America. Before the pilgrims landed at Plymouth, we were here. Before the pen of Jefferson etched across the pages of history the majestic words of the Declaration of Independence, we were here. For more than two centuries our foreparents labored in this country without wages; they made cotton "king"; and they built the homes of their masters in the midst of brutal injustice and shameful humiliation—and yet out of a bottomless vitality they continued to thrive and develop. If the inexpressible cruelties of slavery could not stop us, the opposition we now face will surely fail. We will win our freedom because the sacred heritage of our nation and the eternal will of God are embodied in our echoing demands.

I must close now. But before closing I am impelled to mention one other point in your statement that troubled me profoundly. You warmly commended the Birmingham police force for keeping "order" and "preventing violence." I don't believe you would have so warmly commended the police force if you had seen its angry violent dogs literally biting six unarmed, nonviolent Negroes. I don't believe you would so quickly commend the policemen if you would observe their ugly and inhuman treatment of Negroes here in the city jail; if you would watch them push and curse old Negro women and young Negro girls; if you would see them slap and kick old Negro men and young boys; if you will observe them, as they did on two occasions, refuse to give us food because we wanted to sing our grace together. I'm sorry that I can't join you in your praise for the police department.

It is true that they have been rather disciplined in their public handling of the demonstrators. In this sense they have been rather publicly "nonviolent." But for what purpose? To preserve the evil system of segregation. Over the last few years I have consistently preached that nonviolence demands that the means we use must be as pure as the ends we seek. So I have tried to make it clear that it is wrong to use immoral means to attain moral ends. But now I must affirm that it is just as wrong, or even more so, to use moral means to preserve immoral ends. Maybe Mr. Connor and his policemen have been rather publicly nonviolent, as Chief Pritchett was in Albany, Georgia, but they have used the moral means of nonviolence to maintain the immoral end of flagrant racial injustice. T. S. Eliot has said that there is no greater treason than to do the right deed for the wrong reason.

I wish you had commended the Negro sit-inners and demonstrators of Birmingham for their sublime courage, their willingness to suffer, and their amazing discipline in the midst of the most inhuman provocation. One day the South will recognize its real heroes. They will be the James Merediths, courageously and with a majestic sense of purpose, facing jeering and hostile mobs and with the agonizing loneliness that characterizes the life of the pioneer. They will be old, oppressed, battered Negro women, symbolized in a seventy-two year old woman of Montgomery, Alabama, who rose up with a sense of dignity and with her people decided not to ride the segregated buses, and responded to one who inquired about her tiredness with ungrammatical profundity; "My feet is tired, but my soul is rested." They will be the young high school and college students, young ministers of the gospel and a host of the elders courageously and nonviolently sitting in at lunch counters and willingly going to jail for conscience sake. One day the South will know that when these disinherited children of God sat down at lunch counters they were in reality standing up for the best in the American dream and the most sacred values in our Judeo-Christian heritage, and thus carrying our whole nation back to those great wells of democracy which were dug deep by the founding fathers in the formulation of the Constitution and the Declaration of Independence.

Never before have I written a letter this long, (or should I say a book?). I'm afraid that it is much too long to take your precious time. I can assure you that it would have been much shorter if I had been writing from a comfortable desk, but what else is there to do when you are alone for days in the dull monotony of a narrow jail cell other than write long letters, think strange thoughts, and pray long prayers?

If I have said anything in this letter that is an overstatement of the truth and is indicative of an unreasonable impatience, I beg you to forgive me. If I have said anything in this letter that is an understatement of the truth and is indicative of my having a patience that makes me patient with anything less than brotherhood, I beg God to forgive me.

I hope this letter finds you strong in the faith. I also hope that circumstances will soon make it possible for me to meet each of you, not as an integrationist or a civil rights leader, but as a fellow clergyman and a Christian brother. Let us all hope that the dark clouds of racial prejudice will soon pass away and the deep fog of misunderstanding will be lifted from our fear-drenched communities and in some not too distant tomorrow the radiant stars of love and brotherhood will shine over our great nation with all their scintillating beauty.

Yours for the cause of
Peace and Brotherhood
Martin Luther King, Jr.

from *Don Quixote*

Miguel de Cervantes

CHAPTER XXXIII

Which recounts the novel of The Man Who Was Recklessly Curious [1]

In Florence, a rich and famous Italian city in the province called Tuscany, lived two wealthy, eminent gentlemen who were such good friends that they were known by everyone as the *two friends*. They were bachelors, young men who were of the same age and habits, all of which was sufficient cause for both of them to feel a mutual, reciprocal friendship. True, Anselmo was somewhat more inclined to amorous pursuits than Lotario, whose preferred pastime was the hunt, but when the occasion presented itself, Anselmo would leave his pleasures to follow those of Lotario, and Lotario would leave his to pursue those of Anselmo, and in this fashion their desires were so attuned that a well-adjusted clock did not run as well.

Anselmo was deeply in love with a distinguished and beautiful girl from the same city, the daughter of such excellent parents, and so excellent in and of herself, that he decided, with his friend Lotario's agreement, without which he did nothing, to ask her parents for her hand, which he did; his intermediary was Lotario, and he concluded the arrangements so successfully for his friend that in a short time Anselmo found himself in possession of what he desired; Camila was so happy at having Anselmo for a husband that she unceasingly gave her thanks to heaven, and to Lotario; through whose intervention so much contentment had come to her. In the first days of the nuptial celebrations, which are always filled with joy, Lotario continued to visit the house of his friend Anselmo as he had before, wishing to honor him, congratulate him, and rejoice With him in every way he could, but when the celebrations were over and the frequency of visits and congratulations had diminished, Lotario carefully began to reduce the number of his visits to Anselmo's house, for it seemed to him—as it reasonably would seem to all discerning people—that one should not visit or linger at the houses of married friends as if both were still single; although good and true friendship cannot and should not be suspect for any reason, the honor of the married man is so delicate that it apparently can be offended even by his own brothers, let alone his friends.

Anselmo noticed Lotario's withdrawal and complained to him bitterly, saying that if he had known that matrimony meant they could not communicate as they once had, he never would have married, and if the good relations the two of them had enjoyed when he was a bachelor had earned them the sweet name of *the two friends*, then he would not, merely for the sake of appearing circumspect and for no other reason, permit so well-known and amiable a name to be lost; therefore he begged Lotario, if such a term could legitimately be used between them, that he make Anselmo's house his own again, and come and go as he had before, assuring him that his wife, Camila, had no wish or desire other than what he wanted her to have, and she, knowing how truly the two men had loved each other, was bewildered at seeing him so aloof.

To these and the many other arguments that Anselmo used to persuade Lotario to visit his house as he had in the past, Lotario responded with so much prudence, discretion, and discernment that Anselmo was satisfied with his friend's good intentions, and they agreed that twice a week and on feast days Lotario would eat with Anselmo in his house, and although this was their agreement, Lotario resolved to do no more than what he thought would enhance the honor of his friend, whose reputation he valued more than he did his own. He said, and rightly so, that the man to whom heaven has granted a beautiful wife had to be as careful about the friends he brought home as he was about the women with whom his wife associated, because those things not done or arranged on open squares, or in temples, or at public festivals, or on devotional visits to churches—activities that husbands may not always deny to their wives—can be arranged and expedited in the house of her most trusted friend or kinswoman.

Lotario also said that a married man needed to have a friend who would alert him to any negligence in his behavior, since it often happens that because of the great love the husband has for his wife, and his desire not to distress her, he does not warn or tell her to do or not do certain things that could either redound to his honor or cause his censure, but being advised by his friend, he could easily resolve everything. Where could one find a friend as discerning and loyal and true as the one described by Lotario? Certainly I do not know; Lotario alone was the kind of friend who, with utmost care and solicitude, looked after his friend's honor and wished to lessen, reduce, and diminish the number of days he went to his house so that it would not seem amiss to the idle crowd and its wandering, malicious eyes that a wealthy, noble, and well-born young man, possessing the other good qualities he believed he had, habitually visited the house of a woman as beautiful as Camila; although her virtue and modesty could put a stop to any malicious tongue, he did not want any doubts cast on her good name or his friend's; as a consequence, on most of the visiting days that they had agreed upon, he was occupied and involved in other matters that he claimed were unavoidable, and so a large portion of the time they did spend together was devoted to the complaints of one friend and the excuses of the other.

As it happened, on one of these occasions, when the two men were walking through a meadow outside the city, Anselmo said these words to Lotario:

"Did you think, Lotario my friend, that I cannot respond with gratitude that matches the bounty I have received: the mercies God has shown in making me the son of parents such as mine, and granting me with so generous a hand so many advantages, in what is called nature as well as in fortune, and especially His granting me you as a friend and Camila as my wife, two treasures I esteem, if not as much as I ought to, at least as much as I can? Yet despite all these elements that usually make up the whole that allows men to live happily, I am the most desperate and discontented man in the entire world, because for some days now I have been troubled and pursued by a desire so strange and out of the ordinary that I am amazed at myself, and blame and reprimand myself, and attempt to silence it and hide it away from my thoughts, though I have been no more capable of keeping it secret than if my intention actually had been to reveal it to the entire world. And since, in fact, it must be made public, I want to confide and entrust it to you, certain that with the effort you make, as my true friend, to cure me, I soon shall find myself free of the anguish it causes me, and my joy at your solicitude will be as great as my unhappiness at my own madness."

Anselmo's words left Lotario perplexed, and he did not know where so long an introduction or preamble would lead, and although in his imagination he pondered what the desire could be that was troubling his friend, he never hit the mark of the truth, and in order to quickly end the torment that this uncertainty caused him, Lotario said that it was manifestly insulting to their great friendship for Anselmo to go through so many preliminaries before telling him his most secret thoughts, for he was certain he could promise either the advice that would make them bearable or the remedy that would end them.

"What you say is true," responded Anselmo, "and with that confidence I will tell you, friend Lotario, that the desire that plagues me is my wondering if Camila, my wife, is as good and perfect as I think she is, and I cannot learn the truth except by testing her so that the test reveals the worth of her virtue, as fire shows the worth of gold. Because it seems to me, dear friend, that a woman is not virtuous if she is not solicited, and that she alone is strong who does not bend to promises, gifts, tears, and the constant importunities of lovers who woo her. Why be grateful when a woman is good," he said, "if no one urges her to be bad? Why is it of consequence that she is shy and reserved if she does not have the occasion to lose her restraint and knows she has a husband who, at her first rash act, would take her life? In short, I do not hold the woman who is virtuous because of fear or lack of opportunity in the same esteem as the one who is courted and pursued and emerges wearing the victor's crown. For these reasons, and many others I could mention that support and strengthen this opinion, my desire is for Camila, my wife, to pass through these difficulties, and be refined and prove her value in the fire of being wooed and courted by one worthy of desiring her; and if she emerges, as I believe she will, triumphant from this battle, I shall deem my good fortune unparalleled; I shall be able to say that the cup of my desires is filled to overflowing; I shall say that it fell to me to have a wife strong in virtue, about whom the Wise Man says, 'Who will find her?' And if the outcome is the contrary of what I expect, the pleasure of seeing that I was correct in my opinion will allow me to bear the sorrow that my costly experiment may reasonably cause me. And because you can say many things against my desire but none will succeed in stopping me from realizing it, I want you, my dear friend Lotario, to agree to be the instrument that will effect this plan born of my desire: I shall give you the opportunity to do so, and provide you with everything I think necessary for wooing a woman who is virtuous, honorable, reserved, and not mercenary. Among other reasons, I am moved to entrust you with this arduous undertaking because I know that if Camila is conquered by you, you will not carry the conquest to its conclusion but will do only what has to be done according to our agreement, and I shall not be offended except in desire, and the offense will remain hidden in the virtue of your silence, for I know very well that in any matter having to do with me, it will be as eternal as the silence of death. Therefore, if you want me to have a life that can be called a life, you must enter into this amorous battle, not in a lukewarm or dilatory fashion but with the zeal and diligence that my desire demands, and with the trust assured me by our friendship."

These were the words that Anselmo said to Lotario, who listened so attentively to all of them that, except for those that have been recorded here, none passed his lips until Anselmo had finished; seeing that he had nothing else to say, and after looking at him for a long time as if he were looking at something amazing and terrifying that he had never seen before, Lotario said:

"I cannot persuade myself, O my dear friend Anselmo, that the things you have said are not a joke; if I had thought you were speaking in earnest, I would not have allowed you to go so far, and if I had stopped listening, I would have forestalled your long, impassioned speech. It surely seems to me that you don't know me or I don't know you. But no; I know very well that you are Anselmo, and you know that I am Lotario; the problem is that I think you are not the Anselmo you used to be, and you must have thought I was not the same Lotario, either, because the things you have said to me would not have been said by my friend Anselmo, and what you have asked of me would not have been asked of the Lotario you knew; good friends may test their friends and make use of them, as a poet said, *usque ad aras*,[2] which means that they must not make use of their friendship in things that go against God. If a pagan felt this about friendship, how much more important is it for a Christian to feel the same, for he knows that divine friendship must not be lost for the sake of human friendship. When a friend goes so far as to set aside the demands of heaven in order to respond to those of his friend, it should not be for vain, trivial things but for those on which the honor and life of his friend depend. Well, Anselmo, tell me now which of these is threatened, so that I can dare oblige you and do something as detestable as what you are asking. Neither one, certainly, rather, if I understand you, you are asking me to attempt and endeavor to take away your honor and your life, and mine as well. Because if I attempt to take away your honor, it is obvious that I take away your life, for the man without honor is worse than dead, and if, as you wish, I become the instrument that inflicts so much evil upon you, do I not lose my honor, and, by the same token, my life? Listen, Anselmo my friend, and have the patience not to respond until I finish telling you what I think of the demands your desire has made of you; there will be time for you to reply and for me to listen."

"Gladly," said Anselmo. "Say whatever you wish." And Lotario continued, saying:

"It seems to me, my dear Anselmo, that your mind is now in the state in which the Moors have theirs, for they cannot be made to understand the error of their sect with commentaries from Holy Scripture, or arguments that depend on the rational understanding or are founded on articles of faith; instead, they must be presented with palpable, comprehensible, intelligible, demonstrable, indubitable examples, with mathematical proofs that cannot be denied, as when one says, 'If, from two equal parts, we remove equal parts, those parts that remain are also equal'; if they do not understand the words, as in fact they do not, then it must be shown to them with one's hands, and placed before their eyes, yet even after all this, no one can persuade them of the truths of my holy religion. I must use the same terms and methods with you, because the desire that has been born in you is so misguided and so far beyond everything that has a shred of rationality in it that I think it would be a waste of time to try to make you understand your foolishness; for the moment I do not wish to give it another name. I am even tempted to leave you to your folly as punishment for your wicked desire, but my friendship for you does not permit me to be so harsh that I leave you in obvious danger of perdition. And so that you can see it clearly, tell me, Anselmo: haven't you told me that I have to woo a reserved woman, persuade an honest woman, make offers to an unmercenary woman, serve a prudent woman? Yes, you have said that to me. But if you know you have a wife who is reserved, honest, unmercenary, and prudent, what else do you need to know? And if you believe she will emerge victorious from all my assaults, as she undoubtedly will, what designations do you plan to give her afterward that are better than the ones she has now? What will she be afterward that is better than what she is now? Either your opinion of her is not what you say it is, or you do not know what you are asking. If your opinion of her is not what you say it is, why do you want to test her instead of treating her as an unfaithful woman and chastising her as you see fit? But if she is as virtuous as you believe, it would be reckless to experiment with that truth, for when you have done so, it will still have the same value it had before. Therefore we must conclude that attempting actions more likely to harm us than to benefit us is characteristic of rash minds bereft of reason, especially when they are not forced or compelled to undertake them, and when even from a distance it is obvious that the venture is an act of patent madness.

One attempts extremely difficult enterprises for the sake of God, or for the sake of the world, or both; those attempted for God are the ones undertaken by the saints, who endeavor to live the lives of angels in human bodies; those attempted with the world in mind are undertaken by men who endure such infinite seas, diverse climates, and strange peoples in order to acquire great riches. And those ventured for God and the world together are undertaken by valiant soldiers who, as soon as they see in the enemy defenses an opening no larger than the one made by a cannon ball, set aside all fear, do not consider or notice the clear danger that threatens them, and, borne on the wings of their desire to defend their faith, their nation, and their king, hurl themselves boldly into the midst of the thousand possible deaths that await them. These are perilous actions that are ordinarily ventured; and it is honor, glory, and advantage to attempt them despite the many obstacles and dangers. But the one you say you wish to attempt and put into effect will not win you the glory of God, or great riches, or fame among men; even if the outcome is as you desire, you will not be more content, more wealthy, more honored than you are now, and if it is not, you will find yourself in the greatest misery imaginable; then it will be to no avail to think that no one is aware of the misfortune that has befallen you; your knowing will be enough to make you suffer and grieve.

As confirmation of this truth, I want to recite for you a stanza written by the famous poet Luis Tansilo,[3] at the end of the first part of his *The Tears of St. Peter*, which says:

> There grows grief and there grows shame
> in Peter, when the day has dawned,
> and though he sees no one is near
> he feels a deep shame for his sin:
> for a great heart will be moved
> to shame, even if unseen,
> when it transgresses, shame though
> seen by nought but earth and sky.

In similar fashion, you will not escape sorrow even if it is secret; instead, you will weep constantly, if not tears from your eyes, then tears of blood from your heart, like those shed by the simple doctor who, as our poet recounts, agreed to the test of the goblet,[4] while the prudent and more rational Reinaldos refused; although this is poetic fiction, it contains hidden moral truths worthy of being heeded and understood and imitated, especially if, in light of what I am going to say to you now, you come to realize the magnitude of the error you wish to commit.

Tell me, Anselmo: if heaven, or good luck, had made you the possessor and legitimate owner of a fine diamond whose worth and value satisfied every jeweler who saw it, and all of them were of one opinion and said in one voice that in value, size, and purity it was all that such a stone could be, and you believed this as well, having no knowledge to the contrary, would it be reasonable for you to take that diamond, and place it between an anvil and a hammer, and by dint of powerful blows test if it was as hard and fine as they said? Moreover, in the event you did this, and the stone withstood so foolish a test, it would not, for that reason, gain in value or fame, but if it shattered, which is possible, wouldn't everything be lost? Yes, certainly, and its owner would be thought a fool by everyone.

Then understand, Anselmo my friend, that Camila is a fine diamond, both in your estimation and in that of others, and there is no reason to put her at risk of shattering, for even if she remains whole, she cannot become more precious than she is now; and if she fails and does not resist, consider how you would feel without her, and how correctly you would blame yourself for having been the cause of her ruination and your own. For there is no jewel in the world as valuable as a chaste and honorable woman, and women's honor consists entirely of the good opinion others have of them; since you know that the good opinion people have of your wife is as high as it can be, why do you want to cast doubt upon this truth? Look, my friend: woman is an imperfect creature, and one should not lay down obstacles where she can stumble and fall; instead, one should remove them and clear all impediments from her path so that she may run easily and quickly to reach the perfection she lacks, which consists in being virtuous.

Naturalists tells us that the ermine is an animal with pure white fur, and when hunters want to trap it, they use this trick: knowing the places where it customarily travels and can be found, they obstruct those places with mud, and then they beat the bushes and drive it toward that spot, and when the ermine reaches the mud it stops and lets itself be captured and caught rather than pass through the mire and risk soiling and losing the whiteness that it values more than liberty and life. The honest and chaste woman is the ermine, and the purity of her virtue is whiter and cleaner than snow; the man who wants her not to lose it but to keep and preserve it must treat her in a manner different from the one used with an ermine; he should not place mud before her—I mean the gifts and wooing of importunate lovers—because perhaps, and there is no perhaps about it, she does not have enough virtue and natural strength to overcome and surmount those obstacles by herself; it is necessary to remove them and place before her the purity of virtue and the beauty that lies in a good reputation.

In similar fashion, the chaste woman is like a mirror of clear, shining glass, liable to be clouded and darkened by any breath that touches it. One must treat the virtuous woman as one treats relics: adore them but not touch them. One must protect and esteem the chaste woman as one protects and esteems a beautiful garden filled with flowers and roses; its owner does not permit people to pass through and handle the flowers; it is enough that from a distance, through the iron bars of the fence, they enjoy its fragrance and beauty.

Finally, I want to recite for you some verses that have just come to mind; I heard them in a modern play, and I think they are relevant to what we are discussing. A prudent old man was advising the father of a young girl to shelter her, protect her, and keep her secluded, and among many other reasons, he mentioned these:

> Woman is made of fragile glass;
> but do not put her to the test

to see if she will break,
for that might come to pass.
She is too apt to shatter,
and wisdom is surely ended
if what can ne'er be mended
is put in the way of danger.
What I say to you is true,
and let us all agree;
wherever Danae may be,
showers of gold are there, too.[5]

Everything I have said so far, Anselmo, refers to you; now it is time for you to hear something that has to do with me, and if it takes a long time, forgive me, but it is demanded by the labyrinth into which you have walked and from which you wish me to free you. You consider me your friend, yet you wish to take my honor, which is counter to all friendship; not only that, but you want me to try to take yours. It is clear that you want to take mine, for when Camila sees me wooing her, as you are asking me to do, surely she will look upon me as a man without honor or worth because I am attempting and doing something so far removed from the obligations I have as the man I am, and as your friend. There is no doubt that you want me to take your honor, for when Camila sees me wooing her, she will think that I saw in her some looseness of behavior that gave me the audacity to reveal my evil desire, and thinking herself dishonored, her dishonor affects you, for you are part of her. For this reason people commonly say that the husband of an adulterous woman, even though he has no knowledge of wife's adultery and has given her no reason to be what she should not be, and it was not in his power to prevent his misfortune for he was neither negligent nor careless, yet despite all this he is called and characterized by base names that revile him, and in a certain sense those who know of his wife's wickedness look at him with scornful rather than compassionate eyes, even though responsibility for his difficulties lies not with him but with the desires of his unvirtuous wife.

But I want to tell you why it is reasonable and just for the husband of an immodest woman to be dishonored, even if he does not know about her lack of virtue, and is not responsible for it, and has not been a party to it, or given her reason to be unchaste. And do not grow weary of listening to me; everything will redound to your benefit. When God created our first father in the Earthly Paradise, Holy Scripture says that God put Adam to sleep, and as he slept He took a rib out of his left side and from it He formed our mother Eve; when Adam awoke and saw her, he said: 'This is now bone of my bones, and flesh of my flesh,' and God said: 'Therefore shall a man leave his father and his mother, and cleave unto his wife: and they shall be one flesh.' That was when the divine sacrament of marriage was established, with bonds so strong that death alone can undo them. And this miraculous sacrament is so strong and powerful that it makes one flesh of two different people, and in virtuous spouses it does even more, for although they have two souls, they have only one will. And from this it follows that since the flesh of the wife is one with the flesh of the husband, any stain that besmirches her, or any defect that appears in her, redounds to the flesh of the husband even if he has not given her, as I have said, any reason for her wickedness. Just as discomfort in the foot or any other member of the body is felt throughout the entire body because it is all one flesh, and the head feels the ankle's pain although it has not caused it, so the husband participates in his wife's dishonor because he is one with her. And since honors and dishonors in this world are all born of flesh and blood, and those of the unchaste woman are of this kind, it is unavoidable that the husband is party to them and is considered dishonored even if he has no knowledge of them.

Therefore consider, Anselmo, the danger in which you place yourself by wanting to disturb the tranquility in which your virtuous wife lives; think of how, because of a futile and rash inquisitiveness, you wish to disturb the humors that now rest tranquilly in the bosom of your chaste wife; be aware that what you may gain is little, and what you may lose is so great that I will not even mention it because I lack the words to describe it. But if everything I have said is not enough to dissuade you from your evil purpose, then you can find another instrument for your dishonor and misfortune, for I do not intend to be that instrument, even if I lose your friendship, which is the greatest loss I can imagine."

When he had said this, the virtuous and prudent Lotario fell silent, and Anselmo was left so perplexed and pensive that for some time he could not say a word, but at last he said:

"You have seen, Lotario my friend, how attentively I have listened to everything you wanted to say to me, and in your arguments, examples, and comparisons I have seen the great discernment you possess and the far reaches of your true friendship; I also see and confess that if I do not follow your way of thinking but pursue my own, I am fleeing the good and going after the bad. Assuming this, you must consider that I suffer now from the disease that afflicts some women, filling them with the desire to eat earth, plaster, charcoal, and other things that are even worse, and sickening to look at, let alone to eat; therefore it is necessary to use some artifice to cure me, and this could be done with ease if you simply start, even if indifferently and falsely, to woo Camila, who will not be so fragile that your first encounters will bring down her virtue; I will be content with this simple beginning, and you will have fulfilled what you owe to our friendship, not only by giving me back my life, but by persuading me not to lose my honor. You are obliged to do this for only one reason: being determined, as I am, to make this test a reality, you must not allow me to recount my madness to someone else who would endanger the honor that you insist on my not losing; yours not being as high as it should be, in Camila's opinion, while you woo her, matters little or not at all, for in a very short time, when we see in her the integrity we desire, you will be able to tell her the truth of our scheme, and this will return your standing to where it was before. Since you risk so little and can make me so happy by taking that small risk, do not refuse to do it even if greater obstacles are placed before you; as I have said, if you simply begin, I shall consider the matter concluded."

Seeing Anselmo's resolute will, and not knowing what other examples to cite or arguments to present that would dissuade him, and hearing that he threatened to tell someone else about his wicked desire, and wanting to avoid an even greater evil, Lotario decided to agree and do what Anselmo asked; his purpose and intention was to guide the matter in such a way that Camila's thoughts would not be disturbed and Anselmo would be satisfied, and therefore Lotario told Anselmo not to communicate his thought to anyone else and that he would undertake the enterprise and begin whenever his friend wished. Anselmo embraced him tenderly and lovingly and thanked him for his offer as if Lotario had done him a great favor; the two of them agreed that the plan would begin the following day; Anselmo would give Lotario time and opportunity to speak to Camila alone and also provide him with money and jewels to give and present to her. He advised Lotario to play music for her and write verses in her praise, and if he did not wish to take the trouble to do so, Anselmo would write them himself. Lotario agreed to everything, with intentions quite different from what Anselmo believed them to be.

And having come to this understanding, they went back to Anselmo's house, where they found Camila waiting for her husband, troubled and concerned because he came home later than usual that day.

Lotario returned to his house and Anselmo remained in his, and he was as pleased as Lotario was thoughtful, not knowing what course to follow in order to succeed in that rash affair. But that night he thought of how to deceive Anselmo without offending Camila, and the next day he went to eat with his friend and was welcomed by Camila, who always received and treated him warmly, knowing the good opinion her husband had of him.

They finished eating, the table was cleared, and Anselmo asked Lotario to stay with Camila while he went out to tend to a pressing matter; he said he would be back in an hour and a half. Camila asked him not to leave, and Lotario offered to accompany him, but nothing could sway Anselmo; instead, he urged Lotario to wait until he returned because he had to discuss a matter of great importance with him. He also told Camila not to leave Lotario alone while he was out. In short, he knew so well how to feign the necessity or nonsensicality of his absence that no one could have realized it was mere pretense. Anselmo left, and Camila and Lotario remained alone at the table because the servants had gone to have their own meal. Lotario saw himself placed in precisely the dangerous position that his friend desired, facing an enemy who, with no more than her beauty, could conquer an entire squadron of armed knights: Lotario surely had good reason to fear her.

But what he did was to place his elbow on the arm of his chair and rest his cheek on his open hand, and begging Camila's pardon for his rudeness, he said that he wanted to rest for a while until Anselmo returned. Camila responded that he would be more comfortable in the drawing room than in the chair, and she asked him to go in there to sleep. Lotario refused and dozed in the chair until the return of Anselmo, who found Camila in her bedroom and Lotario asleep and thought that since he had come home so late, they had already had the opportunity to talk and even to sleep; he was impatient for Lotario to awaken so that he could go out again with him and ask if he had been successful.

Everything happened as he wished: Lotario awoke, and they left the house together, and Anselmo asked what he wanted to know, and Lotario replied that he had not thought it a good idea to reveal his intentions completely the first time, and so he had done no more than praise Camila for her loveliness; saying that the sole topic of conversation throughout the city was her beauty and discretion; this had seemed to him a good start to winning her over, disposing her to listen to him with pleasure the next time by using the stratagem the devil uses when he wants to deceive someone who is wary and vigilant; he transforms himself into an angel of light, though he is an angel of darkness, and hides behind an appearance of virtue until finally he reveals his identity and achieves his purpose, unless the deception is discovered at the very start. This pleased Anselmo very much, and he said he would provide the same opportunity every day, because even if he did not leave the house, he would occupy himself with other matters, and Camila would not become aware of the ruse.

Many days went by, and though he did not say a word to Camila, Lotario told Anselmo that he was speaking to her but could never elicit from her the slightest interest in anything unchaste or the smallest shred of hope; on the contrary, he said she had warned him that if he did not rid himself of evil thoughts, she would have to tell her husband.

"Good," said Anselmo. "So far Camila has resisted words; it is necessary to see how she resists actions: tomorrow I shall give you two thousand gold *escudos* to offer her, or even give to her, and another two thousand to buy jewels with which to tempt her; for women, no matter how chaste they are, and especially if they are beautiful, tend to be very fond of dressing well and looking elegant; if she resists this temptation, I will be satisfied and trouble you no more."

Lotario responded that since he had begun it, he would see this undertaking through to its conclusion, although he knew that in the end he would be thwarted and defeated. On the following day he received the four thousand *escudos*, and with them four thousand perplexities, because he did not know what new lies he could tell, but finally he decided to tell Anselmo that Camila was as steadfast in her resistance to gifts and promises of gifts as she was to words, and there was no reason to expend any more effort because it was always a waste of time.

But Fate, which arranged matters differently, decreed that Anselmo, having left Lotario and Camila alone as he had done so many other times before, hid in a small antechamber and watched and listened to them through the keyhole, and he saw that in over half an hour Lotario did not speak a word to Camila and would not have spoken to her if he had been there for a century, and Anselmo realized that everything his friend had told him about Camila's responses was a fiction and a lie. To see if this really was true, he walked out of the antechamber and called Lotario aside, then asked if there was any news and inquired about Camila's mood. Lotario replied that he did not intend to take matters further because her responses had been so harsh and unpleasant; he did not have the heart to say anything else to her.

"Ah," said Anselmo, "Lotario, Lotario, how badly you have fulfilled your duty to me and responded to the trust I put in you! I have been watching through the keyhole of the door to that room, and I have seen that you did not say a word to Camila, which leads me to think you have not said even the first word to her; if this is true, as it undoubtedly is, why have you deceived me, and why do you wish by your actions to take from me the only means I have found to satisfy my desire?"

Anselmo said no more; but what he had said was enough to leave Lotario disconcerted and confused, and taking it almost as a point of honor that he had been discovered in a lie, he swore to Anselmo that from then on he would dedicate himself to satisfying him and not lying to him, as he would see if he were curious enough to spy on him again; Anselmo would not even have to make that effort, however, because Lotario intended to put so much effort into satisfying him that it would eliminate all his suspicions. Anselmo believed him, and in order to give Lotario a more secure and less alarming opportunity, he decided to leave his house for a week and visit a friend who lived in a village not far from the city; Anselmo arranged with this friend to send for him very urgently so that Camila would think there was a reason for his departure.

Oh, Anselmo, how unfortunate and ill-advised! What are you doing? What are you plotting? What are you arranging? Consider that you are acting against yourself, plotting your own dishonor and arranging your own ruination. Camila is a virtuous wife; you possess her in peace and tranquility; no one assails your joy; her thoughts do not go beyond the walls of her house; you are her heaven on earth, the goal of her desires, the fulfillment of her delight, the means by which she measures her will, adjusting it in all things to yours and to that of heaven. If, then, the mine of her honor, beauty, virtue, and modesty gives you, with no effort on your part, all the riches it has, and all that you could wish for, why do you want to dig into the earth and look for more veins of new and unseen treasure, putting yourself in danger of having it all collapse since, after all, it stands on the weak foundations of her frail nature? Remember that if a man seeks the impossible, the possible may justly be denied him; a poet said it better when he wrote:

> I search for life in dread death,
> in fearful disease for health,
> in dark prison for liberty,
> escape in a sealed room,
> in a traitor, loyalty.
> But my own fate from whom
> I ne'er hope for the good
> has with just heaven ruled:
> if the impossible I demand,
> for me the possible is banned.

The next day Anselmo left for the village, having told Camila that during the time he was away, Lotario would come to watch over the house and to eat with her, and that she should be sure to treat him as she would himself. Camila, an intelligent and honorable woman, was distressed by her husband's orders and said he ought to be aware that when he was absent, it was not right for anyone to occupy his seat at the table, and if he was doing this because he had no confidence in her ability to manage his house, he should test her this time and learn through his own experience that she was capable of taking on even greater responsibilities. Anselmo replied that this was his pleasure, and her duty was merely to bow her head and obey. Camila said she would, although it was against her will.

Anselmo left, and on the following day Lotario came to the house, where he was received by Camila with an affectionate and virtuous welcome; she never put herself in a position where Lotario would see her alone; she was always accompanied by her servants, both male and female, especially a maid named Leonela, whom she loved dearly because they had grown up together in the house of Camila's parents, and when she married she brought Leonela with her to Anselmo's house. For the first three days Lotario said nothing to her, although he could have when the table was cleared and the servants left to eat their meal—by Camila's orders, a hasty one. Leonela had also been instructed to eat before Camila did and to never leave her side, but the maid, who had her mind on other affairs more to her liking and needed that time and opportunity to tend to her own pleasures, did not always obey her mistress in this; instead, she left them alone, as if that had been her instructions. But Camila's virtuous presence, the gravity of her countenance, and the modesty of her person were so great that they curbed Lotario's tongue.

But the benefit derived from Camila's many virtues imposing silence on Lotario in fact did harm to them both, because if his tongue was silent, his mind was active and had the opportunity to contemplate, one by one, all the exceptional qualities of virtue and beauty in Camila, which were enough to make a marble statue fall in love, let alone a human heart.

Lotario looked at her when he should have been speaking to her; he thought how worthy she was of being loved, and this thought gradually began an assault on the high regard he had for Anselmo; a thousand times over he wanted to leave the city and go to a place where Anselmo would never see him, and where Lotario would never see Camila, but the pleasure he found in looking at her had already become an impediment to his doing so. He contended and struggled with himself to resist and reject the joy he felt when he looked at her. When he was alone he blamed himself for his folly; he called himself a bad friend, even a bad Christian; he reasoned with himself, making comparisons between himself and Anselmo, and he always concluded by saying that Anselmo's madness and trust had been greater than his own scant fidelity, and if this excused him before God as it did before men for what he intended to do, he would not fear punishment for his crime.

In short, the beauty and virtue of Camila, together with the opportunity that her ignorant husband had placed in his hands, overthrew Lotario's loyalty, and without considering anything but what his longing moved him to do, after three days of Anselmo's absence, days when he was in a constant struggle to resist his desires, Lotario began to compliment Camila with so much passion and such amorous words that Camila was stunned, and all she could do was stand and go to her bedroom without saying a word to him. But not even this brusque behavior could weaken Lotario's hope, for hope is always born at the same time as love; instead, he held Camila in even higher esteem. Having seen in Lotario what she never imagined she would see, Camila did not know what to do, but thinking it would not be safe or proper to give him an opportunity to speak to her again, she resolved that very night to send a servant with a letter for Anselmo, which she did, and in it she wrote these words:

CHAPTER XXXIV

In which the novel of The Man Who Was Recklessly Curious *continues*

> *Just as it is often said that the army without its general seems imperfect, as does the castle without its castellan, I say that the young wife without her husband, when overwhelming reasons do not demand it, seems even worse. I find myself so imperfect without you, and so incapable of enduring this absence, that if you do not return very soon, I shall have to go to the house of my parents for the time you are away, even though I leave yours unguarded, because I believe that the guardian you left for me, if that is what he should be called, is more concerned with his own pleasure than with your interests; since you are clever, I need not say more, nor is it fitting that I do.*

Anselmo received this letter and understood that Lotario had begun his suit and that Camila must have reacted just as he wished; extraordinarily happy at the news, he responded by sending a message to Camila, telling her not to leave his house under any circumstances because he would return very shortly. Camila was astonished by Anselmo's reply, which left her more perplexed than she had been earlier; she did not dare either to remain in her house or to go to the house of her parents; if she remained, her virtue would be at risk, and if she left, she would be disobeying her husband.

In short, she made a choice, and chose badly, for she resolved to remain, determined not to flee Lotario's presence and give the servants reason to gossip; she regretted having written what she wrote to her husband, fearful he would think that Lotario had seen some boldness in her that moved him to treat her with less than proper decorum. But, confident of her virtue, she put her trust in God and in her own innocence and planned to resist with silence everything that Lotario said to her, not informing her husband in order to spare him disputes or difficulties. She even tried to think of a way to excuse Lotario to Anselmo when he asked her the reason for writing that letter. With these thoughts, more honorable than accurate or beneficial, she spent another day listening to Lotario, who was so persistent and persuasive that Camila's resolve began to waver, and it was all her virtue could do to attend to her eyes and keep them from showing any sign of the amorous compassion awakened in her bosom by Lotario's tears and words. Lotario noted all of this, and it all set him ablaze.

Finally, it seemed to him that it was necessary, in the time and circumstance allowed by Anselmo's absence, to tighten the siege around the fortress, and so he launched an attack on her conceit with praises of her beauty, because there is nothing more likely to defeat and bring down the haughty towers of beautiful women's vanity than that same vanity, set in words of adulation. In effect, with utmost diligence, he undermined the rock face of her integrity with such effective tools that even if Camila had been made entirely of bronze, she would have fallen. Lotario wept, pleaded, offered, adored, persisted, and deceived with so much emotion and so many signs of sincerity that he brought down Camila's chastity and won the victory he had least expected and most desired.

Camila surrendered; Camila surrendered, but is that any wonder if the friendship of Lotario could not remain standing? A clear example demonstrating that the only way to defeat the amorous passion is to flee it, that no one should attempt to struggle against so powerful an enemy because divine forces are needed to vanquish its human ones. Only Leonela knew of her mistress's frailty, because the two unfaithful friends and new lovers could not hide it from her. Lotario did not want to tell Camila of Anselmo's scheme, or that Anselmo had provided him with the opportunity to come so far: he did not want her to have a low opinion of his love, or to think he had courted her thoughtlessly and by chance rather than intentionally.

A few days later, Anselmo returned to his house and did not notice what was missing, the thing he had treated most contemptuously and valued most highly. He went to see Lotario immediately and found him at home; the two men embraced, and one asked for the news that would give him either life or death.

"The news I can give you, Anselmo my friend," said Lotario, "is that you have a wife worthy of being the model and paragon of all virtuous women. The words I said to her were carried away by the wind; my offers were scorned, my gifts were refused, and a few feigned tears of mine were mocked beyond measure. In short, just as Camila is the sum total of all beauty, she is the treasure house where chastity dwells and discretion and modesty reside, along with all the virtues that make an honorable woman praiseworthy and fortunate. Here is your money, friend; take it back, for I never had need of it; Camila's integrity does not yield to things as low as presents or promises. Be content, Anselmo, and do not attempt more tests; since you have passed through the sea of difficulties, and suspicions that one often can have about women, and you have kept your feet dry, do not attempt to return to the deep waters of new dangers, or test, with another pilot, the virtue and strength of the ship that heaven has provided to carry you across the seas of this world; realize instead that you are in a safe harbor; drop the anchors of reason and stay in port until you are asked to pay the debt that no human, no matter how noble, can avoid paying."

Anselmo was made very happy by Lotario's words, and he believed them as if they had been spoken by an oracle. Even so, he asked his friend not to abandon the undertaking, if only for the sake of curiosity and amusement, and even if he no longer brought to it the same zeal and urgency as before; he only wanted Lotario to write some verses in praise of Camila, calling her Clori, and Anselmo would tell her that Lotario was in love with a lady to whom he had given this name so that he could celebrate her with the decorum her modesty required. And if Lotario did not wish to take the trouble of writing the verses, Anselmo would do it. "That will not be necessary," said Lotario, "for the Muses are not so antagonistic to me that they do not visit me a few times a year. Tell Camila what you said about my fictitious love, and I shall compose the verses; and if they are not as good as the subject deserves, at least they will be the best I can write."

The reckless man and his traitorous friend agreed to this, and when Anselmo returned to his house, he asked what, to Camila's great surprise, he had not asked before, which was that she tell him the reason she had written him the letter. Camila responded that it had seemed Lotario was looking at her somewhat more boldly than when Anselmo was at home, but she had been mistaken and believed it had been her imagination, because now Lotario avoided seeing her and being alone with her. Anselmo said she could be sure of that, because he knew that Lotario was in love with a noble maiden in the city, whom he celebrated under the name of Clori; even if he were not, there was no reason to doubt Lotario's truthfulness or his great friendship for the two of them. If Lotario had not warned Camila that his love for Clori was all pretense, and that he had told Anselmo about it so that he could spend some time writing praises of Camila herself, she undoubtedly would have been caught in the desperate net of jealousy, but she had been forewarned, and this unexpected piece of news did not trouble her.

The next day, when the three of them were sitting at the table after their meal, Anselmo asked Lotario to recite one of the pieces he had composed for his beloved Clori; since Camila did not know her, he surely could say whatever he wished.

"Even if she did know her," responded Lotario, "I would not hide any-thing, because when a lover praises his lady's beauty and censures her cruelty, he in no way brings dishonor to her good name; but, be that as it may, I can say that yesterday I composed a sonnet to the ingratitude of Clori, and it says:

SONNET

In the deepest quietude of the night,
when gentle sleep embraces mortal men,
I make this poor accounting of my wealth
of woes to heaven, and to Clori mine.
    And at the hour when the sun appears
through rosy-colored portals of the east,
with brokenhearted sighs and halting words
I endlessly renew the old lament.
    And when the sun, from his celestial throne,
hurls burning rays directly down to earth,
my tears flow free and my sobs do increase.
    The night returns; I turn to my sad tale
and once mote find, in wearisome complaint,
that heaven is deaf and Clori cannot hear."

Camila liked the sonnet, but Anselmo liked it even more, for he praised it and said that a lady who did not respond to such evident truths was too cruel. To which Camila said:

"Then, everything said by enamored poets is true?"

"Insofar as they are poets, no," responded Lotario, "but insofar as they are enamored, they are always as lost for words as they are truthful."

"There is no doubt about that," replied Anselmo, simply to support and confirm Lotario's opinions before Camila, who was unaware of Anselmo's stratagem and already in love with Lotario.

And so, with the pleasure she derived from everything relating to him, and with the understanding that his desires and his writings were directed to her, and that she was the real Clori, she asked him to recite another sonnet and more verses, if he knew them by heart.

"I do," responded Lotario, "but I do not believe it is as good as—I mean, it is less bad than—the first. But judge for yourself, because it says:

SONNET

I know I die; and if my word is doubted,
my death's more certain; my body lying dead

at your feet, O cruel beauty, is more certain
than my repenting of my love for you.
　　When I am in the land of the forgotten,
deserted by glory, favor, and by life,
there, in my open bosom, you will see,
a sculpted image of your lovely face.
　　I keep this holy relic for the looming
rigors brought on and caused by my persistence,
made stronger by the harshness of your will.
　　Oh, woe to him who sails 'neath darkened skies
across uncharted seas and dangerous routes
where neither port nor polestar lights the way."

Anselmo praised this second sonnet as he had the first, and in this fashion he was adding, link by link, to the chain that bound and fastened him to his dishonor, for the more Lotario dishonored him, the more honored he said Anselmo was, and every step Camila took in her descent to the very center of disgrace was, in the opinion of her husband, an ascent to the pinnacle of her virtue and good name.

It happened that once, when Camila found herself alone with her maid, she said:

"I am mortified, my dear Leonela, to see how lightly I valued myself, for I did not even oblige Lotario to pay with time for the complete possession of my desire; I gave it to him so quickly, I fear he will judge only my haste or indiscretion, not taking into account that he urged me so strongly I could no longer resist him."

"Do not be concerned, Señora," responded Leonela. "Giving quickly is of little significance, and no reason to lessen esteem, if, in fact, what one gives is good and in itself worthy of esteem. They even say that by giving quickly, one gives twice."

"They also say," said Camila, "that what costs less is valued less."

"The argument doesn't apply to you," responded Leonela, "because love, I've heard it said, sometimes flies and sometimes walks; it runs with one, and goes slowly with another; it cools some and burns others; some it wounds, and others it kills; it begins the rush of its desires at one point, and at the same point it ends and concludes them; in the morning it lays siege to a fortress, and by nightfall it has broken through, because there is no power that can resist it. And this being true, why are you concerned and what do you fear if the same thing must have happened to Lotario, for love used the absence of my master as the instrument for overcoming us.[6] It was inevitable that what love had planned would be concluded before Anselmo could return and prevent the design's completion by his presence, because love has no better minister for carrying out his desires than opportunity: he makes use of opportunity in everything he does, especially at the beginning. I know this very well, more from experience than from hearsay, and one day I'll tell you about it, Señora, for I'm also young and made of flesh and blood. Besides, Señora Camila, you would not have given yourself or surrendered so quickly if you had not first seen in Lotario's eyes, words, sighs, promises, and gifts all his soul, or not seen in it and its virtues how worthy Lotario was of being loved. If this is true, do not allow those qualms and second thoughts to assault your imagination, but be assured that Lotario esteems you as you esteem him, and live contented and satisfied that although you were caught in the snare of love, it is he who tightens it around you with his admiration and esteem. He not only has the four Ss[7] that people say good lovers need to have, but a whole alphabet as well; if you don't believe me, just listen and you'll see how I can recite it to you by heart. He is, as I see it and in my opinion, Amiable, Benevolent, Courteous, Dignified, Enamored, Firm, Gallant, Honorable, Illustrious, Loyal, Manly, Noble, Openhearted, Pleasing, Quick-witted, Rich, the Ss that everybody knows, and then Truthful, Valiant, X isn't included because it's a harsh letter, Y is the same as I, and Z is Zealous in protecting your honor."

Camila laughed at her maid's alphabet and considered her more experienced in matters of love than she said; in fact, she confessed to this, revealing to Camila her love for a wellborn young man from their city; this troubled Camila, for she feared that here was where her honor could be endangered. She pressed Leonela to find out if their love had gone beyond words. With little shame and a good deal of audacity, she responded that it had. For it is certainly true that negligence in ladies destroys shame in their maids: when they see their mistresses stumble, they do not care if they stumble, too, or if anyone knows about it.

All that Camila could do was to implore Leonela not to say anything about her mistress's affair to the man she said was her lover, and to keep her own secret so that it would not come to the attention of either Anselmo or Lotario. Leonela responded that she would, but she kept her word in a way that affirmed Camila's fear that she would lose her reputation because of her maid, for the immodest and brazen Leonela, when she saw that her mistress's behavior was not what it had once been, dared to bring her lover into the house and keep him there, confident that even if Camila saw him, she would not venture to reveal it; this is one of the many misfortunes caused by the sins of ladies: they become the slaves of their own servants and are obliged to conceal their maids' immodest and base behavior, which is what happened to

Camila; although she often saw Leonela with her lover in one of the rooms of her house, she not only did not dare to reprimand her, but provided Leonela with the opportunity to hide him, clearing away every obstacle so that he would not be seen by her husband.

But she could not keep Lotario from seeing him one day as he left the house at dawn; Lotario did not know who he was and at first thought it was a ghost, but when he saw him walk, and muffle his face, and conceal himself with care and caution, he abandoned his simple idea and took up another that would have meant the ruin of them all if Camila had not rectified it. Lotario thought that the man he had seen leaving Anselmo's house at so unusual an hour had not gone there because of Leonela; he did not even remember that there was a Leonela in the world; he believed only that Camila, who had been easy and loose with him, was being just as easy and loose with another man, for the immorality of the immoral woman brings with it this effect: she loses her good name and honor with the very man to whose entreaties and entice-ments she succumbed; he believes she surrenders more easily to other men and takes as absolute truth any suspicion of the kind that may occur to him. It cer-tainly seems that at this point Lotario lost his good sense and forgot all his skillful reasoning; without a second or even a rational thought, filled with impatience and blinded by the jealous rage gnawing at his entrails and driving him to take his revenge on Camila, who in no way had offended him, he went to see Anselmo, who was still in bed, and said:

"You should know, Anselmo, that for many days I have been struggling with myself, forcing myself not to tell you what it is no longer possible or fair to keep from you. You should know that the fortress of Camila has surrendered and submitted to everything I wished, and if I have delayed in disclosing this to you, it was to see if it was a passing whim, or if she was testing me to see if I was serious about the love I had, with your permission, begun to declare for her. I also believed that if she was as virtuous as she should have been and as we both thought she was, she would already have told you about my solicita-tions; seeing that she has not, I realize that the promises she has made to me are true, and that the next time you are absent from you house, she will speak to me in the antechamber where you keep your jewels and treasure"—it was true that Camila usually spoke to him there—"but I do not want you to rush off to take your revenge, because the sin has not yet been committed except in thought, and it may be that when the time comes to turn the thought into action, Camila will have changed her mind and replaced the thought with repentance. Therefore, since you have always followed my advice, completely or in part, take the counsel I will give you now, so that prudently forewarned, and with no chance of being deceived, you may be satisfied regarding the best course of action to follow. Pretend that you are leaving for two or three days, as you have in the past, but stay hidden in your antechamber, where there are tapestries and other things that can conceal you very comfortably; then you will see with your own eyes, and I with mine, exactly what Camila wants; and if it is the immorality that may be feared but is not expected, then silently, wisely, and discreetly you can punish the offense committed against you."

Anselmo was bewildered, perplexed, and astonished by Lotario's words, for they came at the moment when he least expected to hear them: he now considered Camila to be victorious over the feigned assaults of Lotario, and he was beginning to enjoy the glory of her triumph. He said nothing for a long time, staring at the floor, not blinking an eye, and then at last he spoke, saying:

"You have done, Lotario, what I expected of your friendship; I shall follow your advice in everything; arrange matters as you wish and keep the secret as it should be kept in so unexpected a circumstance."

Lotario promised he would, and as he left the room, he repented completely for everything he had said, and he saw how foolishly he had behaved, since he could take his own revenge on Camila and not in so cruel and dishonorable a way. He cursed his lack of intelligence, denounced his hasty decision, and did not know by what means he could undo what he had done or give it a more reasonable outcome. Finally, he decided to tell Camila everything, and since there was no lack of opportunity, he found her alone that same day, and as soon as she saw that she could speak freely, she said to him:

"You should know, friend Lotario, that my heart aches so much it seems it is about to break inside my bosom, and it will be a miracle if it does not, for Leonela's shamelessness has grown so great that she brings her lover into this house every night, and is with him until daybreak, putting my reputation at the greatest risk if anyone were to see him leaving my house at that hour. What troubles me is that I cannot punish or reprimand her: she is privy to our affair, and that has curbed my speech and forced me to be silent about hers, and I am afraid this will give rise to some misfortune."

When Camila first began to speak, Lotario believed it was a ruse to convince him that the man he had seen was Leonela's lover, not hers, but when he saw her weep, and grieve, and ask for his help, he believed the truth and then felt completely bewildered and remorseful. Despite this, however, he told Camila not to worry, saying he would devise a plan to put an end to Leonela's insolence. He also told her what, in his jealous rage, he had said to Anselmo, and how it had been agreed that Anselmo would hide in the antechamber and see her lack of fidelity for himself. He begged her forgiveness for this act of madness and asked her advice on how to repair the damage he had done and emerge safely from the intricate labyrinth into which his foolish talk had led them.

Camila was horrified to hear what Lotario was saying, and with a good deal of anger and many well-chosen words, she reproached him, denouncing his wicked thoughts and the simpleminded and wrong-headed decision he had made; but since a woman naturally has a quicker wit for both good and evil than a man, though it tends to fail her when she embarks on any kind of deliberate reasoning, Camila soon found a way to repair the apparently irreparable situation, and she told Lotario to have Anselmo hide the next day in the place he had mentioned, because from his concealment she intended to derive an advantage that would allow the two of them to take their pleasure from then on with no fear of being surprised; not telling him all of her idea, she warned Lotario to be sure, when Anselmo was hidden, to come in as soon as Leonela called him and respond to everything she said as he would if he did not know Anselmo was listening. Lotario insisted she tell him her plan so that he would do everything he needed to do with greater certainty and care.

"I tell you," said Camila, "that there is nothing for you to do except answer the questions I ask you." Camila did not want to tell him beforehand what she planned to do, fearful he would not go along with what she thought was a very good plan but instead would follow or look for others that could not possibly be as good.

At this, Lotario left the house; the next day, using the excuse that he was going to the village where his friend lived, Anselmo went away and then came back to hide, which he did with no trouble since Camila and Leonela had arranged to give him the opportunity.

And so Anselmo hid, feeling, as one can imagine, the agitation of a man who expected to see with his own eyes the very heart of his honor exposed and to lose the supreme treasure he had thought he possessed in his beloved Camila. When Camila and Leonela were absolutely sure and certain that Anselmo was hiding, they walked into the antechamber, and as soon as Camila stepped in, she heaved a great sigh and said:

"Oh Leonela, my friend! Before I carry out my plan, which I do not want you to know about in the event you attempt to prevent it, would it not be better for you to take Anselmo's dagger, the one I asked you to bring, and with it pierce this ignoble bosom of mine? But no, do not; it would not be reasonable for me to bear responsibility for another's crime. First I want to know what the bold and immoral eyes of Lotario saw in me that gave him the audacity to reveal a desire as wicked as the one he has revealed to me, one that shows disdain for his friend and dishonors me. Go, Leonela, to that window and call him; undoubtedly he is in the street, waiting to put his evil intention into effect. But first I shall carry out mine, as cruel as it is honorable."

"Oh, Señora!" responded the clever and forewarned Leonela. "What is it that you want to do with this dagger? Do you by chance wish to take your own life, or that of Lotario? Either action will discredit your name and reputation. It is better for you to hide the offense; do not give that wicked man the opportunity to enter this house and find us alone. Think, Señora: we are women, and weak, and he is a man, and determined; since he comes with his wicked intention, blind with passion, perhaps before you can put your plan into effect, he'll do the thing that would be worse than taking your life. Confound Señor Anselmo for allowing that insolent knave to do so much evil in his house! And if, Señora, you kill him, as I think you intend to do, what will we do with him when he's dead?"

"What will we do, my friend?" responded Camila. "We will leave him for Anselmo to bury, for he will rightly consider it a restful task to put his own infamy under the ground. Call Lotario, once and for all; the more I delay taking my legitimate revenge for the offense, the more I seem to offend the loyalty I owe my husband."

Anselmo listened to all of this, and each word Camila said changed his thoughts, but when he realized that she had determined to kill Lotario, he wanted to come out and show himself and prevent her from doing that; he was held back, however, by his desire to see the outcome of so gallant and virtuous a resolve, although he intended to come out in time to stop it.

Just then Camila fell into a deep swoon, and laying her down on a bed that was in the chamber, Leonela began to cry very bitterly, saying: "Oh, woe is me if I am so unfortunate and she dies here in my arms: the flower of the world's modesty, the crown of virtuous women, the exemplar of all chastity . . . !"

She said other things similar to these, and no one who heard her would not have taken her for the most aggrieved and loyal maid in the world and her mistress for a second persecuted Penelope. Camila soon recovered from her swoon, and when she did, she said:

"Why do you not go, Leonela, and call the most loyal friend ever seen by the sun or hidden by night? Go, run, hurry, make haste; do not allow delay to cool the flames of rage that I feel or the righteous vengeance I hope for to dwindle into mere threats and curses."

"I am going now to call him, Señora," said Leonela, "but first you must give me the dagger, so that while I am gone you do not do something that will leave all those who love you weeping for the rest of our lives."

"You may go, Leonela my friend, certain that I shall not," responded Camila, "because although in your opinion it is rash and foolish of me to defend my honor, I shall not go as far as that Lucretia who, they say, killed herself even though she had done no wrong, and without first killing the one responsible for her misfortune. I shall die, if I must; but I have to take my revenge and exact satisfaction from the man who has brought me to this place to weep over the insolence of his actions, for which I am blameless."

Leonela had to be asked many more times before she went out to call Lotario, but finally she left, and while she was gone, Camila said, as if talking to herself:

"Lord save me! Would it not have been better to reject Lotario, as I have so many times before, rather than give him reason to think, as I have done now, that I am immodest and unchaste, even for this short time that I must wait until I make him aware of his error? No doubt it would have been better, but then I would not be avenged, nor my husband's honor satisfied if, with clean hands, he could walk away so easily from the situation to which his wicked thoughts have brought him. Let the traitor pay with his life for what his lascivious desire attempted to do; let the world know, if it ever does come to light, that Camila not only remained faithful to her husband, but took revenge on the one who dared offend him. Even so, I believe it would have been better to tell Anselmo, but I tried in the letter I wrote to him when he was in the village, and I think his not coming to remedy the harm I pointed out to him must have been because he is so good and trusting, he would not or could not believe that the bosom of so firm a friend could harbor any thoughts detrimental to his honor; not even I believed it afterward, not for many days, and I never would have believed it if his insolence had not grown so great, and if his open offers of gifts and exaggerated promises and constant tears had not made it clear to me. But why do I even think about this now? Does a gallant resolve have need of more counsel? Of course not. Away traitors, come revenge! Let the deceiver enter, let him come, let him arrive, let him die and be finished with, let whatever happens happen! I was pure when I came into possession of the man heaven gave me for my own; I shall be pure when I leave it behind, even if I am bathed in my own chaste blood and the impure blood of the falsest friend that friendship has ever known."

And saying this, she paced the room with the dagger unsheathed, making such disordered and extravagant movements and gestures that she appeared to have lost her mind and seemed not a fragile woman but a desperate ruffian.

Anselmo watched it all, concealed behind the tapestries where he had hidden; he was astonished by everything, and it seemed to him that what he had seen and heard was enough to allay the greatest suspicions, and he would have liked to forego the proofs that would come with Lotario's arrival, fearing some dreadful mishap. He was about to show himself and come out of hiding to embrace and reassure his wife, but he stopped when he saw Leonela return, leading Lotario by the hand, and as soon as Camila saw him she drew a line on the floor with the dagger and said:

"Lotario, listen to what I am saying: if by some chance you dare to cross this line, or even approach it, at the very moment I see what you are attempting, I shall plunge the dagger I am holding into my breast. And before you say a word in response, I want you to listen to a few more of mine, and then you can say whatever you wish. First, I want you to tell me, Lotario, if you know my husband Anselmo, and what opinion you have of him; second, I also want to know if you know me. Answer me this, and do not be confused or think too much about how you will reply, for my questions are not difficult."

Lotario was not so simpleminded that he had not realized what Camila intended from the moment she told him to have Anselmo hide, and he responded so cleverly and so appropriately to her intention that the two of them made the lie appear to be the absolute truth, and so he replied to Camila in this fashion:

"I did not think, O beautiful Camila, that you called me in order to ask me things so far from the intention with which I come here. If you are doing this in order to delay granting me the promised favor, you should have done so from a greater distance, for the nearer we are to the object of our desire, the greater our hope of possessing it; but, so that you cannot say I do not answer your questions, I will say that I know your husband, Anselmo, and he and I have known each other since we were children; I do not want to say what you know all too well about our friendship, so that I do not bear witness to the offense that love, which is a powerful excuse for even greater crimes, forces me to commit against him. I know you and hold you in the same high esteem that he does; otherwise, I would not, for any lesser prize, violate what I owe my own person and the holy laws of true friendship, infringed and broken by me on account of an enemy as powerful as love."

"If you confess to that," responded Camila, "mortal enemy of all that justly deserves to be loved, how do you dare appear before the one who, as you know, is the mirror that reflects him? If you looked in it carefully, you would see how little justification you have for offending him. But oh, woe is me, now I realize what has made you disregard what you owe to yourself: it must have been negligence on my part; I do not wish to call it immodesty, since it did not follow from a deliberate decision but from the sort of careless act that women often commit inadvertently when they think they have no reason to be cautious. Otherwise tell me, O traitor, when did I ever respond to your entreaties with a word or gesture that could have awakened in you even the shadow of a hope of satisfying your base desires? When were your amorous words not rejected and reproached with severity and harshness? When were your many promises and gifts ever believed or accepted? But since it seems to me that no one can persevere in his amorous intention for very long if he is not sustained by some hope, I shall blame myself for your impertinence, for no doubt some negligence on my part has sustained your desire for so long, and therefore I shall impose the punishment and penalty on myself that your crime deserves. And so that you may see that if I am cruel with myself, I could be no less cruel with you, I wanted to bring you here to be a witness to the sacrifice I intend to make to the insulted honor of my honorable husband; you offended him with all possible deliberation, as I offended him by my carelessness in giving you the opportunity, if in fact I gave you one, that would favor and condone your wicked intentions. I say again: the suspicion I have that some carelessness of mine engendered those monstrous thoughts in you troubles me greatly; it is what I desire to punish with my own hands, for if another punished me, perhaps my crime would be made public; but before I do that, I want to kill as I die, and take with me the one who will finally satisfy my desire for the vengeance I hope for, and that I shall have when I see, in the next world, the penalty imposed by a disinterested justice that does not bend before the one who has brought me to such desperate straits."

And having said this, with incredible strength and speed she attacked Lotario with the unsheathed dagger, showing such clear intentions of wanting to plunge it into his bosom that he was not certain if her displays were false or true, for he had to use his skill and strength to keep Camila from stabbing him. She was acting out that strange deception and lie so vividly that in order to give it the appearance of truth, she tried to color it with her own blood; seeing that she could not reach Lotario, or pretending that she could not, she said:

"Fate does not wish to satisfy completely my righteous desire, but it will not be strong enough to keep me from satisfying it in part, at least." And struggling to free from Lotario's grasp the hand that held the dagger, she finally succeeded, aimed the point at a part of her body that she could wound, but not deeply, and plunged it in above her left armpit, near the shoulder; then she dropped to the floor as if she had fallen into a faint.

Leonela and Lotario were dumbfounded, astonished at what had just happened and still doubting its reality although Camila lay on the floor, bathed in blood. Lotario, horrified and breathless, rushed over to her to pull out the dagger, and when he saw how small the wound was, he stopped being afraid and once again marveled at the great sagacity, prudence, and intelligence of the beautiful Camila; in order to comply with his obligations, he began a long, melancholy lamentation over Camila's body, as if she were dead, and he cursed not only himself but the man who had placed her in that situation. And since he knew that his friend Anselmo was listening, he said things that would move anyone to pity him much more than Camila, even if he did think she was dead.

Leonela took her in her arms and laid her on the bed, pleading with Lotario to go and find someone who would heal Camila in secret; she also asked his advice and opinion regarding what they would tell Anselmo about her mistress's wound in the event he came home before she was healed. He replied that they should say whatever they wanted, for he was not the one to give any useful advice; he would say only that she should try to stop the bleeding because he was going where no one would see him again. Displaying great grief and emotion, he left the house, and when he found himself alone, in a place where no one could see him, he could not stop crossing himself as he marveled at Camila's stratagem and Leonela's clever responses. He considered how certain Anselmo would be that his wife was a second Portia, and he wished he could meet with him so they could both celebrate the most hidden truth and concealed lie that anyone could ever imagine.

Leonela staunched her mistress's blood, which was no more than what was necessary to make the lie believable, and washing the wound with a little wine, she bandaged it the best she could, and as she treated her she said words that would have been enough, even if nothing had been said before, to persuade Anselmo that he had in Camila the very image and example of virtue.

Added to Leonela's words were those of Camila, who called herself a craven coward for not having the courage, when she needed it most, to take her own life, which she despised. She asked her maid if she should tell her dear husband about what had happened; Leonela advised her not to, because that would oblige him to take his revenge on Lotario, which would be very dangerous, and it was the duty of a good wife not to give her husband reasons for disputes but to save him from as many as possible. Camila responded that her advice seemed very good, and she would follow it, but in any case they ought to decide what they would tell Anselmo about the reason for the wound, which he would be bound to see; to which Leonela replied that she did not know how to lie, even as a joke.

"Well, my friend," replied Camila, "then what shall I do if I would not dare create or sustain a lie even if my life depended on it? If we cannot find our way out of this, it would be better to tell him the unadorned truth rather than have him discover us in a falsehood."

"Don't be sad, Señora; by tomorrow," responded Leonela, "I'll think of what we should say, and perhaps because of where the wound is, you'll be able to hide it and he won't see it, and heaven will be merciful and favor our just and honorable thoughts. Be calm, Señora, and try to stay calm so that my master doesn't find you troubled, and you can leave the rest to me, and to God, who always comes to the aid of virtuous desires." Anselmo had been very attentive as he heard and watched the performance of the tragedy of the death of his honor, which had been performed with such unusual and convincing effects by the actors that they seemed to have been transformed into the very parts they were playing. He longed for night to fall, when he would be able to leave his house, and go to see his good friend Lotario, and celebrate with him the precious pearl he had discovered in the revelation of his wife's virtue. The two women were careful to give him the opportunity to leave, and he did not miss that opportunity, and he left and went to find Lotario, and when he had found him, it is difficult to recount the number of embraces he gave him, the things he said about his joy, his praises of Camila. Lotario listened to all of this and could give no indications of happiness because he thought of how deceived his friend was and how unjustly he had wronged him. And although Anselmo saw that Lotario was not happy, he thought it was because he had left Camila wounded when he had been the reason for the wound; among other things, he even told him not to grieve over what had happened to Camila, because the wound was surely superficial since the two women had agreed to hide it from him; therefore there was nothing to fear, and from now on Lotario should rejoice and celebrate with him because through his efforts, Anselmo found himself lifted to the highest happiness he could ever desire, and he wanted to do nothing else but write verses in praise of Camila that would make her live forever in the memory of future ages. Lotario praised his decision and said that he, for his part, would help him raise so noble an edifice.

And so Anselmo was the most deliriously deceived man in the world: he himself led into his house the man who was the ruination of his name, believing he had been the instrument of his glory. Camila received him with an apparently crestfallen expression, although her soul rejoiced. This deception lasted some months until Fortune spun her wheel, the wickedness they had concealed with so much skill was made public, and Anselmo's reckless curiosity cost him his life.

CHAPTER XXXV

In which the novel of The Man Who Was Recklessly Curious *is concluded*

• • •

And so, because of Anselmo's certainty regarding Camila's virtue, he led a carefree and contented life, and Camila intentionally showed coldness to Lotario so that Anselmo would believe her feelings toward him were the opposite of what they truly were; to give this even more weight, Lotario asked permission not to visit his friend's house anymore since it was clear that the sight of him troubled Camila a great deal, but the deluded Anselmo said that under no circumstances would he allow any such thing; in this way, in a thousand ways, Anselmo constructed his own dishonor, believing that he was creating his own delight.

In the meantime, the delight Leonela took in freely engaging in her love affair went so far that she cared about nothing else and pursued it without restraint, certain that her mistress would conceal what she did and even advise her how to carry on an affair without arousing too much suspicion. Finally, one night, Anselmo heard footsteps in Leonela's bedroom, and when he tried to go in to see whose they were, he found the door closed against him, which gave him an even greater desire to open it; he pushed so hard that it opened, and as he went in he saw a man leaping out the window to the street, and when he tried to hurry out to catch him or see who he was, he could do neither because Leonela threw her arms around him, saying:

"Be calm, Señor, don't be angry, you don't need to follow the man who left here; it really is my affair; in fact, he's my husband."

Anselmo did not believe her; instead, blind with rage, he took out his dagger and tried to stab Leonela, saying that if she did not tell him the truth, he would kill her. She was terrified, and not knowing what she was saying, she cried:

"Don't kill me, Señor, and I'll tell you things that are more important than you can imagine."

"Tell me now," said Anselmo, "or you're a dead woman."

"I can't now," said Leonela, "I'm too upset; wait until tomorrow, and then you'll hear things that will amaze you; but you can be sure that the man who jumped out the window is a young man of this city who has given his promise to marry me."

Anselmo grew calmer and was willing to wait the period of time she requested, for he did not think he would hear anything against Camila, he was so certain and sure of her virtue; so he went out of Leonela's bedroom and left her locked inside, saying she would not leave until she told him what she had to tell him.

Then he went to see Camila, and told her everything that had occurred, and said that her maid had promised to tell him great, important things. It goes without saying that Camila became alarmed, fearing, and with reason, that Leonela would tell Anselmo everything she knew about her infidelity; she did not have the courage to wait and see if her suspicions were true, and that same night, when she thought Anselmo was asleep, she gathered together the most precious jewels she had, and some money, and without being detected by anyone, she left her house and went to Lotario's; she told him what had happened and asked that he hide her, or that the two of them go where they would both be safe from Anselmo. Camila threw Lotario into such confusion that he could not say a word, much less decide what to do.

Finally, he decided to take Camila to a convent where one of his sisters was prioress. Camila agreed, and with the speed the situation demanded, Lotario took her to the convent and left her there, and he himself abandoned the city and told no one of his departure.

At dawn, Anselmo's desire to hear what Leonela wanted to tell him was so great, he did not even notice that Camila was not at his side but got up and went to the room where he had left the maid. He unlocked the door and went in but did not find Leonela there; he found only some sheets knotted together and tied to the window, a clear sign that she had used them to climb down and leave the house. Then he walked back to his own room very mournfully to tell Camila and was stunned not to find her in bed or anywhere in the house. He questioned the servants, but no one could answer his questions.

As he was looking for Camila, he happened to see the open chests and saw too that most of her jewels were missing from them, and this was when he became aware of the calamity and knew that Leonela was not the cause of his affliction. He did not even bother to finish dressing, but just as he was, sad and melancholy, he went to tell his friend Lotario about his misfortune. But when he did not find him, and the servants said Lotario had left in the night and taken with him all the money he had, Anselmo thought he would go mad. As a final blow, when he returned home all of the servants had gone, and his house was empty and deserted.

He did not know what to think, what to say, or what to do, but slowly his judgment began to return. He reflected on what had happened and saw himself deprived, in an instant, of his wife, his friend, and his servants, abandoned, it seemed to him, by heaven, and, above all, bereft of honor, for in Camila's absence he saw his ruination.

Finally he resolved, after a long while, to go to the village where he had stayed with his friend when he gave them the opportunity to devise that misfortune. He locked the doors of his house, mounted his horse, and set out with weakening courage; when he had traveled only half the distance, he was overwhelmed by his thoughts and had to dismount; he tied his horse's reins to a tree and dropped to the ground beneath it, heaving tender, pitiful sighs, and lay there until it was almost dark; then he saw a man on horseback riding toward him from the city, and after greeting him, he asked what the news was in Florence. The citizen responded:

"The strangest heard there in many days, because it is being said publicly that Lotario, the great friend of Anselmo the rich man, who lived near San Giovanni, ran off last night with Camila, Anselmo's wife, and Anselmo is nowhere to be found. All of this was disclosed by one of Camila's maids, who was discovered last night by the governor as she climbed down a sheet hanging from a window in Anselmo's house. The fact is that I don't know exactly how everything turned out; all I know is that the whole city is astonished by what happened, since it was not what anybody expected from their great friendship, for they were so close that people called them the two friends."

"Do you know, by any chance," said Anselmo, "where Lotario and Camila went?"

"I have no idea," said the Florentine, "although the governor has made every effort to find them."

"Then God go with you, Señor," said Anselmo.

"And with you," responded the Florentine, and he rode away. At such calamitous news, Anselmo was on the verge not only of losing his mind but of ending his life. He struggled to his feet and reached the house of his friend, who still knew nothing of his misfortune, but when he saw Anselmo come in looking pallid, exhausted, and drawn, he realized that something very serious had happened. Anselmo immediately asked to be helped to his bed and to be given writing materials. This was done, and he was left lying in bed, the door closed, as he had requested. When he found himself alone, his mind became so burdened with thoughts of his misfortune that he knew his life was coming to an end, and so he decided to leave some explanation of his strange death; he began to write, but before he had finished putting down everything he wanted to say, his breath failed, and he yielded up his life to the grief caused by his reckless curiosity.

The master of the house, seeing that it was late and Anselmo had not called for him, decided to go in to find out if he was feeling better, and he found him facedown, half his body in bed and the other half slumped over the writing desk, the paper he had been writing on unsealed and the pen still in his hand. His host came over to him, having first called his name, and when Anselmo did not answer he grasped his hand, found it cold, and knew that he was dead. Shocked and grief-stricken, his friend summoned the household to see the misfortune that had befallen Anselmo, and finally he read the paper, written by Anselmo's own hand, which said:

> *A foolish and reckless desire took my life. If news of my death should reach Camila, she must know that I forgive her, for she was not obliged to perform miracles, and I had no need to ask her to; since I constructed my own dishonor, there is no reason to . . .*

Anselmo wrote this far, making it clear that before he could end his thought, his life came to an end. The following day, his friend informed Anselmo's kin of his death; they already knew of his misfortune and of the convent where Camila was almost at the point of joining her husband on that inevitable journey, not on account of her husband's death, but because of what she had heard about her absent lover. It was said that although a widow, she did not wish to leave the convent, much less take vows to be a nun; then, a few days later, the news reached her that Lotario had died in the battle between Monsieur de Lautrec and the Great Captain Gonzalo Fernández de Córdoba, which had just taken place in the kingdom of Naples, where Anselmo's friend, repentant too late, had fled;[8] when Camila learned this, she took her vows, and not long afterward her life ended in the pitiless embrace of sorrow and melancholy. This was the end met by the three and born of such rash beginnings.

"This novel seems fine," said the priest, "but I cannot persuade myself that it is true; if it is invented, the author invented badly, because no one can imagine any husband foolish enough to conduct the costly experiment that Anselmo did. If this occurred between a lover and his lady, it might be plausible, but between a husband and his wife it seems impossible; as for the manner in which it was told, I did not find it displeasing."

Notes

[1] This is the first of what are called the interpolated novels (in contemporary terms, they are novellas) in the first part of *Don Quixote*; the story is derived from an episode in Canto 43 of Ariosto's *Orlando furioso*. There are indications in the second part of *Don Quixote* that Cervantes was criticized for these "interruptions" of the action.

[2] Plutarch attributes the phrase to Pericles.

3 An Italian poet of the sixteenth century (1510–1568).

4 An allusion to the story, recounted in *Orlando furioso*, of a magic goblet that indicated if the women who drank from it were faithful.

5 Danae was confined in a tower by her father, King Acrisius, when an oracle stated that her son would kill him. Zeus transformed himself into a shower of gold, visited her, and fathered Perseus.

6 As Martin de Riquer points out, Leonela says "us" because she was complicit in their affair.

7 The four Ss that a lover needed to be were *sabio* ("wise"), *solo* ("alone"), *solícito* ("solicitous"), and *secreto* ("secretive"). This conceit was popular during the Renaissance, as were the ABCs of love cited by many authors. The W is omitted from Leonela's ABC because it is not part of the Spanish alphabet.

8 This appears to refer to the battle of Cerignola, in 1503, when the defeat of the French made the kingdom of Naples a Spanish province.

What You Pawn I Will Redeem

Sherman Alexie

Noon

One day you have a home and the next you don't, but I'm not going to tell you my particular reasons for being homeless, because it's my secret story, and Indians have to work hard to keep secrets from hungry white folks.

I'm a Spokane Indian boy, an Interior Salish, and my people have lived within a one-hundred-mile radius of Spokane, Washington, for at least ten thousand years. I grew up in Spokane, moved to Seattle twenty-three years ago for college, flunked out within two semesters, worked various blue- and bluer-collar jobs for many years, married two or three times, fathered two or three kids, and then went crazy. Of course, "crazy" is not the official definition of my mental problem, but I don't think "asocial disorder" fits it, either, because that makes me sound like I'm a serial killer or something. I've never hurt another human being, or at least not physically. I've broken a few hearts in my time, but we've all done that, so I'm nothing special in that regard. I'm a boring heartbreaker, at that, because I've never abandoned one woman for another. I never dated or married more than one woman at a time. I didn't break hearts into pieces overnight. I broke them slowly and carefully. I didn't set any land-speed records running out the door. Piece by piece, I disappeared. And I've been disappearing ever since. But I'm not going to tell you any more about my brain or my soul.

I've been homeless for six years. If there's such a thing as being an effective homeless man, I suppose I'm effective. Being homeless is probably the only thing I've ever been good at. I know where to get the best free food. I've made friends with restaurant and convenience-store managers who let me use their bathrooms. I don't mean the public bathrooms, either. I mean the employees' bathrooms, the clean ones hidden in the back of the kitchen or the pantry or the cooler. I know it sounds strange to be proud of, but it means a lot to me, being truthworthy enough to piss in somebody else's clean bathroom. Maybe you don't understand the value of a clean bathroom, but I do.

Probably none of this interests you. I probably don't interest you much. Homeless Indians are everywhere in Seattle. We're common and boring, and you walk right on by us, with maybe a look of anger or disgust or even sadness at the tenable fate of the noble savage. But we have dreams and families. I'm friends with a homeless Plains Indian man whose son is the editor of a big-time newspaper back east. That's his story, but we Indians are great storytellers and liars and mythmakers, so maybe that Plains Indian hobo is a plain old everyday Indian. I'm kind of suspicious of him, because he describes himself only as Plains Indian, a generic term, and not by a specific tribe. When I asked him why he wouldn't tell me exactly what he is, he said, "Do any of us know exactly what we are?" Yeah, great, a philosophizing Indian. "Hey," I said, "you got to have a home to be that homely." He laughed and flipped me the eagle and walked away. But you probably want to know more about the story I'm really trying to tell you.

I wander the streets with a regular crew, my teammates, my defenders, and my posse. It's Rose of Sharon, Junior, and me. We matter to one another if we don't matter to anybody else. Rose of Sharon is a big woman, about seven feet tall if you're measuring overall effect, and about five feet tall if you're talking about the physical. She's a Yakama Indian of the Wishram variety. Junior is a Colville, but there are about 199 tribes that make up the Colville, so he could be anything. He's good-looking, though, like he just stepped out of some "Don't Litter the Earth" public-service advertisement. He's got those great big cheekbones that are like planets, you know, with little moons orbiting around them. He gets me jealous, jealous, and jealous. If you put Junior and me next to each other, he's the Before Columbus Arrived Indian, and I'm the After Columbus Arrived Indian. I am living proof of the horrible damage that colonialism has done to us Skins. But I'm not going to let you know how scared I sometimes get of history and its ways. I'm a strong man, and I know that silence is the best way of dealing with white folks.

This whole story started at lunchtime, when Rose of Sharon, Junior, and I were panning the handle down at Pike Place Market. After about two hours of negotiating, we earned five dollars, good enough for a bottle of fortified courage from the most beautiful 7–Eleven in the world. So we headed over that way, feeling like warrior drunks, and we walked past this pawnshop I'd never noticed before. And that was strange, because we Indians have built-in pawnshop radar. But the strangest thing was the old powwow-dance regalia I saw hanging in the window.

"That's my grandmother's regalia," I said to Rose of Sharon and Junior.

"How do you know for sure?" Junior asked.

I didn't know for sure, because I hadn't seen that regalia in person ever. I'd seen only photographs of my grandmother dancing in it. And that was before somebody stole it from her fifty years ago. But it sure looked like my memory of it, and it had all the same colors of feathers and beads that my family always sewed into their powwow regalia.

"There's only one way to know for sure," I said.

So Rose of Sharon, Junior, and I walked into the pawnshop and greeted the old white man working behind the counter.

"How can I help you?" he asked.

"That's my grandmother's powwow regalia in your window," I said. "Somebody stole it from her fifty years ago, and my family has been looking for it ever since."

The pawnbroker looked at me like I was a liar. I understood. Pawnshops are filled with liars.

"I'm not lying," I said. "Ask my friends here. They'll tell you."

"He's the most honest Indian I know," Rose of Sharon said.

"All right, honest Indian," the pawnbroker said. "I'll give you the benefit of the doubt. Can you prove it's your grandmother's regalia?"

Because they don't want to be perfect, because only God is perfect, Indian people sew flaws into their powwow regalia. My family always sewed one yellow bead somewhere on their regalia. But we always hid it where you had to search hard to find it.

"If it really is my grandmother's," I said, "there will be one yellow bead hidden somewhere on it."

"All right, then," the pawnbroker said. "Let's take a look."

He pulled the regalia out of the window, laid it down on his glass counter, and we searched for that yellow bead and found it hidden beneath the armpit.

"There it is," the pawnbroker said. He didn't sound surprised. "You were right. This is your grandmother's regalia."

"It's been missing for fifty years," Junior said.

"Hey, Junior," I said. "It's my family's story. Let me tell it:"

"All right," he said. "I apologize. You go ahead."

"It's been missing for fifty years," I said.

"That's his family's sad story," Rose of Sharon said. "Are you going to give it back to him?"

"That would be the right thing to do," the pawnbroker said. "But I can't afford to do the right thing. I paid a thousand dollars for this. I can't give away a thousand dollars."

"We could go to the cops and tell them it was stolen," Rose of Sharon said.

"Hey," I said to her, "don't go threatening people."

The pawnbroker sighed. He was thinking hard about the possibilities.

"Well, I suppose you could go to the cops," he said. "But I don't think they'd believe a word you said."

He sounded sad about that. Like he was sorry for taking advantage of our disadvantages.

"What's your name?" the pawnbroker asked me.

"Jackson," I said.

"Is that first or last?" he asked.

"Both."

"Are you serious?"

"Yes, it's true. My mother and father named me Jackson Jackson. My family nickname is Jackson Squared. My family is funny."

"All right, Jackson Jackson," the pawnbroker said. "You wouldn't happen to have a thousand dollars, would you?"

"We've got five dollars total," I said.

"That's too bad," he said and thought hard about the possibilities. "I'd sell it to you for a thousand dollars if you had it. Heck, to make it fair, I'd sell it to you for nine hundred and ninety-nine dollars. I'd lose a dollar. It would be the moral thing to do in this case. To lose a dollar would be the right thing."

"We've got five dollars total," I said again.

"That's too bad," he said again and thought harder about the possibilities. "How about this? I'll give you twenty-four hours to come up with nine hundred and ninety-nine dollars. You come back here at lunchtime tomorrow with the money, and I'll sell it back to you. How does that sound?"

"It sounds good," I said.

"All right, then," he said. "We have a deal. And I'll get you started. Here's twenty bucks to get you started."

He opened up his wallet and pulled out a crisp twenty-dollar bill and gave it to me. Rose of Sharon, Junior, and I walked out into the daylight to search for nine hundred and seventy-four more dollars.

1:00 P.M.

Rose of Sharon, Junior, and I carried our twenty-dollar bill and our five dollars in loose change over to the 7–Eleven and spent it to buy three bottles of imagination. We needed to figure out how to raise all that money in one day. Thinking hard, we huddled in an alley beneath the Alaska Way Viaduct and finished off those bottles one, two, and three.

2:00 P.M.

Rose of Sharon was gone when I woke. I heard later she had hitchhiked back to Toppenish and was living with her sister on the reservation.

Junior was passed out beside me, covered in his own vomit, or maybe somebody else's vomit, and my head hurt from thinking, so I left him alone and walked down to the water. I loved the smell of ocean water. Salt always smells like memory.

When I got to the wharf, I ran into three Aleut cousins who sat on a wooden bench and stared out at the bay and cried. Most of the homeless Indians in Seattle come from Alaska. One by one, each of them hopped a big working boat in Anchorage or Barrow or Juneau, fished his way south to Seattle, jumped off the boat with a pocketful of cash to party hard at one of the highly sacred and traditional Indian bars, went broke and broker, and has been trying to find his way back to the boat and the frozen north ever since.

These Aleuts smelled like salmon, I thought, and they told me they were going to sit on that wooden bench until their boat came back.

"How long has your boat been gone?" I asked.

"Eleven years," the elder Aleut said.

I cried with them for a while.

"Hey," I said. "Do you guys have any money I can borrow?"

They didn't.

3:00 P.M.

I walked back to Junior. He was still passed out. I put my face down near his mouth to make sure he was breathing. He was alive, so I dug around in his blue-jean pockets and found half a cigarette. I smoked it all the way down and thought about my grandmother.

Her name was Agnes, and she died of breast cancer when I was fourteen. My father thought Agnes caught her tumors from the uranium mine on the reservation. But my mother said the disease started when Agnes was walking back from the powwow one night and got run over by a motorcycle. She broke three ribs, and my mother said those ribs never healed right, and tumors always take over when you don't heal right.

Sitting beside Junior, smelling the smoke and salt and vomit, I wondered if my grandmother's cancer had started when somebody stole her powwow regalia. Maybe the cancer started in her broken heart and then leaked out into her breasts. I know it's crazy, but I wondered if I could bring my grandmother back to life if I bought back her regalia.

I needed money, big money, so I left Junior and walked over to the Real Change office.

4:00 P.M.

"Real Change is a multifaceted organization that publishes a newspaper, supports cultural projects that empower the poor and homeless, and mobilizes the public around poverty issues. Real Change's mission is to organize, educate, and build alliances to create solutions to homelessness and poverty. They exist to provide a voice to poor people in our community."

I memorized Real Change's mission statement because I sometimes sell the newspaper on the streets. But you have to stay sober to sell it, and I'm not always good at staying sober. Anybody can sell the newspaper. You buy each copy for thirty cents and sell it for a dollar and keep the net profit.

"I need one thousand four hundred, and thirty papers," I said to the Big Boss.

"That's a strange number," he said. "And that's a lot of papers."

"I need them."

The Big Boss pulled out the calculator and did the math. "It will cost you four hundred and twenty-nine dollars for that many," he said.

"If I had that kind of money, I wouldn't need to sell the papers."

"What's going on, Jackson-to-the-Second-Power?" he asked. He is the only one who calls me that. He is a funny and kind man.

I told him about my grandmother's powwow regalia and how much money I needed to buy it back.

"We should call the police," he said.

"I don't want to do that," I said. "It's a quest now. I need to win it back by myself."

"I understand," he said. "And to be honest, I'd give you the papers to sell if I thought it would work. But the record for most papers sold in a day by one vendor is only three hundred and two."

"That would net me about two hundred bucks," I said.

The Big Boss used his calculator. "Two hundred and eleven dollars and forty cents," he said. "That's not enough," I said.

"The most money anybody has made in one day is five hundred and twenty-five. And that's because somebody gave Old Blue five hundred-dollar bills for some dang reason. The average daily net is about thirty dollars."

"This isn't going to work."

"No."

"Can you lend me some money?"

"I can't do that," he said. "If I lend you money, I have to lend money to everybody."

"What can you do?"

"I'll give you fifty papers for free. But don't tell anybody I did it."

"Okay," I said.

He gathered up the newspapers and handed them to me. I held them to my chest. He hugged me. I carried the newspapers back toward the water.

5:00 P.M.

Back on the wharf, I stood near the Bainbridge Island Terminal and tried to sell papers to business commuters walking onto the ferry.

I sold five in one hour, dumped the other forty-five into a garbage can, and walked into the McDonald's, ordered four cheeseburgers for a dollar each, and slowly ate them.

After eating, I walked outside and vomited on the sidewalk. I hated to lose my food so soon after eating it. As an alcoholic Indian with a busted stomach, I always hope I can keep enough food in my stomach to stay alive.

6:00 P.M.

With one dollar in my pocket, I walked back to Junior. He was still passed out, so I put my ear to his chest and listened for his heartbeat. He was alive, so I took off his shoes and socks and found one dollar in his left sock and fifty cents in his right sock. With two dollars and fifty cents in my hand, I sat beside Junior and thought about my grandmother and her stories.

When I was sixteen, my grandmother told me a story about World War II. She was a nurse at a military hospital in Sydney, Australia. Over the course of two years, she comforted and healed U.S. and Australian soldiers.

One day, she tended to a wounded Maori soldier. He was very dark-skinned. His hair was black and curly, and his eyes were black and warm. His face with covered with bright tattoos.

"Are you Maori?" he asked my grandmother.

"No," she said. "I'm Spokane Indian. From the United States."

"Ah, yes," he said. "I have heard of your tribes. But you are the first American Indian I have ever met."

"There's a lot of Indian soldiers fighting for the United States," she said. "I have a brother still fighting in Germany, and I lost another brother on Okinawa."

"I am sorry," he said. "I was on Okinawa as well. It was terrible." He had lost his legs to an artillery attack.

"I am sorry about your legs," my grandmother said.

"It's funny, isn't it?" he asked.

"What's funny?"

"How we brown people are killing other brown people so white people will remain free."

"I hadn't thought of it that way."

"Well, sometimes I think of it that way. And other times, I think of it the way they want me to think of it. I get confused."

She fed him morphine.

"Do you believe in heaven?" he asked.

"Which heaven?" she asked.

"I'm talking about the heaven where my legs are waiting for me."

They laughed.

"Of course," he said, "my legs will probably run away from me when I get to heaven. And how will I ever catch them?"

"You have to get your arms strong," my grandmother said. "So you can run on your hands."

They laughed again.

Sitting beside Junior, I laughed with the memory of my grandmother's story. I put my hand close to Junior's mouth to make sure he was still breathing. Yes, Junior was alive, so I took his two dollars and fifty cents and walked to the Korean grocery store over in Pioneer Square.

7:00 P.M.

In the Korean grocery store, I bought a fifty-cent cigar and two scratch lottery tickets for a dollar each. The maximum cash prize was five hundred dollars a ticket. If I won both, I would have enough money to buy back the regalia.

I loved Kay, the young Korean woman who worked the register. She was the daughter of the owners and sang all day.

"I love you," I said when I handed her the money.

"You always say you love me," she said.

"That's because I will always love you."

"You are a sentimental fool."

"I'm a romantic old man."

"Too old for me."

"I know I'm too old for you, but I can dream."

"Okay," she said. "I agree to be a part of your dreams, but I will only hold your hand in your dreams. No kissing and no sex. Not even in your dreams."

"Okay," I said. "No sex. Just romance."

"Good-bye, Jackson Jackson, my love, I will see you soon."

I left the store, walked over to Occidental Park, sat on a bench, and smoked my cigar all the way down.

Ten minutes after I finished the cigar, I scratched my first lottery ticket and won nothing. So I could win only five hundred dollars now, and that would be just half of what I needed.

Ten minutes later, I scratched my other lottery ticket and won a free ticket, a small consolation and one more chance to win money. I walked back to Kay.

"Jackson Jackson," she said. "Have you come back to claim my heart?"

"I won a free ticket," I said.

"Just like a man," she said. "You love money and power more than you love me."

"It's true," I said. "And I'm sorry it's true."

She gave me another scratch ticket, and I carried it outside. I liked to scratch my tickets in private. Hopeful and sad, I scratched that third ticket and won real money. I carried it back inside to Kay. "I won a hundred dollars," I said.

She examined the ticket and laughed. "That's a fortune," she said and counted out five twenties. Our fingertips touched as she handed me the money. I felt electric and constant.

"Thank you," I said and gave her one of the bills.

"I can't take that," she said. "It's your money."

No, it's tribal. It's an Indian thing. When you win, you're supposed to share with your family."

"I'm not your family."

"Yes, you are."

She smiled. She kept the money. With eighty dollars in my pocket, I said good-bye to my dear Kay and walked out into the cold night air.

8:00 P.M.

I wanted to share the good news with Junior. I walked back to him, but he was gone. I later heard he had hitchhiked down to Portland, Oregon, and died of exposure in an alley behind the Hilton Hotel.

9:00 P.M.

Lonely for Indians, I carried my eighty dollars over to Big Heart's in South Downtown. Big Heart's is an all-Indian bar. Nobody knows how or why Indians migrate to one bar and turn it into an official Indian bar. But Big Heart's has been an Indian bar for twenty-three years. It used to be way up on Aurora Avenue, but a crazy Lummi Indian burned that one down, and the owners moved to the new location, a few blocks south of Safeco Field.

I walked inside Big Heart's and counted fifteen Indians, eight men and seven women. I didn't know any of them, but Indians like to belong, so we all pretended to be cousins.

"How much for whiskey shots?" I asked the bartender, a fat white guy.

"You want the bad stuff or the badder stuff?"

"As bad as you got."

"One dollar a shot."

I laid my eighty dollars on the bar top.

"All right," I said. "Me and all my cousins here are going to be drinking eighty shots. How many is that apiece?"

"Counting you," a woman shouted from behind me, "that's five shots for everybody."

I turned to look at her. She was a chubby and pale Indian sitting with a tall and skinny Indian man.

"All right, math genius," I said to her and then shouted for the whole bar to hear. "Five drinks for everybody!"

All of the other Indians rushed the bar, but I sat with the mathematician and her skinny friend. We took our time with our whiskey shots.

"What's your tribe?" I asked them.

"I'm Duwamish," she said. "And he's Crow."

"You're a long way from Montana," I said to him.

"I'm Crow," he said. "I flew here."

"What's your name?" I asked them.

"I'm Irene Muse," she said. "And this is Honey Boy."

She shook my hand hard, but he offered his hand like I was supposed to kiss it. So I kissed it. He giggled and blushed as well as a dark-skinned Crow can blush.

"You're one of them two-spirits, aren't you?" I asked him.

"I love women," he said. "And I love men."

"Sometimes both at the same time," Irene said.

We laughed.

"Man," I said to Honey Boy. "So you must have about eight or nine spirits going on inside of you, enit?"

"Sweetie," he said, "I'll be whatever you want me to be."

"Oh, no," Irene said. "Honey Boy is falling in love."

"It has nothing to do with love," he said.

We laughed.

"Wow," I said. "I'm flattered, Honey Boy, but I don't play on your team."

"Never say never," he said.

"You better be careful," Irene said. "Honey Boy knows all sorts of magic. He always makes straight boys fall for him."

"Honey Boy," I said, "you can try to seduce me. And Irene, you can try with him. But my heart belongs to a woman named Kay."

"Is your Kay a virgin?" Honey Boy asked.

We laughed.

We drank our whiskey shots until they were gone. But the other Indians bought me more whiskey shots because I'd been so generous with my money. Honey Boy pulled out his credit card, and I drank and sailed on that plastic boat.

After a dozen shots, I asked Irene to dance. And she refused. But Honey Boy shuffled over to the jukebox, dropped in a quarter, and selected Willie Nelson's "Help Me Make It Through the Night." As Irene and I sat at the table and laughed and drank more whiskey, Honey Boy danced a slow circle around us and sang along with Willie.

"Are you serenading me?" I asked him.

He kept singing and dancing.

"Are you serenading me?" I asked him again.

"He's going to put a spell on you," Irene said.

I leaned over the table, spilling a few drinks, and kissed Irene hard. She kissed me back.

10:00 P.M.

Irene pushed me into the women's bathroom, into a stall, shut the door behind us, and shoved her hand down my pants. She was short, so I had to lean over to kiss her. I grabbed and squeezed her everywhere I could reach, and she was wonderfully fat and every part of her body felt like a large, warm, and soft breast.

Midnight

Nearly blind with alcohol, I stood alone at the bar and swore I'd been standing in the bathroom with Irene only a minute ago.

"One more shot!" I yelled at the bartender.

"You've got no more money!" he yelled.

"Somebody buy me a drink!" I shouted.

"They've got no more money!"

"Where's Irene and Honey Boy?"

"Long gone!"

2:00 A.M.

"Closing time!" the bartender shouted at the three or four Indians still drinking hard after a long hard day of drinking. Indian alcoholics are either sprinters or marathon runners.

"Where's Irene and Honey Bear?" I asked.

"They've been gone for hours," the bartender said.

"Where'd they go?"

"I told you a hundred times, I don't know."

"What am I supposed to do?"

"It's closing time. I don't care where you go, but you're not staying here."

"You are an ungrateful bastard. I've been good to you."

"You don't leave right now, I'm going to kick your ass."

"Come on, I know how to fight."

He came for me. I don't remember what happened after that.

4:00 A.M.

I emerged from the blackness and discovered myself walking behind a big warehouse. I didn't know where I was. My face hurt. I touched my nose and decided it might be broken. Exhausted and cold, I pulled a plastic tarp from a truck bed, wrapped it around me like a faithful lover, and fell asleep in the dirt.

6:00 A.M.

Somebody kicked me in the ribs. I opened my eyes and looked up at a white cop.

"Jackson," said the cop. "Is that you?"

"Officer Williams," I said. He was a good cop with a sweet tooth. He'd given me hundreds of candy bars over the years. I wonder if he knew I was diabetic.

"What the hell are you doing here?" he asked.

"I was cold and sleepy," I said. "So I laid down."

"You dumb-ass, you passed out on the railroad tracks."

I sat up and looked around. I was lying on the railroad tracks. Dockworkers stared at me. I should have been a railroad-track pizza, a double Indian pepperoni with extra cheese. Sick and scared, I leaned over and puked whiskey.

"What the hell's wrong with you?" Officer Williams asked. "You've never been this stupid."

"It's my grandmother," I said. "She died."

"I'm sorry, man. When did she die?"

"1972."

"And you're killing yourself now?"

"I've been killing myself ever since she died."

He shook his head. He was sad for me. Like I said, he was a good cop.

"And somebody beat the hell out of you," he said. "You remember who?"

"Mr. Grief and I went a few rounds."

"It looks like Mr. Grief knocked you out."

"Mr. Grief always wins."

"Come on," he said, "let's get you out of here."

He helped me stand and led me over to his squad car. He put me in the back. "You throw up in there," he said, "and you're cleaning it up."

"That's fair," I said.

He walked around the car and sat in the driver's seat. "I'm taking you over to detox," he said.

"No, man, that place is awful," I said. "It's full of drunk Indians."

We laughed. He drove away from the docks.

"I don't know how you guys do it," he said.

"What guys?" I asked.

"You Indians. How the hell do you laugh so much? I just picked your ass off the railroad tracks, and you're making jokes. Why the hell do you do that?"

"The two funniest tribes I've ever been around are Indians and Jews, so I guess that says something about the inherent humor of genocide."

We laughed.

"Listen to you, Jackson. You're so smart. Why the hell are you on the streets?"

"Give me a thousand dollars, and I'll tell you."

"You bet I'd give you a thousand dollars if I knew you'd straighten up your life."

He meant it. He was the second-best cop I'd ever known.

"You're a good cop," I said.

"Come on, Jackson," he said. "Don't blow smoke up my ass."

"No, really, you remind me of my grandfather."

"Yeah, that's what you Indians always tell me."

"No, man, my grandfather was a tribal cop. He was a good cop. He never arrested people. He took care of them. Just like you."

"I've arrested hundreds of scumbags, Jackson. And I've shot a couple in the ass."

"It don't matter. You're not a killer."

"I didn't kill them. I killed their asses. I'm an ass-killer."

We drove through downtown. The missions and shelters had already released their overnighters. Sleepy homeless men and women stood on corners and stared up at the gray sky. It was the morning after the night of the living dead.

"Did you ever get scared?" I asked Officer Williams.

"What do you mean?"

"I mean, being a cop, is it scary?"

He thought about that for a while. He contemplated it. I liked that about him.

"I guess I try not to think too much about being afraid," he said. "If you think about fear, then you'll be afraid. The job is boring most of the time. Just driving and looking into dark corners, you know, and seeing nothing. But then things get heavy. You're chasing somebody or fighting them or walking around a dark house and you just know some crazy guy is hiding around a corner, and hell yes, it's scary."

"My grandfather was killed in the line of duty," I said.

"I'm sorry. How'd it happen?"

I knew he'd listen closely to my story.

"He worked on the reservation. Everybody knew everybody. It was safe. We aren't like those crazy Sioux or Apache or any of those other warrior tribes. There's only been three murders on my reservation in the last hundred years."

"That is safe."

"Yeah, we Spokane, we're passive, you know? We're mean with words. And we'll cuss out anybody. But we don't shoot people. Or stab them. Not much, anyway."

"So what happened to your grandfather?"

"This man and his girlfriend were fighting down by Little Falls."

"Domestic dispute. Those are the worst."

"Yeah, but this guy was my grandfather's brother. My great-uncle."

"Oh, no."

"Yeah, it was awful. My grandfather just strolled into the house. He'd been there a thousand times. And his brother and his girlfriend were all drunk and beating on each other. And my grandfather stepped between them just like he'd done a hundred times before. And the girlfriend tripped or something. She fell down and hit her head and started crying. And my grandfather knelt down beside her to make sure she was all right. And for some reason, my great-uncle reached down, pulled my grandfather's pistol out of the holster, and shot him in the head."

"That's terrible. I'm sorry."

"Yeah, my great-uncle could never figure out why he did it. He went to prison forever, you know, and he always wrote these long letters. Like fifty pages of tiny little handwriting. And he was always trying to figure out why he did it. He'd write and write and write and try to figure it out. He never did. It's a great big mystery."

"Do you remember your grandfather?"

"A little bit. I remember the funeral. My grandmother wouldn't let them bury him. My father had to drag her away from the grave."

"I don't know what to say."

"I don't, either."

We stopped in front of the detox center.

"We're here," Officer Williams said.

"I can't go in there," I said.

"You have to."

"Please, no. They'll keep me for twenty-four hours. And then it will be too late."

"Too late for what?"

I told him about my grandmother's regalia and the deadline for buying it back.

"If it was stolen," he said, "then you need to file reports. I'll investigate it myself. If that thing is really your grandmother's, I'll get it back for you. Legally."

"No," I said. "That's not fair. The pawnbroker didn't know it was stolen. And besides, I'm on a mission here. I want to be a hero, you know? I want to win it back like a knight."

"That's romantic crap."

"It might be. But I care about it. It's been a long time since I really cared about something."

Officer Williams turned around in his seat and stared at me. He studied me.

"I'll give you some money," he said. "I don't have much. Only thirty bucks. I'm short until payday. And it's not enough to get back the regalia. But it's something."

"I'll take it," I said.

"I'm giving it to you because I believe in what you believe. I'm hoping, and I don't know why I'm hoping it, but I hope you can turn thirty bucks into a thousand somehow."

"I believe in magic."

"I believe you'll take my money and get drunk on it." *fuel*

"Then why are you giving it to me?"

"There ain't no such thing as an atheist cop."

"Sure there is."

"Yeah, well, I'm not an atheist cop."

He let me out of the car, handed me two fives and a twenty, and shook my hand. "Take care of yourself, Jackson," he said. "Stay off the railroad tracks."

"I'll try," I said.

He drove away. Carrying my money, I headed back toward the water.

8:00 A.M.

On the wharf, those three Aleut men still waited on the wooden bench.

"Have you seen your ship?" I asked.

"Seen a lot of ships," the elder Aleut said. "But not our ship."

I sat on the bench with them. We sat in silence for a long time. I wondered whether we would fossilize if we sat there long enough.

I thought about my grandmother. I'd never seen her dance in her regalia. More than anything, I wished I'd seen her dance at a powwow.

"Do you guys know any songs?" I asked the Aleuts.

"I know all of Hank Williams," the elder Aleut said.

"How about Indian songs?"

"Hank Williams is Indian."

"How about sacred songs?"

"Hank Williams is sacred."

"I'm talking about ceremonial songs, you know, religious ones. The songs you sing back home when you're wishing and hoping."

"What are you wishing and hoping for?"

"I'm wishing my grandmother was still alive." ✓

"Every song I know is about that."

"Well, sing me as many as you can."

The Aleuts sang their strange and beautiful songs. I listened. They sang about my grandmother and their grandmothers. They were lonely for the cold and snow. I was lonely for everybody.

10:00 A.M.

After the Aleuts finished their last song, we sat in silence. Indians are good at silence.

"Was that the last song?" I asked.

"We sang all the ones we could," the elder Aleut said. "All the others are just for our people."

I understood. We Indians have to keep our secrets. And these Aleuts were so secretive that they didn't refer to themselves as Indians.

"Are you guys hungry?" I asked.

They looked at one another and communicated without talking.

"We could eat," the elder Aleut said.

11:00 A.M.

The Aleuts and I walked over to Mother's Kitchen, a greasy diner in the International District. I knew they served homeless Indians who'd lucked in to money.

"Four for breakfast?" the waitress asked when we stepped inside.

"Yes, we're very hungry," the elder Aleut said.

She sat us in a booth near the kitchen. I could smell the food cooking. My stomach growled.

"You guys want separate checks?" the waitress asked.

"No, I'm paying for it," I said.

"Aren't you the generous one," she said.

"Don't do that," I said.

"Do what?" she asked.

"Don't ask me rhetorical questions. They scare me."

She looked puzzled, and then she laughed. "Okay, Professor," she said. "I'll only ask you real questions from now on."

"Thank you."

"What do you guys want to eat?"

"That's the best question anybody can ask anybody," I said.

"How much money you got?" she asked.

"Another good question," I said. "I've got twenty-five dollars I can spend. Bring us all the breakfast you can, plus your tip."

She knew the math.

"All right, that's four specials and four coffees and fifteen percent for me."

The Aleuts and I waited in silence. Soon enough, the waitress returned and poured us four coffees, and we sipped at them until she returned again with four plates of food. Eggs, bacon, toast, hash-brown potatoes. It is amazing how much food you can buy for so little money.

Grateful, we feasted.

Noon

I said farewell to the Aleuts and walked toward the pawnshop. I later heard the Aleuts had waded into the saltwater near Dock 47 and disappeared. Some Indians said the Aleuts walked on the water and headed north. Other Indians saw the Aleuts drown. I don't know what happened to them.

I looked for the pawnshop and couldn't find it. I swear it wasn't located in the place where it had been before. I walked twenty or thirty blocks looking for the pawnshop, turned corners and bisected intersections, looked up its name in the phone books, and asked people walking past me if they'd ever heard of it. But that pawnshop seemed to have sailed away from me like a ghost ship. I wanted to cry. Right when I'd given up, when I turned one last corner and thought I might die if I didn't find that pawnshop, there it was, located in a space I swore it hadn't been filling up a few minutes before.

I walked inside and greeted the pawnbroker, who looked a little younger than he had before.

"It's you," he said.

"Yes, it's me," I said.

"Jackson Jackson."

"That is my name."

"Where are your friends?"

"They went traveling. But it's okay. Indians are everywhere."

"Do you have my money?"

"How much do you need again?" I asked and hoped the price had changed.

"Nine hundred and ninety-nine dollars."

It was still the same price. Of course it was the same price. Why would it change?

"I don't have that," I said.

"What do you have?"

"Five dollars."

I set the crumpled Lincoln on the countertop. The pawnbroker studied it.

"Is that the same five dollars from yesterday?"

"No, it's different."

He thought about the possibilities.

"Did you work hard for this money?" he asked.

"Yes," I said.

He closed his eyes and thought harder about the possibilities. Then he stepped into his back room and returned with my grandmother's regalia.

"Take it," he said and held it out to me.

"I don't have the money."

"I don't want your money."

"But I wanted to win it."

"You did win it. Now, take it before I change my mind."

Do you know how many good men live in this world? Too many to count!

I took my grandmother's regalia and walked outside. I knew that solitary yellow bead was part of me. I knew I was that yellow bead in part. Outside, I wrapped myself in my grandmother's regalia and breathed her in. I stepped off the sidewalk and into the intersection. Pedestrians stopped. Cars stopped. The city stopped. They all watched me dance with my grandmother. I was my grandmother, dancing. *Meaning what?*

323 U.S. 214
Korematsu v. United States

Supreme Court of The United States

Certiorari to The Circuit Court of Appeals for the Ninth Court

No. 22 Argued: October 11, 12, 1944—Decided: December 18, 1944

MR. JUSTICE BLACK delivered the opinion of the Court.

The petitioner, an American citizen of Japanese descent, was convicted in a federal district court for remaining in San Leandro, California, a "Military Area," contrary to Civilian Exclusion Order No. 34 of the Commanding General [p216] of the Western Command, U.S. Army, which directed that, after May 9, 1942, all persons of Japanese ancestry should be excluded from that area. No question was raised as to petitioner's loyalty to the United States. The Circuit Court of Appeals affirmed[1] and the importance of the constitutional question involved caused us to grant certiorari.

It should be noted, to begin with, that all legal restrictions which curtail the civil rights of a single racial group are immediately suspect. That is not to say that all such restrictions are unconstitutional. It is to say that courts must subject them to the most rigid scrutiny. Pressing public necessity may sometimes justify the existence of such restrictions; racial antagonism never can.

In the instant case, prosecution of the petitioner was begun by information charging violation of an Act of Congress, of March 21, 1942, 56 Stat. 173, which provides that

> . . . whoever shall enter, remain in, leave, or commit any act in any military area or military zone prescribed, under the authority of an Executive order of the President, by the Secretary of War, or by any military commander designated by the Secretary of War, contrary to the restrictions applicable to any such area or zone or contrary to the order of the Secretary of War or any such military commander, shall, if it appears that he knew or should have known of the existence and extent of the restrictions or order and that his act was in violation thereof, be guilty of a misdemeanor

and upon conviction shall be liable to a fine of not to exceed $5,000 or to imprisonment for not more than one year, or both, for each offense.

Exclusion Order No. 34, which the petitioner knowingly and admittedly violated, was one of a number of military orders and proclamations, all of which were substantially [p217] based upon Executive Order No. 9066, 7 Fed.Reg. 1407. That order, issued after we were at war with Japan, declared that

the successful prosecution of the war requires every possible protection against espionage and against sabotage to national defense material, national defense premises, and national defense utilities. . . .

One of the series of orders and proclamations, a curfew order, which, like the exclusion order here, was promulgated pursuant to Executive Order 9066, subjected all persons of Japanese ancestry in prescribed West Coast military areas to remain in their residences from 8 p.m. to 6 a.m. As is the case with the exclusion order here, that prior curfew order was designed as a "protection against espionage and against sabotage." In *Hirabayashi v. United States*, 320 U.S. 81, we sustained a conviction obtained for violation of the curfew order. The Hirabayashi conviction and this one thus rest on the same 1942 Congressional Act and the same basic executive and military orders, all of which orders were aimed at the twin dangers of espionage and sabotage.

The 1942 Act was attacked in the *Hirabayashi* case as an unconstitutional delegation of power; it was contended that the curfew order and other orders on which it rested were beyond the war powers of the Congress, the military authorities, and of the President, as Commander in Chief of the Army, and, finally, that to apply the curfew order against none but citizens of Japanese ancestry amounted to a constitutionally prohibited discrimination solely on account of race. To these questions, we gave the serious consideration which their importance justified. We upheld the curfew order as an exercise of the power of the government to take steps necessary to prevent espionage and sabotage in an area threatened by Japanese attack.

In the light of the principles we announced in the *Hirabayashi* case, we are unable to conclude that it was beyond the war power of Congress and the Executive to exclude [p218] those of Japanese ancestry from the West Coast war area at the time they did. True, exclusion from the area in which one's home is located is a far greater deprivation than constant confinement to the home from 8 p.m. to 6 a.m. Nothing short of apprehension by the proper military authorities of the gravest imminent danger to the public safety can constitutionally justify either. But exclusion from a threatened area, no less than curfew, has a definite and close relationship to the prevention of espionage and sabotage. The military authorities, charged with the primary responsibility of defending our shores, concluded that curfew provided inadequate protection and ordered exclusion. They did so, as pointed out in our Hirabayashi opinion, in accordance with Congressional authority to the military to say who should, and who should not, remain in the threatened areas.

In this case, the petitioner challenges the assumptions upon which we rested our conclusions in the *Hirabayashi* case. He also urges that, by May, 1942, when Order No. 34 was promulgated, all danger of Japanese invasion of the West Coast had disappeared. After careful consideration of these contentions, we are compelled to reject them.

Here, as in the *Hirabayashi* case, *supra*, at p. 99,

> . . . we cannot reject as unfounded the judgment of the military authorities and of Congress that there were disloyal members of that population, whose number and strength could not be precisely and quickly ascertained. We cannot say that the war-making branches of the Government did not have ground for believing that, in a critical hour, such persons could not readily be isolated and separately dealt with, and constituted a menace to the national defense and safety which demanded that prompt and adequate measures be taken to guard against it.

Like curfew, exclusion of those of Japanese origin was deemed necessary because of the presence of an unascertained number of disloyal members of the group, most of [p219] whom we have no doubt were loyal to this country. It was because we could not reject the finding of the military authorities that it was impossible to bring about an immediate segregation of the disloyal from the loyal that we sustained the validity of the curfew order as applying to the whole group. In the instant case, temporary exclusion of the entire group was rested by the military on the same ground. The judgment that exclusion of the whole group was, for the same reason, a military imperative answers the contention that the exclusion was in the nature of group punishment based on antagonism to those of Japanese origin. That there were members of the group who retained loyalties to Japan has been confirmed by investigations made subsequent to the exclusion. Approximately five thousand American citizens of Japanese ancestry refused to swear unqualified allegiance to the United States and to renounce allegiance to the Japanese Emperor, and several thousand evacuees requested repatriation to Japan.[2]

We uphold the exclusion order as of the time it was made and when the petitioner violated it. *Cf. Chastleton Corporation v. Sinclair*, 264 U.S. 543, 547; *Block v. Hirsh*, 256 U.S. 135, 155. In doing so, we are not unmindful of the hardships imposed by it upon a large group of American citizens. *Cf. Ex parte*

Being treated as non-citizen is part of war? Whites are so treated?

Kawato, 317 U.S. 69, 73. But hardships are part of war, and war is an aggregation of hardships. All citizens alike, both in and out of uniform, feel the impact of war in greater or lesser measure. Citizenship has its responsibilities, as well as its privileges, and, in time of war, the burden is always heavier. Compulsory [p220] exclusion of large groups of citizens from their homes, except under circumstances of direst emergency and peril, is inconsistent with our basic governmental institutions. But when, under conditions of modern warfare, our shores are threatened by hostile forces, the power to protect must be commensurate with the threatened danger.

It is argued that, on May 30, 1942, the date the petitioner was charged with remaining in the prohibited area, there were conflicting orders outstanding, forbidding him both to leave the area and to remain there. Of course, a person cannot be convicted for doing the very thing which it is a crime to fail to do. But the outstanding orders here contained no such contradictory commands.

There was an order issued March 27, 1942, which prohibited petitioner and others of Japanese ancestry from leaving the area, but its effect was specifically limited in time "until and to the extent that a future proclamation or order should so permit or direct." 7 Fed.Reg. 2601. That "future order," the one for violation of which petitioner was convicted, was issued May 3, 1942, and it did "direct" exclusion from the area of all persons of Japanese ancestry before 12 o'clock noon, May 9; furthermore, it contained a warning that all such persons found in the prohibited area would be liable to punishment under the March 21, 1942, Act of Congress. Consequently, the only order in effect touching the petitioner's being in the area on May 30, 1942, the date specified in the information against him, was the May 3 order which prohibited his remaining there, and it was that same order which he stipulated in his trial that he had violated, knowing of its existence. There is therefore no basis for the argument that, on May 30, 1942, he was subject to punishment, under the March 27 and May 3 orders, whether he remained in or left the area.

It does appear, however, that, on May 9, the effective date of the exclusion order, the military authorities had [p221] already determined that the evacuation should be effected by assembling together and placing under guard all those of Japanese ancestry at central points, designated as "assembly centers," in order

> to insure the orderly evacuation and resettlement of Japanese voluntarily migrating from Military Area No. 1, to restrict and regulate such migration.

Public Proclamation No. 4, 7 Fed.Reg. 2601. And on May 19, 1942, eleven days before the time petitioner was charged with unlawfully remaining in the area, Civilian Restrictive Order No. 1, 8 Fed.Reg. 982, provided for detention of those of Japanese ancestry in assembly or relocation centers. It is now argued that the validity of the exclusion order cannot be considered apart from the orders requiring him, after departure from the area, to report and to remain in an assembly or relocation center. The contention is that we must treat these separate orders as one and inseparable; that, for this reason, if detention in the assembly or relocation center would have illegally deprived the petitioner of his liberty, the exclusion order and his conviction under it cannot stand.

We are thus being asked to pass at this time upon the whole subsequent detention program in both assembly and relocation centers, although the only issues framed at the trial related to petitioner's remaining in the prohibited area in violation of the exclusion order. Had petitioner here left the prohibited area and gone to an assembly center, we cannot say, either as a matter of fact or law, that his presence in that center would have resulted in his detention in a relocation center. Some who did report to the assembly center were not sent to relocation centers, but were released upon condition that they remain outside the prohibited zone until the military orders were modified or lifted. This illustrates that they pose different problems, and may be governed by different principles. The lawfulness of one does not necessarily determine the lawfulness of the others. This is made clear [p222] when we analyze the requirements of the separate provisions of the separate orders. These separate requirements were that those of Japanese ancestry (1) depart from the area; (2) report to and temporarily remain in an assembly center; (3) go under military control to a relocation center, there to remain for an indeterminate period until released conditionally or unconditionally by the military authorities. Each of these requirements, it will be noted, imposed distinct duties in connection with the separate steps in a complete evacuation program. Had Congress directly incorporated into one Act the language of these separate orders, and provided sanctions for their violations, disobedience of any one would have constituted a separate offense. *Cf. Blockburger v. United States*, 284 U.S. 299, 304. There is no reason why violations of these orders, insofar as they were promulgated pursuant to Congressional enactment, should not be treated as separate offenses.

The *Endo* case, *post*, p. 283, graphically illustrates the difference between the validity of an order to exclude and the validity of a detention order after exclusion has been effected.

Since the petitioner has not been convicted of failing to report or to remain in an assembly or relocation center, we cannot in this case determine the validity of those separate provisions of the order. It is sufficient here for us to pass upon the order which petitioner violated. To do more would be to go beyond the issues raised, and to decide momentous questions not contained within the framework of the pleadings or the evidence in this case. It will be time enough to decide the serious constitutional issues which petitioner seeks to raise when an assembly or relocation order is applied or is certain to be applied to him, and we have its terms before us.

Some of the members of the Court are of the view that evacuation and detention in an Assembly Center were inseparable. After May 3, 1942, the date of Exclusion [p223] Order No. 34, Korematsu was under compulsion to leave the area not as he would choose, but via an Assembly Center. The Assembly Center was conceived as a part of the machinery for group evacuation. The power to exclude includes the power to do it by force if necessary. And any forcible measure must necessarily entail some degree of detention or restraint, whatever method of removal is selected. But whichever view is taken, it results in holding that the order under which petitioner was convicted was valid.

It is said that we are dealing here with the case of imprisonment of a citizen in a concentration camp solely because of his ancestry, without evidence or inquiry concerning his loyalty and good disposition towards the United States. Our task would be simple, our duty clear, were this a case involving the imprisonment of a loyal citizen in a concentration camp because of racial prejudice. Regardless of the true nature of the assembly and relocation centers—and we deem it unjustifiable to call them concentration camps, with all the ugly connotations that term implies—we are dealing specifically with nothing but an exclusion order. To cast this case into outlines of racial prejudice, without reference to the real military dangers which were presented, merely confuses the issue. Korematsu was not excluded from the Military Area because of hostility to him or his race. He was excluded because we are at war with the Japanese Empire, because the properly constituted military authorities feared an invasion of our West Coast and felt constrained to take proper security measures, because they decided that the military urgency of the situation demanded that all citizens of Japanese ancestry be segregated from the West Coast temporarily, and, finally, because Congress, reposing its confidence in this time of war in our military leaders—as inevitably it must—determined that they should have the power to do just this. There was evidence of disloyalty on the part of some, the military authorities considered that the need for [p224] action was great, and time was short. We cannot—by availing ourselves of the calm perspective of hindsight—now say that, at that time, these actions were unjustified.

Affirmed.

Notes

[1] 140 F.2d 289.

[2] Hearings before the Subcommittee on the National War Agencies Appropriation Bill for 1945, Part II, 608–726; *Final Report, Japanese Evacuation from the West Coast,* 1942, 309–327; Hearings before the Committee on Immigration and Naturalization, House of Representatives, 78th Cong., 2d Sess., on H.R. 2701 and other bills to expatriate certain nationals of the United States, pp. 37–42, 49–58.

MR. JUSTICE FRANKFURTER, concurring.

According to my reading of Civilian Exclusion Order No. 34, it was an offense for Korematsu to be found in Military Area No. 1, the territory wherein he was previously living, except within the bounds of the established Assembly Center of that area. Even though the various orders issued by General DeWitt be deemed a comprehensive code of instructions, their tenor is clear, and not contradictory. They put upon Korematsu the obligation to leave Military Area No. 1, but only by the method prescribed in the instructions, *i.e.,* by reporting to the Assembly Center. I am unable to see how the legal considerations that led to the decision in *Hirabayashi v. United States,* 320 U.S. 81, fail to sustain the military order which made the conduct now in controversy a crime. And so I join in the opinion of the Court, but should like to add a few words of my own.

The provisions of the Constitution which confer on the Congress and the President powers to enable this country to wage war are as much part of the Constitution as provisions looking to a nation at peace. And we have had recent occasion to quote approvingly the statement of former Chief Justice Hughes that the war power of the Government is "the power to wage war successfully." *Hirabayashi v. United States, supra,* at 93, and see *Home Bldg. & L. Assn. v. Blaisdell,* 290 U.S. 398, 426. Therefore, the validity of action under the war power must be judged wholly in the context of war. That action is not to be stigmatized as lawless because like action in times of peace would be lawless. To talk about a military order that expresses an allowable judgment of war needs by those entrusted with the duty of conducting war as "an [p225] unconstitutional order" is to suffuse a part of the Constitution with an atmosphere of unconstitutionality. The respective spheres of action of military authorities and of judges are, of course, very different. But, within their sphere, military authorities are no more outside the bounds of obedience to the Constitution than are judges within theirs. "The war power of the United States, like its other powers . . . is subject to applicable constitutional limitations," *Hamilton v. Kentucky Distilleries* Co., 251 U.S. 146, 156. To recognize that military orders are "reasonably expedient military precautions" in time of war, and yet to deny them constitutional legitimacy, makes of the Constitution an instrument for dialectic subtleties not reasonably to be attributed to the hard-headed Framers, of whom a majority had had actual participation in war. If a military order such as that under review does not transcend the means appropriate for conducting war, such action by the military is as constitutional as would be any authorized action by the Interstate Commerce Commission within the limits of the constitutional power to regulate commerce. And, being an exercise of the war power explicitly granted by the Constitution for safeguarding the national life by prosecuting war effectively, I find nothing in the Constitution which denies to Congress the power to enforce such a valid military order by making its violation an offense triable in the civil courts. Compare *Interstate Commerce Commission v. Brimson*, 154 U.S. 447; 155 U.S. 3, and *Monongahela Bridge Co. v. United States*, 216 U.S. 177. To find that the Constitution does not forbid the military measures now complained of does not carry with it approval of that which Congress and the Executive did. That is their business, not ours.

MR. JUSTICE ROBERTS.

I dissent, because I think the indisputable facts exhibit a clear violation of Constitutional rights.

This is not a case of keeping people off the streets at night, as was *Hirabayashi v. United States*, 320 U.S. 81, [p226] nor a case of temporary exclusion of a citizen from an area for his own safety or that of the community, nor a case of offering him an opportunity to go temporarily out of an area where his presence might cause danger to himself or to his fellows. On the contrary, it is the case of convicting a citizen as a punishment for not submitting to imprisonment in a concentration camp, based on his ancestry, and solely because of his ancestry, without evidence or inquiry concerning his loyalty and good disposition towards the United States. If this be a correct statement of the facts disclosed by this record, and facts of which we take judicial notice, I need hardly labor the conclusion that Constitutional rights have been violated.

The Government's argument, and the opinion of the court, in my judgment, erroneously divide that which is single and indivisible, and thus make the case appear as if the petitioner violated a Military Order, sanctioned by Act of Congress, which excluded him from his home by refusing voluntarily to leave, and so knowingly and intentionally defying the order and the Act of Congress.

The petitioner, a resident of San Leandro, Alameda County, California, is a native of the United States of Japanese ancestry who, according to the uncontradicted evidence, is a loyal citizen of the nation.

A chronological recitation of events will make it plain that the petitioner's supposed offense did not, in truth, consist in his refusal voluntarily to leave the area which included his home in obedience to the order excluding him therefrom. Critical attention must be given to the dates and sequence of events.

December 8, 1941, the United States declared war on Japan.

February 19, 1942, the President issued Executive Order No. 9066,[1] which, after stating the reason for issuing the [p227] order as "protection against espionage and against sabotage to national defense material, national defense premises, and national defense utilities," provided that certain Military Commanders might, in their discretion, "prescribe military areas" and define their extent,

> from which any or all persons may be excluded, and with respect to which the right of any person to enter, remain in, or leave shall be subject to whatever restrictions

the "Military Commander may impose in his discretion."

February 20, 1942, Lieutenant General DeWitt was designated Military Commander of the Western Defense Command embracing the westernmost states of the Union—about one-fourth of the total area of the nation.

March 2, 1942, General DeWitt promulgated Public Proclamation No. 1,[2] which recites that the entire Pacific Coast is "particularly subject to attack, to attempted invasion . . . , and, in connection therewith, is subject to espionage and acts of sabotage." It states that, "as a matter of military necessity," certain military areas and zones are established known as Military Areas Nos. 1 and 2. It adds that "[s]uch persons or classes of persons as the situation may require" will, by subsequent orders, "be excluded from all of Military Area No. 1" and from certain zones in Military Area No. 2. Subsequent proclamations were made which, together with Proclamation No. 1, included in such areas and zones all of California, Washington, Oregon, Idaho, Montana, Nevada and Utah, and the southern portion of Arizona. The orders required that, if any person of Japanese, German or Italian ancestry residing in Area No. 1 desired to change his habitual residence, he must execute and deliver to the authorities a Change of Residence Notice.

San Leandro, the city of petitioner's residence, lies in Military Area No. 1. [p228]

On March 2, 1942, the petitioner, therefore, had notice that, by Executive Order, the President, to prevent espionage and sabotage, had authorized the Military to exclude him from certain areas and to prevent his entering or leaving certain areas without permission. He was on notice that his home city had been included, by Military Order, in Area No. 1, and he was on notice further that, at sometime in the future, the Military Commander would make an order for the exclusion of certain persons, not described or classified, from various zones including that, in which he lived.

March 21, 1942, Congress enacted[3] that anyone who knowingly

> shall enter, remain in, leave, or commit any act in any military area or military zone prescribed . . . by any military commander . . . contrary to the restrictions applicable to any such area or zone or contrary to the order of . . . any such military commander

shall be guilty of a misdemeanor. This is the Act under which the petitioner was charged.

March 24, 1942, General DeWitt instituted the curfew for certain areas within his command, by an order the validity of which was sustained in *Hirabayashi v. United States, supra.*

March 24, 1942, General DeWitt began to issue a series of exclusion orders relating to specified areas.

March 27, 1942, by Proclamation No. 4,[4] the General recited that

> it is necessary, in order to provide for the welfare and to insure the orderly evacuation and resettlement of Japanese voluntarily migrating from Military Area No. 1, to restrict and regulate such migration, and ordered that, as of March 29, 1942,

> all alien Japanese and persons of Japanese ancestry who are within the limits of Military Area No. 1, be and they are hereby [p229] prohibited from leaving that area for any purpose until and to the extent that a future proclamation or order of this headquarters shall so permit or direct.[5]

No order had been made excluding the petitioner from the area in which he lived. By Proclamation No. 4, he was, after March 29, 1942, confined to the limits of Area No. 1. If the Executive Order No. 9066 and the Act of Congress meant what they said, to leave that area, in the face of Proclamation No. 4, would be to commit a misdemeanor.

May 3, 1942, General DeWitt issued Civilian Exclusion Order No. 34[6] providing that, after 12 o'clock May 8, 1942, all persons of Japanese ancestry, both alien and nonalien, were to be excluded from a described portion of Military Area No. 1, which included the County of Alameda, California. The order required a responsible member of each family and each individual living alone to report, at a time set, at a Civil Control Station for instructions to go to an Assembly Center, and added that any person failing to comply with the provisions of the order who was found in the described area after the date set would be liable to prosecution under the Act of March 21, 1942, *supra*. It is important to note that the order, by its express terms, had no application to persons within the bounds "of an established Assembly Center pursuant to instructions from this Headquarters . . ." The obvious purpose of the orders made, taken together, was to drive all citizens of Japanese ancestry into Assembly Centers within the zones of their residence, under pain of criminal prosecution. [p230]

The predicament in which the petitioner thus found himself was this: he was forbidden, by Military Order, to leave the zone in which he lived; he was forbidden, by Military Order, after a date fixed, to be found within that zone unless he were in an Assembly Center located in that zone. General DeWitt's report to the Secretary of War concerning the programme of evacuation and relocation of Japanese makes it entirely clear, if it were necessary to refer to that document—and, in the light of the above recitation, I think it is not,—that an Assembly Center was a euphemism for a prison. No person within such a center was permitted to leave except by Military Order.

In the dilemma that he dare not remain in his home, or voluntarily leave the area, without incurring criminal penalties, and that the only way he could avoid punishment was to go to an Assembly Center and submit himself to military imprisonment, the petitioner did nothing.

June 12, 1942, an Information was filed in the District Court for Northern California charging a violation of the Act of March 21, 1942, in that petitioner had knowingly remained within the area covered by Exclusion Order No. 34. A demurrer to the information having been overruled, the petitioner was tried under a plea of not guilty, and convicted. Sentence was suspended, and he was placed on probation for five years. We know, however, in the light of the foregoing recitation, that he was at once taken into military custody and lodged in an Assembly Center. We further know that, on March 18, 1942, the President had promulgated Executive Order No. 9102,[7] establishing the War Relocation Authority under which so-called Relocation Centers, a euphemism for concentration camps, were established pursuant to cooperation between the military authorities of the Western Defense Command and the Relocation Authority, and that the petitioner has [p231] been confined either in an Assembly Center within the zone in which he had lived or has been removed to a Relocation Center where, as the facts disclosed in *Ex parte Endo* (post, p. 283) demonstrate, he was illegally held in custody.

The Government has argued this case as if the only order outstanding at the time the petitioner was arrested and informed against was Exclusion Order No. 34, ordering him to leave the area in which he resided, which was the basis of the information against him. That argument has evidently been effective. The opinion refers to the *Hirabayashi case, supra,* to show that this court has sustained the validity of a curfew order in an emergency. The argument, then, is that exclusion from a given area of danger, while somewhat more sweeping than a curfew regulation, is of the same nature—a temporary expedient made necessary by a sudden emergency. This, I think, is a substitution of an hypothetical case for the case actually before the court. I might agree with the court's disposition of the hypothetical case.[8] The liberty of every American citizen freely to come and to go must frequently, in the face of sudden danger, be temporarily limited or suspended. The civil authorities must often resort to the expedient of excluding citizens temporarily from a locality. The drawing of fire lines in the case of a conflagration, the removal of persons from the area where a pestilence has broken out, are familiar examples. If the exclusion worked by Exclusion Order No. 34 were of that nature, the *Hirabayashi* case would be authority for sustaining it. [p232] But the facts above recited, and those set forth in *Ex parte Endo, supra,* show that the exclusion was but a part of an overall plan for forceable detention. This case cannot, therefore, be decided on any such narrow ground as the possible validity of a Temporary Exclusion Order under which the residents of an area are given an opportunity to leave and go elsewhere in their native land outside the boundaries of a military area. To make the case turn on any such assumption is to shut our eyes to reality.

As I have said above, the petitioner, prior to his arrest, was faced with two diametrically contradictory orders given sanction by the Act of Congress of March 21, 1942. The earlier of those orders made him a criminal if he left the zone in which he resided; the later made him a criminal if he did not leave.

I had supposed that, if a citizen was constrained by two laws, or two orders having the force of law, and obedience to one would violate the other, to punish him for violation of either would deny him due process of law. And I had supposed that, under these circumstances, a conviction for violating one of the orders could not stand.

We cannot shut our eyes to the fact that, had the petitioner attempted to violate Proclamation No. 4 and leave the military area in which he lived, he would have been arrested and tried and convicted for violation of Proclamation No. 4. The two conflicting orders, one which commanded him to stay and the other which commanded him to go, were nothing but a cleverly devised trap to accomplish the real purpose of the military authority, which was to lock him up in a concentration camp. The only course by which the petitioner could avoid arrest and prosecution was to go to that camp according to instructions to be given him when he reported at a Civil Control Center. We know that is the fact. Why should we set up a figmentary and artificial situation, instead of addressing ourselves to the actualities of the case? [p233]

These stark realities are met by the suggestion that it is lawful to compel an American citizen to submit to illegal imprisonment on the assumption that he might, after going to the Assembly Center, apply for his discharge by suing out a writ of habeas corpus, as was done in the *Endo* case, *supra*. The answer, of course, is that, where he was subject to two conflicting laws, he was not bound, in order to escape violation of one or the other, to surrender his liberty for any period. Nor will it do to say that the detention was a necessary part of the process of evacuation, and so we are here concerned only with the validity of the latter.

Again, it is a new doctrine of constitutional law that one indicted for disobedience to an unconstitutional statute may not defend on the ground of the invalidity of the statute, but must obey it though he knows it is no law, and, after he has suffered the disgrace of conviction and lost his liberty by sentence, then, and not before, seek, from within prison walls, to test the validity of the law.

Moreover, it is beside the point to rest decision in part on the fact that the petitioner, for his own reasons, wished to remain in his home. If, as is the fact, he was constrained so to do, it is indeed a narrow application of constitutional rights to ignore the order which constrained him in order to sustain his conviction for violation of another contradictory order.

I would reverse the judgment of conviction.

Notes

[1] 17 Fed.Reg. 1407.

[2] 7 Fed.Reg. 2320

[3] 56 Stat. 173.

[4] 7 Fed.Reg. 2601.

[5] The italics in the quotation are mine. The use of the word "voluntarily" exhibits a grim irony probably not lost on petitioner and others in like case. Either so or its use was a disingenuous attempt to camouflage the compulsion which was to be applied.

[6] 7 Fed.Reg. 3967.

[7] 7 Fed.Reg. 2165.

[8] My agreement would depend on the definition and application of the terms "temporary" and "emergency." No pronouncement of the commanding officer can, in my view, preclude judicial inquiry and determination whether an emergency ever existed and whether, if so, it remained at the date of the restraint out of which the litigation arose. *Cf. Chastleton Corp. v. Sinclair*, 264 U.S. 543.

MR. JUSTICE MURPHY, dissenting.

This exclusion of "all persons of Japanese ancestry, both alien and non-alien," from the Pacific Coast area on a plea of military necessity in the absence of martial law ought not to be approved. Such exclusion goes over "the very brink of constitutional power," and falls into the ugly abyss of racism.

In dealing with matters relating to the prosecution and progress of a war, we must accord great respect and consideration [p234] to the judgments of the military authorities who are on the scene and who have full knowledge of the military facts. The scope of their discretion must, as a matter of necessity and common sense, be wide. And their judgments ought not to be overruled lightly by those whose training and duties ill-equip them to deal intelligently with matters so vital to the physical security of the nation.

At the same time, however, it is essential that there be definite limits to military discretion, especially where martial law has not been declared. Individuals must not be left impoverished of their constitutional rights on a plea of military necessity that has neither substance nor support. Thus, like other claims conflicting with the asserted constitutional rights of the individual, the military claim must subject itself to the judicial process of having its reasonableness determined and its conflicts with other interests reconciled.

> What are the allowable limits of military discretion, and whether or not
> they have been overstepped in a particular case, are judicial questions.

Sterling v. Constantin, 287 U.S. 378, 401.

The judicial test of whether the Government, on a plea of military necessity, can validly deprive an individual of any of his constitutional rights is whether the deprivation is reasonably related to a public danger that is so "immediate, imminent, and impending" as not to admit of delay and not to permit the intervention of ordinary constitutional processes to alleviate the danger. *United States v. Russell*, 13 Wall. 623, 627–628; *Mitchell v. Harmony*, 13 How. 115, 134–135; *Raymond v. Thomas*, 91 U.S. 712, 716. Civilian Exclusion Order No. 34, banishing from a prescribed area of the Pacific Coast "all persons of Japanese ancestry, both alien and non-alien," clearly does not meet that test. Being an obvious racial discrimination, the [p235] order deprives all those within its scope of the equal protection of the laws as guaranteed by the Fifth Amendment. It further deprives these individuals of their constitutional rights to live and work where they will, to establish a home where they choose and to move about freely. In excommunicating them without benefit of hearings, this order also deprives them of all their constitutional rights to procedural due process. Yet no reasonable relation to an "immediate, imminent, and impending" public danger is evident to support this racial restriction, which is one of the most sweeping and complete deprivations of constitutional rights in the history of this nation in the absence of martial law.

It must be conceded that the military and naval situation in the spring of 1942 was such as to generate a very real fear of invasion of the Pacific Coast, accompanied by fears of sabotage and espionage in that area. The military command was therefore justified in adopting all reasonable means necessary to combat these dangers. In adjudging the military action taken in light of the then apparent dangers, we must not erect too high or too meticulous standards; it is necessary only that the action have some reasonable relation to the removal of the dangers of invasion, sabotage and espionage. But the exclusion, either temporarily or permanently, of all persons with Japanese blood in their veins has no such reasonable relation. And that relation is lacking because the exclusion order necessarily must rely for its reasonableness upon the assumption that all persons of Japanese ancestry may have a dangerous tendency to commit sabotage and espionage and to aid our Japanese enemy in other ways. It is difficult to believe that reason, logic, or experience could be marshalled in support of such an assumption.

That this forced exclusion was the result in good measure of this erroneous assumption of racial guilt, rather than [p236] *bona fide* military necessity is evidenced by the Commanding General's Final Report on the evacuation from the Pacific Coast area. In it, he refers to all individuals of Japanese descent as "subversive," as belonging to "an enemy race" whose "racial strains are undiluted," and as constituting "over 112,000 potential enemies . . . at large today" along the Pacific Coast.[2] In support of this blanket condemnation of all persons of Japanese descent, however, no reliable evidence is cited to show that such individuals were generally disloyal,[3] or had generally so conducted themselves in this area as to constitute a special menace to defense installations or war industries, or had otherwise, by their behavior, furnished reasonable ground for their exclusion as a group.

Justification for the exclusion is sought, instead, mainly upon questionable racial and sociological grounds not [p237] ordinarily within the realm of expert military judgment, supplemented by certain semi-military conclusions drawn from an unwarranted use of circumstantial evidence. Individuals of Japanese ancestry are condemned because they are said to be "a large, unassimilated, tightly knit racial group, bound to an enemy nation by strong ties of race, culture, custom and religion."[4] They are claimed to be given to "emperor worshipping ceremonies,"[5] and to "dual citizenship."[6] Japanese language schools and allegedly pro-Japanese organizations are cited as evidence of possible group disloyalty,[7] together with facts as to [p238] certain persons being educated and residing at length in Japan.[8] It is intimated that many of these individuals deliberately resided "adjacent to strategic points," thus enabling them

> to carry into execution a tremendous program of sabotage on a mass scale should any considerable number of them have been inclined to do so.[9]

The need for protective custody is also asserted. The report refers, without identity, to "numerous incidents of violence," as well as to other admittedly unverified or cumulative incidents. From this, plus certain other events not shown to have been connected with the Japanese Americans, it is concluded that the "situation was fraught with danger to the Japanese population itself," and that the general public "was ready to take matters into its own hands."[10] Finally, it is intimated, though not directly [p239] charged or proved, that persons of Japanese ancestry were responsible for three minor isolated shellings and bombings of the Pacific Coast area,[11] as well as for unidentified radio transmissions and night signaling.

The main reasons relied upon by those responsible for the forced evacuation, therefore, do not prove a reasonable relation between the group characteristics of Japanese Americans and the dangers of invasion, sabotage and espionage. The reasons appear, instead, to be largely an accumulation of much of the misinformation, half-truths and insinuations that for years have been directed against Japanese Americans by people with racial and economic prejudices—the same people who have been among the foremost advocates of the evacuation.[12] A military judgment [p240] based upon such racial and sociological considerations is not entitled to the great weight ordinarily given the judgments based upon strictly military considerations. Especially is this so when every charge relative to race, religion, culture, geographical location, and legal and economic status has been substantially discredited by independent studies made by experts in these matters.[13]

The military necessity which is essential to the validity of the evacuation order thus resolves itself into a few intimations that certain individuals actively aided the enemy, from which it is inferred that the entire group of Japanese Americans could not be trusted to be or remain loyal to the United States. No one denies, of course, that there were some disloyal persons of Japanese descent on the Pacific Coast who did all in their power to aid their ancestral land. Similar disloyal activities have been engaged in by many persons of German, Italian and even more pioneer stock in our country. But to infer that examples of individual disloyalty prove group disloyalty and justify discriminatory action against the entire group is to deny that, under our system of law, individual guilt is the sole basis for deprivation of rights. Moreover, this inference, which is at the very heart of the evacuation orders, has been used in support of the abhorrent and despicable treatment of minority groups by the dictatorial tyrannies which this nation is now pledged to destroy. To give constitutional sanction to that inference in this case, however well intentioned may have been the military command on the Pacific Coast, is to adopt one of the cruelest of the rationales used by our enemies to destroy the dignity of the individual and to encourage and open the door to discriminatory actions against other minority groups in the passions of tomorrow. [p241]

No adequate reason is given for the failure to treat these Japanese Americans on an individual basis by holding investigations and hearings to separate the loyal from the disloyal, as was done in the case of persons of German and Italian ancestry. *See* House Report No. 2124 (77th Cong., 2d Sess.) 247–52. It is asserted merely that the loyalties of this group "were unknown and time was of the essence."[14] Yet nearly four months elapsed after Pearl Harbor before the first exclusion order was issued; nearly eight months went by until the last order was issued, and the last of these "subversive" persons was not actually removed until almost eleven months had elapsed. Leisure and deliberation seem to have been more of the essence than speed. And the fact that conditions were not such as to warrant a declaration of martial law adds strength to the belief that the factors of time and military necessity were not as urgent as they have been represented to be.

Moreover, there was no adequate proof that the Federal Bureau of Investigation and the military and naval intelligence services did not have the espionage and sabotage situation well in hand during this long period. Nor is there any denial of the fact that not one person of Japanese ancestry was accused or convicted of espionage or sabotage after Pearl Harbor while they were still free,[15] a fact which is some evidence of the loyalty of the vast majority of these individuals and of the effectiveness of the established methods of combatting these evils. It [p242] seems incredible that, under these circumstances, it would have been impossible to hold loyalty hearings for the mere 112,000 persons involved—or at least for the 70,000 American citizens— especially when a large part of this number represented children and elderly men and women.[16] Any inconvenience that may have accompanied an attempt to conform to procedural due process cannot be said to justify violations of constitutional rights of individuals.

I dissent, therefore, from this legalization of racism. Racial discrimination in any form and in any degree has no justifiable part whatever in our democratic way of life. It is unattractive in any setting, but it is utterly revolting among a free people who have embraced the principles set forth in the Constitution of the United States. All residents of this nation are kin in some way by blood or culture to a foreign land. Yet they are primarily and necessarily a part of the new and distinct civilization of the United States. They must, accordingly, be treated at all times as the heirs of the American experiment, and as entitled to all the rights and freedoms guaranteed by the Constitution.

Notes

[1] *Final Report, Japanese Evacuation from the West Coast,* 1942, by Lt.Gen. J. L. DeWitt. This report is dated June 5, 1943, but was not made public until January, 1944.

[2] Further evidence of the Commanding General's attitude toward individuals of Japanese ancestry is revealed in his voluntary testimony on April 13, 1943, in San Francisco before the House Naval Affairs Subcommittee to Investigate Congested Areas, Part 3, pp. 739 40 (78th Cong., 1st Sess.):

I don't want any of them [persons of Japanese ancestry] here. They are a dangerous element. There is no way to determine their loyalty. The west coast contains too many vital installations essential to the defense of the country to allow any Japanese on this coast. . . . The danger of the Japanese was, and is now—if they are permitted to come back—espionage and sabotage. It makes no difference whether he is an American citizen, he is still a Japanese. American citizenship does not necessarily determine loyalty. . . . But we must worry about the Japanese all the time until he is wiped off the map. Sabotage and espionage will make problems as long as he is allowed in this area. . . .

[3] *The Final Report,* p. 9, casts a cloud of suspicion over the entire group by saying that, "while it was believed that some were loyal, it was known that many were not." (Italics added.)

[4] *Final Report,* p. vii; see also pp. 9, 17. To the extent that assimilation is a problem, it is largely the result of certain social customs and laws of the American general public. Studies demonstrate that persons of Japanese descent are readily susceptible to integration in our society if given the opportunity. Strong, *The Second-Generation Japanese Problem* (1934); Smith, *Americans in Process* (1937); Mears, Resident *Orientals on the American Pacific Coast* (1928); Millis, *The Japanese Problem in the United States* (1942). The failure to accomplish an ideal status of

assimilation, therefore, cannot be charged to the refusal of these persons to become Americanized, or to their loyalty to Japan. And the retention by some persons of certain customs and religious practices of their ancestors is no criterion of their loyalty to the United States.

[5] *Final Report*, pp. 10–11. No sinister correlation between the emperor worshipping activities and disloyalty to America was shown.

[6] *Final Report*, p. 22. The charge of "dual citizenship" springs from a misunderstanding of the simple fact that Japan, in the past, used the doctrine of jus sanguinis, as she had a right to do under international law, and claimed as her citizens all persons born of Japanese nationals wherever located. Japan has greatly modified this doctrine, however, by allowing all Japanese born in the United States to renounce any claim of dual citizenship and by releasing her claim as to all born in the United States after 1925. See Freeman, "Genesis, Exodus, and Leviticus: Genealogy, Evacuation, and Law," 28 *Cornell L.Q.* 414, 447–8, and authorities there cited; McWilliams, *Prejudice*, 123–4 (1944).

[7] *Final Report*, pp. 12–13. We have had various foreign language schools in this country for generations without considering their existence as ground for racial discrimination. No subversive activities or teachings have been shown in connection with the Japanese schools. McWilliams, *Prejudice*, 121–3 (1944).

[8] *Final Report*, pp. 13–15. Such persons constitute a very small part of the entire group, and most of them belong to the Kibei movement—the actions and membership of which are well known to our Government agents.

[9] *Final Report*, p. 10; see also pp. vii, 9, 15–17. This insinuation, based purely upon speculation and circumstantial evidence, completely overlooks the fact that the main geographic pattern of Japanese population was fixed many years ago with reference to economic, social and soil conditions. Limited occupational outlets and social pressures encouraged their concentration near their initial points of entry on the Pacific Coast. That these points may now be near certain strategic military and industrial areas is no proof of a diabolical purpose on the part of Japanese Americans. See McWilliams, *Prejudice*, 119–121 (1944); *House Report No. 2124* (77th Cong., 2d Sess.), 59–93.

[10] *Final Report*, pp. 8–9. This dangerous doctrine of protective custody, as proved by recent European history, should have absolutely no standing as an excuse for the deprivation of the rights of minority groups. See *House Report No. 1911* (77th Cong., 2d Sess.) 1–2. Cf. *House Report No. 2124* (77th Cong., & Sess.) 145–7. In this instance, moreover, there are only two minor instances of violence on record involving persons of Japanese ancestry. McWilliams, *What About Our Japanese-Americans?* Public Affairs Pamphlets, No. 91, p. 8 (1944).

[11] *Final Report*, p. 18. One of these incidents (the reputed dropping of incendiary bombs on an Oregon forest) occurred on Sept. 9, 1942—a considerable time after

the Japanese Americans had been evacuated from their homes and placed in Assembly Centers. See *New York Times*, Sept. 15, 1942, p. 1, col. 3.

[12] Special interest groups were extremely active in applying pressure for mass evacuation. See *House Report No. 2124* (77th Cong., 2d Sess.) 154–6; McWilliams, *Prejudice*, 128 (1944). Mr. Austin E. Anson, managing secretary of the Salinas Vegetable Grower-Shipper Association, has frankly admitted that

> We're charged with wanting to get rid of the Japs for selfish reasons. . . . We do. It's a question of whether the white man lives on the Pacific Coast or the brown men. They came into this valley to work, and they stayed to take over. . . . They undersell the white man in the markets. . . . They work their women and children while the white farmer has to pay wages for his help. If all the Japs were removed tomorrow, we'd never miss them in two weeks, because the white farmers can take over and produce everything the Jap grows. And we don't want them back when the war ends, either.

Quoted by Taylor in his article "The People Nobody Wants," 214 *Sat.Eve.Post* 24, 66 (May 9, 1942).

[13] See notes 4–12, supra.

[14] *Final Report*, p. vii; see also p. 18.

[15] *The Final Report*, p. 34, makes the amazing statement that, as of February 14, 1942, "The very fact that no sabotage has taken place to date is a disturbing and confirming indication that such action will be taken." Apparently, in the minds of the military leaders, there was no way that the Japanese Americans could escape the suspicion of sabotage.

[16] During a period of six months, the 112 alien tribunals or hearing boards set up by the British Government shortly after the outbreak of the present war summoned and examined approximately 74,000 German and Austrian aliens. These tribunals determined whether each individual enemy alien was a real enemy of the Allies or only a "friendly enemy." About 64,000 were freed from internment and from any special restrictions, and only 2,000 were interned. Kempner, "The Enemy Alien Problem in the Present War," 34 *Amer. Journ. of Int. Law* 443, 414–416; *House Report No. 2124* (77th Cong., 2d Sess.), 280–281.

MR. JUSTICE JACKSON, dissenting.

Korematsu was born on our soil, of parents born in Japan. The Constitution makes him a citizen of the United States by nativity, and a citizen of California by [p243] residence. No claim is made that he is not loyal to this country. There is no suggestion that, apart from the matter involved here, he is not law-abiding and well disposed. Korematsu, however, has been convicted of an act not commonly a crime. It consists merely of being present in the state whereof he is a citizen, near the place where he was born, and where all his life he has lived.

Even more unusual is the series of military orders which made this conduct a crime. They forbid such a one to remain, and they also forbid him to leave. They were so drawn that the only way Korematsu could avoid violation was to give himself up to the military authority. This meant submission to custody, examination, and transportation out of the territory, to be followed by indeterminate confinement in detention camps.

A citizen's presence in the locality, however, was made a crime only if his parents were of Japanese birth. Had Korematsu been one of four—the others being, say, a German alien enemy, an Italian alien enemy, and a citizen of American-born ancestors, convicted of treason but out on parole—only Korematsu's presence would have violated the order. The difference between their innocence and his crime would result, not from anything he did, said, or thought, different than they, but only in that he was born of different racial stock.

Now, if any fundamental assumption underlies our system, it is that guilt is personal and not inheritable. Even if all of one's antecedents had been convicted of treason, the Constitution forbids its penalties to be visited upon him, for it provides that "no attainder of treason shall work corruption of blood, or forfeiture except during the life of the person attainted." But here is an attempt to make an otherwise innocent act a crime merely because this prisoner is the son of parents as to whom he had no choice, and belongs to a race from which there is no way to resign. If Congress, in peacetime legislation, should [p244] enact such a criminal law, I should suppose this Court would refuse to enforce it.

But the "law" which this prisoner is convicted of disregarding is not found in an act of Congress, but in a military order. Neither the Act of Congress nor the Executive Order of the President, nor both together, would afford a basis for this conviction. It rests on the orders of General DeWitt. And it is said that, if the military commander had reasonable military grounds for promulgating the orders, they are constitutional, and become law, and the Court is required to enforce them. There are several reasons why I cannot subscribe to this doctrine.

It would be impracticable and dangerous idealism to expect or insist that each specific military command in an area of probable operations will conform to conventional tests of constitutionality. When an area is so beset that it must be put under military control at all, the paramount consideration is that its measures be successful, rather than legal. The armed services must protect a society, not merely its Constitution. The very essence of the military job is to marshal physical force, to remove every obstacle to its effectiveness, to give it every strategic advantage. Defense measures will not, and often should not, be held within the limits that bind civil authority in peace. No court can require such a commander in such circumstances to act as a reasonable man; he may be unreasonably cautious and exacting. Perhaps he should be. But a commander, in temporarily focusing the life of a community on defense, is carrying out a military program; he is not making law in the sense the courts know the term. He issues orders, and they may have a certain authority as military commands, although they may be very bad as constitutional law.

But if we cannot confine military expedients by the Constitution, neither would I distort the Constitution to approve all that the military may deem expedient. That is [p245] what the Court appears to be doing, whether consciously or not. I cannot say, from any evidence before me, that the orders of General DeWitt were not reasonably expedient military precautions, nor could I say that they were. But even if they were permissible military procedures, I deny that it follows that they are constitutional. If, as the Court holds, it does follow, then we may as well say that any military order will be constitutional, and have done with it.

The limitation under which courts always will labor in examining the necessity for a military order are illustrated by this case. How does the Court know that these orders have a reasonable basis in necessity? No evidence whatever on that subject has been taken by this or any other court. There is sharp controversy as to the credibility of the DeWitt report. So the Court, having no real evidence before it, has no choice but to accept General DeWitt's own unsworn, self-serving statement, untested by any cross-examination, that what he did was reasonable. And thus it will always be when courts try to look into the reasonableness of a military order.

In the very nature of things, military decisions are not susceptible of intelligent judicial appraisal. They do not pretend to rest on evidence, but are made on information that often would not be admissible and on assumptions that could not be proved. Information in support of an order could not be disclosed to courts without danger that it would reach the enemy. Neither can courts act on communications made in confidence. Hence, courts can never have any real alternative to accepting the mere declaration of the authority that issued the order that it was reasonably necessary from a military viewpoint.

Much is said of the danger to liberty from the Army program for deporting and detaining these citizens of Japanese extraction. But a judicial construction of the due process clause that will sustain this order is a far more

[p246] subtle blow to liberty than the promulgation of the order itself. A military order, however unconstitutional, is not apt to last longer than the military emergency. Even during that period, a succeeding commander may revoke it all. But once a judicial opinion rationalizes such an order to show that it conforms to the Constitution, or rather rationalizes the Constitution to show that the Constitution sanctions such an order, the Court for all time has validated the principle of racial discrimination in criminal procedure and of transplanting American citizens. The principle then lies about like a loaded weapon, ready for the hand of any authority that can bring forward a plausible claim of an urgent need. Every repetition imbeds that principle more deeply in our law and thinking and expands it to new purposes. All who observe the work of courts are familiar with what Judge Cardozo described as "the tendency of a principle to expand itself to the limit of its logic."[1] A military commander may overstep the bounds of constitutionality, and it is an incident. But if we review and approve, that passing incident becomes the doctrine of the Constitution. There it has a generative power of its own, and all that it creates will be in its own image. Nothing better illustrates this danger than does the Court's opinion in this case.

It argues that we are bound to uphold the conviction of Korematsu because we upheld one in *Hirabayashi v. United States*, 320 U.S. 81, when we sustained these orders insofar as they applied a curfew requirement to a citizen of Japanese ancestry. I think we should learn something from that experience.

In that case, we were urged to consider only the curfew feature, that being all that technically was involved, because it was the only count necessary to sustain Hirabayashi's conviction and sentence. We yielded, and the Chief Justice guarded the opinion as carefully as language [p247] will do. He said:

> Our investigation here does not go beyond the inquiry whether, in the light of all the relevant circumstances preceding and attending their promulgation, the challenged orders and statute *afforded a reasonable basis for the action taken in imposing the curfew.*

320 U.S. at 101.

> We decide only the issue as we have defined it—we decide only that the *curfew order*, as applied, and at the time it was applied, was within the boundaries of the war power.

320 U.S. at 102. And again: "It is unnecessary to consider whether or to what extent *such findings would support orders differing from the curfew order.*" 320 U.S. at 105. (Italics supplied.) However, in spite of our limiting words, we did validate a discrimination on the basis of ancestry for mild and temporary

deprivation of liberty. Now the principle of racial discrimination is pushed from support of mild measures to very harsh ones, and from temporary deprivations to indeterminate ones. And the precedent which it is said requires us to do so is *Hirabayashi*. The Court is now saying that, in *Hirabayashi*, we did decide the very things we there said we were not deciding. Because we said that these citizens could be made to stay in their homes during the hours of dark, it is said we must require them to leave home entirely, and if that, we are told they may also be taken into custody for deportation, and, if that, it is argued, they may also be held for some undetermined time in detention camps. How far the principle of this case would be extended before plausible reasons would play out, I do not know.

I should hold that a civil court cannot be made to enforce an order which violates constitutional limitations even if it is a reasonable exercise of military authority. The courts can exercise only the judicial power, can apply only law, and must abide by the Constitution, or they cease to be civil courts and become instruments of military policy. [p248]

Of course, the existence of a military power resting on force, so vagrant, so centralized, so necessarily heedless of the individual, is an inherent threat to liberty. But I would not lead people to rely on this Court for a review that seems to me wholly delusive. The military reasonableness of these orders can only be determined by military superiors. If the people ever let command of the war power fall into irresponsible and unscrupulous hands, the courts wield no power equal to its restraint. The chief restraint upon those who command the physical forces of the country, in the future as in the past, must be their responsibility to the political judgments of their contemporaries and to the moral judgments of history.

My duties as a justice, as I see them, do not require me to make a military judgment as to whether General DeWitt's evacuation and detention program was a reasonable military necessity. I do not suggest that the courts should have attempted to interfere with the Army in carrying out its task. But I do not think they may be asked to execute a military expedient that has no place in law under the Constitution. I would reverse the judgment and discharge the prisoner.

Note

[1] *Nature of the Judicial Process*, p. 51.

from *History of the Peloponnesian War*

Thucydides

Who Thucydides narrates

In 427 B.C., having put down a revolt by the city state of Mytilene, the Athenian assembly decided initially to execute all Mytilenian citizens. The next day, the assembly reconsiders.

The Mytilenian Debate

heart of the moment

When Salaethus and the other prisoners reached Athens, the Athenians immediately put Salaethus to death in spite of the fact that he undertook, among other things, to have the Peloponnesians withdrawn from Plataea, which was still being besieged. They then discussed what was to be done with the other prisoners and, in their angry mood, decided to put to death not only those now in their hands but also the entire adult male population of Mytilene, and to make slaves of the women and children. What they held against Mytilene was the fact that it had revolted even though it was not a subject state, like the others, and the bitterness of their feelings was considerably increased by the fact that the Peloponnesian feet had actually dared to cross over to Ionia to support the revolt. This, it was thought, could never have happened unless the revolt had been long premeditated. So they sent a trireme to Paches to inform him of what had been decided, with orders to put the Mytilenians to death immediately.

Next day, however, there was a sudden change of feeling and people began to think how cruel and how unprecedented such a decision was—to destroy not only the guilty, but the entire population of a state. Observing this, the deputation from Mytilene which was in Athens and the Athenians who were supporting them approached the authorities with a view to having the question debated again. They won their point the more easily because the authorities themselves saw clearly that most of the citizens were wanting someone to give them a chance of reconsidering the matter. So an assembly was called at once. Various opinions were expressed on both sides, and Cleon, the son of *Speaker* Cleaenetus, spoke again. It was he who had been responsible for passing the original motion for putting the Mytilenians to death. He was remarkable

trireme [L. triremis fr - three + remus oar] ancient galley with three ranks of oars one above another, used chiefly as a warship

among the Athenians for the violence of his character, and at this time he exercised far the greatest influence over the people.[1] He spoke as follows:

'Personally I have had occasion often enough already to observe that a democracy is incapable of governing others, and I am all the more convinced of this when I see how you are now changing your minds about the Mytilenians. Because fear and conspiracy play no part in your daily relations with each other, you imagine that the same thing is true of your allies, and you fail to see that when you allow them to persuade you to make a mistaken decision and when you give way to your own feelings of compassion you are being guilty of a kind of weakness which is dangerous to you and which will not make them love you any more. What you do not realize is that your empire is a tyranny exercised over subjects who do not like it and who are always plotting against you; you will not make them obey you by injuring your own interests in order to do them a favour; your leadership depends on superior strength and not on any goodwill of theirs. And this is the very worst thing—to pass measures and then not to abide by them. We should realize that a city is better off with bad laws, so long as they remain fixed, than with good laws that are constantly being altered, that lack of learning combined with sound common sense is more helpful than the kind of cleverness that gets out of hand, and that as a general rule states are better governed by the man in the street than by intellectuals. These are the sort of people who want to appear wiser than the laws, who want to get their own way in every general discussion, because they feel that they cannot show off their intelligence in matters of greater importance, and who, as a result, very often bring ruin on their country. But the other kind—the people who are not so confident in their own intelligence—are prepared to admit that the laws are wiser than they are and that they lack the ability to pull to pieces a speech made by a good speaker; they are unbiased judges, and not people taking part in some kind of a competition; so things usually go well when they are in control. We statesmen, too, should try to be like them, instead of being carried away by mere cleverness and a desire to show off our intelligence and so giving you, the people, advice which we do not really believe in ourselves.

'As for me, I have not altered my opinion, and I am amazed at those who have proposed a reconsideration of the question of Mytilene, thus causing a delay which is all to the advantage of the guilty party. After a lapse of time the injured party will lose the edge of his anger when he comes to act against those who have wronged him; whereas the best punishment and the one most fitted to the crime is when reprisals follow immediately. I shall be amazed, too, if anyone contradicts me and attempts to prove that the harm done to us by

Mytilene is really a good thing for us, or that when we suffer ourselves we are somehow doing harm to our allies. It is obvious that anyone who is going to say this must either have such confidence in his powers as an orator that he will struggle to persuade you that what has been finally settled was, on the contrary, not decided at all, or else he must have been bribed to put together some elaborate speech with which he will try to lead you out of the right track. But in competitions of this sort the prizes go to others and the state takes all the danger for herself. The blame is yours, for stupidly instituting these competitive displays. You have become regular speech-goers, and as for action, you merely listen to accounts of it; if something is to be done in the future you estimate the possibilities by hearing a good speech on the subject, and as for the past you rely not so much on the facts which you have seen with your own eyes as on what you have heard about them in some clever piece of verbal criticism. Any novelty in an argument deceives you at once, but when the argument is tried and proved you become unwilling to follow it; you look with suspicion on what is normal and are the slaves of every paradox that comes your way. The chief wish of each one of you is to be able to make a speech himself, and, if you cannot do that, the next best thing is to compete with those who can make this sort of speech by not looking as though you were at all out of your depth while you listen to the views put forward, by applauding a good point even before it is made, and by being as quick at seeing how an argument is going to be developed as you are slow at understanding what in the end it will lead to. What you are looking for all the time is something that is, I should say, outside the range of ordinary experience, and yet you cannot even think straight about the facts of life that are before you. You are simply victims of your own pleasure in listening, and are more like an audience sitting at the feet of a professional lecturer than a parliament discussing matters of state.

'I am trying to stop you behaving like this, and I say that no single city has ever done you the harm that Mytilene has done. Personally I can make allowances for those who revolt because they find your rule intolerable or because they have been forced into it by enemy action. Here, however, we have the case of people living on an island, behind their own fortifications, with nothing to fear from our enemies except an attack by sea against which they were adequately protected by their own force of triremes; they had their own independent government and they were treated by us with the greatest consideration. Now, to act as they acted is not what I should call a revolt (for people only revolt when they have been badly treated); it is a case of calculated aggression, of deliberately taking sides with our bitterest enemies in order to destroy us. And this is far worse than if they had made war against us simply to increase their own power. They learned nothing from the fate of those of their neighbours who had already revolted and been subdued; the prosperity which they enjoyed did not make them hesitate before running into danger; confident in the future, they declared war on us, with hopes that indeed extended beyond their means, though still fell short of their desires. They made up their minds to put might first and right second, choosing the moment when they thought they would win, and then making their unprovoked attack upon us.

'The fact is that when great prosperity comes suddenly and unexpectedly to a state, it usually breeds arrogance; in most cases it is safer for people to enjoy an average amount of success rather than something which is out of all proportion; and it is easier, I should say, to ward off hardship than to maintain happiness. What we should have done long ago with the Mytilenians was to treat them in exactly the same way as all the rest; then they would never have grown so arrogant; for it is a general rule of human nature that people despise those who treat them well and look up to those who make no concessions. Let them now therefore have the punishment which their crime deserves. Do not put the blame on the aristocracy and say that the people were innocent. The fact is that the whole lot of them attacked you together, although the people might have come over to us and, if they had, would now be back again in control of their city. Yet, instead of doing this, they thought it safer to share the dangers, and join in the revolt of the aristocracy.

'Now think of your allies. If you are going to give the same punishment to those who are forced to revolt by your enemies and those who do so of their own accord, can you not see that they will all revolt upon the slightest pretext, when success means freedom and failure brings no very dreadful consequences? Meanwhile we shall have to spend our money and risk our lives against state after state; if our efforts are successful, we shall recover a city that is in ruins, and so lose the future revenue from it, on which our strength is based; and if we fail to subdue it, we shall have more enemies to deal with in addition to those we have already, and we shall spend the time which ought to be used in resisting our present foes in making war on our own allies.

'Let there be no hope, therefore, held out to the Mytilenians that we, either as a result of a good speech or a large bribe, are likely to forgive them on the grounds that it is only human to make mistakes. There was nothing involuntary about the harm they did us; they knew what they were about and they planned it all beforehand; and one only forgives actions that were not deliberate. As for me, just as I was at first, so I am now, and I shall continue to impress on you the importance of not altering your previous decisions. To feel pity, to be carried away by the pleasure of hearing a clever argument, to listen to the claims of decency are three things that are entirely against the interests of an imperial power. Do not be guilty of them. As for compassion, it is proper to feel it in the case of people who are like ourselves and who will pity us in their turn, not in the case of those who, so far from having the same feelings towards us, must always and inevitably be our enemies. As for the speech-makers who give such pleasure by their arguments, they should hold their competitions on subjects which are less important, and not on a question where the state may have to pay a heavy penalty for its light pleasure, while the speakers themselves will no doubt be enjoying splendid rewards for their splendid arguments. And a sense of decency is only felt towards those who are going to be our friends in future, not towards those who remain just as they were and as much our enemies as they ever have been.

'Let me sum the whole thing up. I say that, if you follow my advice, you will be doing the right thing as far as Mytilene is concerned and at the same time will be acting in your own interests; if you decide differently, you will not win them over, but you will be passing judgement on yourselves. For if they were justified in revolting, you must be wrong in holding power. If, however, whatever the rights or wrongs of it may be, you propose to hold power all the same, then your interest demands that these too, rightly or wrongly, must be punished. The only alternative is to surrender your empire, so that you can afford to go in for philanthropy. Make up your minds, therefore, to pay them back in their own coin, and do not make it look as though you who escaped their machinations are less quick to react than they who started them. Remember how they would have been likely to have treated you, if they had won, especially as they were the aggressors. Those who do wrong to a neighbour when there is no reason to do so are the ones who persevere to the point of destroying him, since they see the danger involved in allowing their enemy to survive. For he who has suffered for no good reason is a more dangerous enemy, if he escapes, than the one who has both done and suffered injury.

'I urge you, therefore, not to be traitors to your own selves. Place yourselves in imagination at the moment when you first suffered and remember how then you would have given anything to have them in your power. Now pay them back for it, and do not grow soft just at this present moment, forgetting meanwhile the danger that hung over your heads then. Punish them as they deserve, and make an example of them to your other allies, plainly showing that revolt will be punished by death. Once they realize this, you will not have so often to neglect the war with your enemies because you are fighting with your own allies.'

So Cleon spoke. After him Diodotus, the son of Eucrates, who in the previous assembly also had vigorously opposed the motion to put the Mytilenians to death, came forward again on this occasion and spoke as follows:

'I do not blame those who have proposed a new debate on the subject of Mytilene, and I do not share the view which we have heard expressed, that it is a bad thing to have frequent discussions on matters of importance. Haste and anger are, to my mind, the two greatest obstacles to wise counsel—haste, that usually goes with folly, anger, that is the mark of primitive and narrow minds. And anyone who maintains that words cannot be a guide to action must be either a fool or one with some personal interest at stake; he is a fool, if he imagines that it is possible to deal with the uncertainties of the future by any other medium, and he is personally interested if his aim is to persuade you into some disgraceful action, and, knowing that he cannot make a good speech in a bad cause, he tries to frighten his opponents and his hearers by some good-sized pieces of misrepresentation. Then still more intolerable are those who go further and accuse a speaker of making a kind of exhibition of himself, because he is paid for it. If it was only ignorance with which he was being charged, a speaker who failed to win his case could retire from the debate and still be thought an honest man, if not a very intelligent one. But when corruption is imputed, he will be suspect if he wins his case, and if he loses it, will be regarded as dishonest and stupid at the same time. This sort of thing does the city no good; her counsellors will be afraid to speak and she will be deprived of their services. Though certainly it would be the best possible thing for the city if these gentlemen whom I have been describing lacked the power to express themselves; we should not then be persuaded into making so many mistakes.

'The good citizen, instead of trying to terrify the opposition, ought to prove his case in fair argument; and a wise state, without giving special honours to its best counsellors, will certainly not deprive them of the honour they already enjoy; and when a man's advice is not taken, he should not even be disgraced, far less penalized. In this way successful speakers will be less likely to pursue further honours by speaking against their own convictions in order to make themselves popular, and unsuccessful speakers, too, will not struggle to win over the people by the same acts of flattery. What we do here, however, is exactly the opposite. Then, too, if a man gives the best possible advice but is under the slightest suspicion of being influenced by his own private profit, we are so embittered by the idea (a wholly unproved one) of this profit of his, that we do not allow the state to receive the certain benefit of his good advice. So a state of affairs has been reached where a good proposal honestly put forward is just as suspect as something thoroughly bad, and the result is that just as the speaker who advocates some monstrous measure has to win over the people by deceiving them, so also a man with good advice to give has to tell lies if he expects to be believed. And because of this refinement in intellectuality, the state is put into a unique position; it is only she to whom no one can ever do a good turn openly and without deception. For if one openly performs a patriotic action, the reward for one's pains is to be thought to have made something oneself on the side. Yet in spite of all this we are discussing matters of the greatest importance, and we who give you our advice ought to be resolved to look rather further into things than you whose attention is occupied only with the surface—especially as we can be held to account for the advice we give, while you are not accountable for the way in which you receive it. For indeed you would take rather more care over your decisions, if the proposer of a motion and those who voted for it were all subject to the same penalties. As it is, on the occasions when some emotional impulse on your part has led you into disaster, you turn upon the one man who made the original proposal and you let yourself off, in spite of the fact that you are many and in spite of the fact that you were just as wrong as he was.

'However, I have not come forward to speak about Mytilene in any spirit of contradiction or with any wish to accuse anyone. If we are sensible people, we shall see that the question is not so much whether they are guilty as whether we are making the right decision for ourselves. I might prove that they are the most guilty people in the world, but it does not follow that I shall propose the death penalty, unless that is in your interests; I might argue that they deserve to be forgiven, but should not recommend forgiveness unless that seemed to me the best thing for the state.

'In my view our discussion concerns the future rather than the present. One of Cleon's chief points is that to inflict the death penalty will be useful to us in the future as a means for deterring other cities from revolt; but I, who am just as concerned as he is with the future, am quite convinced that this is not so. And I ask you not to reject what is useful in my speech for the sake of what is specious in his. You may well find his speech attractive, because it fits in better with your present angry feelings about the Mytilenians; but this is not a law-court, where we have to consider what is fit and just; it is a political assembly, and the question is how Mytilene can be most useful to Athens.

'Now, in human societies the death penalty has been laid down for many offences less serious than this one. Yet people still take risks when they feel sufficiently confident. No one has ever yet risked committing a crime which he thought he could not carry out successfully. The same is true of states. None has ever yet rebelled in the belief that it had insufficient resources, either in itself or from its allies, to make the attempt. Cities and individuals alike, all are by nature disposed to do wrong, and there is no law that will prevent it, as is shown by the fact that men have tried every kind of punishment, constantly adding to the list, in the attempt to find greater security from criminals. It is likely that in early times the punishments even for the greatest crimes were not as severe as they are now, but the laws were still broken, and in the course of time the death penalty became generally introduced. Yet even with this, the laws are still broken. Either, therefore, we must discover some fear more potent than the fear of death, or we must admit that here certainly we have not got an adequate deterrent. So long as poverty forces men to be bold, so long as the insolence and pride of wealth nourish their ambitions, and in the other accidents of life they are continually dominated by some incurable master passion or another, so long will their impulses continue to drive them into danger. Hope and desire persist throughout and cause the greatest calamities—one leading and the other following, one conceiving the enterprise, and the other suggesting that it will be successful—invisible factors, but more powerful than the terrors that are obvious to our eyes. Then too, the idea that fortune will be on one's side plays as big a part as anything else in creating a mood of over-confidence; for sometimes she does come unexpectedly to one's aid, and so she tempts men to run risks for which they are inadequately prepared. And this is particularly true in the case of whole peoples, because they are playing for the highest stakes—either for their own freedom or for the power to control others—and each individual, when acting as part of a community, has the irrational opinion that his own powers are greater than in fact they are. In a word it is impossible (and only the most simple-minded will deny this) for human nature, when once seriously set upon a certain course, to be prevented from following that course by the force of law or by any other means of intimidation whatever.

'We must not, therefore, come to the wrong conclusions through having too much confidence in the effectiveness of capital punishment, and we must not make the condition of rebels desperate by depriving them of the possibility of repentance and of a chance of atoning as quickly as they can for what they did. Consider this now: at the moment, if a city has revolted and realizes that the revolt cannot succeed, it will come to terms while it is still capable of paying an indemnity and continuing to pay tribute afterwards. But if Cleon's method is adopted, can you not see that every city will not only make much more careful preparations for revolt, but will also hold out against siege to the very end, since to surrender early or late means just the same thing? This is, unquestionably, against our interests—to spend money on a siege because of the impossibility of coming to terms, and, if we capture the place, to take over a city that is in ruins so that we lose the future revenue from it. And it is just on this revenue that our strength in war depends.

'Our business, therefore, is not to injure ourselves by acting like a judge who strictly examines a criminal; instead we should be looking for a method by which, employing moderation in our punishments, we can in future secure for ourselves the full use of those cities which bring us important contributions. And we should recognize that the proper basis of our security is in good administration rather than in the fear of legal penalties. As it is, we do just the opposite: when we subdue a free city, which was held down by force and has, as we might have expected, tried to assert its independence by revolting, we think that we ought to punish it with the utmost severity. But the right way to deal with free people is this—not to inflict tremendous punishments on them after they have revolted, but to take tremendous care of them before this point is reached, to prevent them even contemplating the idea of revolt, and, if we do have to use force with them, to hold as few as possible of them responsible for this.

'Consider what a mistake you would be making on this very point, if you took Cleon's advice. As things are now, in all the cities the democracy is friendly to you; either it does not join in with the oligarchies in revolting, or, if it is forced to do so, it remains all the time hostile to the rebels, so that when you go to war with them, you have the people on your side. But if you destroy the democratic party at Mytilene, who never took any hand in the revolt and who, as soon as they got arms, voluntarily gave the city up to you, you will first of all be guilty of killing those who have helped you, and, secondly, you will be doing exactly what the reactionary classes want most. For now, when they start a revolt, they will have the people on their side from the beginning, because you have already made it clear that the same punishment is laid down both for the guilty and the innocent. In fact, however, even if they were guilty, you should pretend that they were not, in order to keep on your side the one element that is still not opposed to you. It is far more useful to us, I think, in preserving our empire, that we should voluntarily put up with injustice than that we should justly put to death the wrong people. As for Cleon's point—that in this act of vengeance both justice and self-interest are combined—this is not a case where such a combination is at all possible.

'I call upon you, therefore, to accept my proposal as the better one. Do not be swayed too much by pity or by ordinary decent feelings. I, no more than Cleon, wish you to be influenced by such emotions. It is simply on the basis of the argument which you have heard that I ask you to be guided by me, to try at your leisure the men whom Paches has considered guilty and sent to

Athens, and to allow the rest to live in their own city. In following this course you will be acting wisely for the future and will be doing something which will make your enemies fear you now. For those who make wise decisions are more formidable to their enemies than those who rush madly into strong action.'

This was the speech of Diodotus. And now, when these two motions, each so opposed to each, had been put forward, the Athenians, in spite of the recent change of feeling, still held conflicting opinions, and at the show of hands the votes were nearly equal. However, the motion of Diodotus was passed.

Immediately another trireme was sent out in all haste, since they feared that, unless it overtook the first trireme, they would find on their arrival that the city had been destroyed. The first trireme had a start of about twenty-four hours. The ambassadors from Mytilene provided wine and barley for the crew and promised great rewards if they arrived in time, and so the men made such speed on the voyage that they kept on rowing while they took their food (which was barley mixed with oil and wine) and rowed continually, taking it in turn to sleep. Luckily they had no wind against them, and as the first ship was not hurrying on its distasteful mission, while they were pressing on with such speed, what happened was that the first ship arrived so little ahead of them that Paches had just had time to read the decree and to prepare to put it into force, when the second ship put in to the harbour and prevented the massacre. So narrow had been the escape of Mytilene.

The other Mytilenians whom Paches had sent to Athens as being the ones chiefly responsible for the revolt were, on the motion of Cleon, put to death by the Athenians. There were rather more than 1,000 of them. The Athenians also destroyed the fortifications of Mytilene and took over their navy. Afterwards, instead of imposing a tribute on Lesbos, they divided all the land, except that belonging to the Methymnians, into 3,000 holdings, 300 of which were set apart as sacred for the gods, while the remainder was distributed by lot to Athenian shareholders, who were sent out to Lesbos. The Lesbians agreed with these shareholders to pay a yearly rent of two minae for each holding, and cultivated the land themselves. The Athenians also took over all the towns on the mainland that had been under the control of Mytilene. So for the future the Mytilenians became subjects of Athens. This completes the account of what took place in Lesbos.

Note

[1] This wording is echoed by Thucydides in VI, 35 when he introduces the Syracusan 'demagogue' Athenagoras.

from *History of the Peloponnesian War*

Thucydides

In 416 B.C., Athenian attempts at coercing Melos to join its alliance failed, so Athens sent an expedition to subjugate the island state. The expedition's generals argue with the Melian government that Melos should surrender rather than resist militarily.

The Melian Dialogue

Next summer Alcibiades sailed to Argos with twenty ships and seized 300 Argive citizens who were still suspected of being pro-Spartan. These were put by the Athenians into the nearby islands under Athenian control.

The Athenians also made an expedition against the island of Melos. They had thirty of their own ships, six from Chios, and two from Lesbos; 1,200 hoplites, 300 archers, and twenty mounted archers, all from Athens; and about 1,500 hoplites from the allies and the islanders.

The Melians are a colony from Sparta. They had refused to join the Athenian empire like the other islanders, and at first had remained neutral without helping either side; but afterwards, when the Athenians had brought force to bear on them by laying waste their land, they had become open enemies of Athens.

Now the generals Cleomedes, the son of Lycomedes, and Tisias, the son of Tisimachus, encamped with the above force in Melian territory and, before doing any harm to the land, first of all sent representatives to negotiate. The Melians did not invite these representatives to speak before the people, but asked them to make the statement for which they had come in front of the governing body and the few. The Athenian representatives then spoke as follows:

'So we are not to speak before the people, no doubt in case the mass of the people should hear once and for all and without interruption an argument from us which is both persuasive and incontrovertible, and should so be led astray. This, we realize, is your motive in bringing us here to speak before the few. Now suppose that you who sit here should make assurance doubly sure. Suppose that you, too, should refrain from dealing with every point in detail in a set speech, and should instead interrupt us whenever we say something

149

controversial and deal with that before going on to the next point? Tell us first whether you approve of this suggestion of ours.'

The Council of the Melians replied as follows:

'No one can object to each of us putting forward our own views in a calm atmosphere. That is perfectly reasonable. What is scarcely consistent with such a proposal is the present threat, indeed the certainty, of your making war on us. We see that you have come prepared to judge the argument yourselves, and that the likely end of it all will be either war, if we prove that we are in the right, and so refuse to surrender, or else slavery.'

Athenians: If you are going to spend the time in enumerating your suspicions about the future, or if you have met here for any other reason except to look the facts in the face and on the basis of these facts to consider how you can save your city from destruction, there is no point in our going on with this discussion. If, however, you will do as we suggest, then we will speak on.

Melians: It is natural and understandable that people who are placed as we are should have recourse to all kinds of arguments and different points of view. However, you are right in saying that we are met together here to discuss the safety of our country and, if you will have it so, the discussion shall proceed on the lines that you have laid down.

Athenians: Then we on our side will use no fine phrases saying, for example, that we have a right to our empire because we defeated the Persians, or that we have come against you now because of the injuries you have done us—a great mass of words that nobody would believe. And we ask you on your side not to imagine that you will influence us by saying that you, though a colony of Sparta, have not joined Sparta in the war, or that you have never done us any harm. Instead we recommend that you should try to get what it is possible for you to get, taking into consideration what we both really do think; since you know as well as we do that, when these matters are discussed by practical people, the standard of justice depends on the equality of power to compel and that in fact the strong do what they have the power to do and the weak accept what they have to accept.

Melians: Then in our view (since you force us to leave justice out of account and to confine ourselves to self-interest)—in our view it is at any rate useful that you should not destroy a principle that is to the general good of all men—namely, that in the case of all who fall into danger there should be such a thing as fair play and just dealing, and that such people should be allowed to use and to profit by arguments that fall short of a mathematical accuracy. And this is a principle which affects you as much as anybody, since your own fall would be visited by the most terrible vengeance and would be an example to the world.

Athenians: As for us, even assuming that our empire does come to an end, we are not despondent about what would happen next. One is not so much frightened of being conquered by a power which rules over others, as Sparta does (not that we are concerned with Sparta now), as of what would happen if a ruling power is attacked and defeated by its own subjects. So far as this point is concerned, you can leave it to us to face the risks involved. What we shall do now is to show you that it is for the good of our own empire that we are here and that it is for the preservation of your city that we shall say what we are going to say. We do not want any trouble in bringing you into our empire, and we want you to be spared for the good both of yourselves and of ourselves.

Melians: And how could it be just as good for us to be the slaves as for you to be the masters?

Athenians: You, by giving in, would save yourselves from disaster; we, by not destroying you, would be able to profit from you.

Melians: So you would not agree to our being neutral, friends instead of enemies, but allies of neither side?

Athenians: No, because it is not so much your hostility that injures us; it is rather the case that, if we were on friendly terms with you, our subjects would regard that as a sign of weakness in us, whereas your hatred is evidence of our power.

Melians: Is that your subjects' idea of fair play—that no distinction should be made between people who are quite unconnected with you and people who are mostly your own colonists or else rebels whom you have conquered?

Athenians: So far as right and wrong are concerned they think that there is no difference between the two, that those who still preserve their independence do so because they are strong, and that if we fail to attack them it is because we are afraid. So that by conquering you we shall increase not only the size but the security of our empire. We rule the sea and you are islanders, and weaker islanders too than the others; it is therefore particularly important that you should not escape.

Melians: But do you think there is no security for you in what we suggest? For here again, since you will not let us mention justice, but tell us to give in to your interests, we, too, must tell you what our interests are and, if yours and ours happen to coincide, we must try to persuade you of the fact. Is it not certain that you will make enemies of all states who are at present neutral, when they see what is happening here and naturally conclude that in course of time you will attack them too? Does not this mean that you are strengthening the enemies you have already and are forcing others to become your enemies even against their intentions and their inclinations?

Athenians: As a matter of fact we are not so much frightened of states on the continent. They have their liberty, and this means that it will be a long time before they begin to take precautions against us. We are more concerned about islanders like yourselves, who are still unsubdued, or subjects who have already become embittered by the constraint which our empire imposes on them. These are the people who are most likely to act in a reckless manner and to bring themselves and us, too, into the most obvious danger.

Melians: Then surely, if such hazards are taken by you to keep your empire and by your subjects to escape from it, we who are still free would show ourselves great cowards and weaklings if we failed to face everything that comes rather than submit to slavery.

Athenians: No, not if you are sensible. This is no fair fight, with honour on one side and shame on the other. It is rather a question of saving your lives and not resisting those who are far too strong for you.

Melians: Yet we know that in war fortune sometimes makes the odds more level than could be expected from the difference in numbers of the two sides. And if we surrender, then all our hope is lost at once, whereas, so long as we remain in action, there is still a hope that we may yet stand upright.

Athenians: Hope, that comforter in danger! If one already has solid advantages to fall back upon, one can indulge in hope. It may do harm, but will not destroy one. But hope is by nature an expensive commodity, and those who are risking their all on one cast find out what it means only when they are already ruined; it never fails them in the period when such a knowledge would enable them to take precautions. Do not let this happen to you, you who are weak and whose fate depends on a single movement of the scale. And do not be like those people who, as so commonly happens, miss the chance of saving themselves in a human and practical way, and, when every clear and distinct hope has left them in their adversity, turn to what is blind and vague, to prophecies and oracles and such things which by encouraging hope lead men to ruin.

Melians: It is difficult, and you may be sure that we know it, for us to oppose your power and fortune, unless the terms be equal. Nevertheless we trust that the gods will give us fortune as good as yours, because we are standing for what is right against what is wrong; and as for what we lack in power, we trust that it will be made up for by our alliance with the Spartans, who are bound, if for no other reason, then for honour's sake, and because we are their kinsmen, to come to our help. Our confidence, therefore, is not so entirely irrational as you think.

Athenians: So far as the favour of the gods is concerned, we think we have as much right to that as you have. Our aims and our actions are perfectly consistent with the beliefs men hold about the gods and with the principles which govern their own conduct. Our opinion of the gods and our knowledge of men lead us to conclude that it is a general and necessary law of nature to rule whatever one can. This is not a law that we made ourselves, nor were we the first to act upon it when it was made. We found it already in existence, and we shall leave it to exist for ever among those who come after us. We are merely acting in accordance with it, and we know that you or anybody else with the same power as ours would be acting in precisely the same way. And therefore, so far as the gods are concerned, we see no good reason why we should fear to be at a disadvantage. But with regard to your views about Sparta and your confidence that she, out of a sense of honour, will come to your aid, we must say that we congratulate you on your simplicity but do not envy you your folly. In matters that concern themselves or their own constitution the Spartans are quite remarkably good; as for their relations with others, that is a long story, but it can be expressed shortly and clearly by saying that of all people we know the Spartans are most conspicuous for believing that what they like doing is honourable and what suits their interests is just. And this kind of attitude is not going to be of much help to you in your absurd quest for safety at the moment.

Melians: But this is the very point where we can feel most sure. Their own self-interest will make them refuse to betray their own colonists, the Melians, for that would mean losing the confidence of their friends among the Hellenes and doing good to their enemies.

Athenians: You seem to forget that if one follows one's self-interest one wants to be safe, whereas the path of justice and honour involves one in danger. And, where danger is concerned, the Spartans are not, as a rule, very venturesome.

Melians: But we think that they would even endanger themselves for our sake and count the risk more worth taking than in the case of others, because we are so close to the Peloponnese that they could operate more easily, and because they can depend on us more than on others, since we are of the same race and share the same feelings.

Athenians: Goodwill shown by the party that is asking for help does not mean security for the prospective ally. What is looked for is a positive preponderance of power in action. And the Spartans pay attention to this point even more than others do. Certainly they distrust their own native resources so much that when they attack a neighbour they bring a great army of allies with them. It is hardly likely therefore that, while we are in control of the sea, they will cross over to an island.

Melians: But they still might send others. The Cretan sea is a wide one, and it is harder for those who control it to intercept others than for those who want to slip through to do so safely. And even if they were to fail in this, they would turn against your own land and against those of your allies left unvisited by Brasidas. So, instead of troubling about a country which has nothing to do with you, you will find trouble nearer home, among your allies, and in your own country.

Athenians: It is a possibility, something that has in fact happened before. It may happen in your case, but you are well aware that the Athenians have never yet relinquished a single siege operation through fear of others. But we are somewhat shocked to find that, though you announced your intention of discussing how you could preserve yourselves, in all this talk you have said absolutely nothing which could justify a man in thinking that he could be preserved. Your chief points are concerned with what you hope may happen in the future, while your actual resources are too scanty to give you a chance of survival against the forces that are opposed to you at this moment. You will therefore be showing an extraordinary lack of common sense if, after you have asked us to retire from this meeting, you still fail to reach a conclusion wiser than anything you have mentioned so far. Do not be led astray by a false sense of honour—a thing which often brings men to ruin when they are faced with an obvious danger that somehow affects their pride. For in many cases men have still been able to see the dangers ahead of them, but this thing called dishonour, this word, by its own force of seduction, has drawn them into a state where they have surrendered to an idea, while in fact they have fallen voluntarily into irrevocable disaster, in dishonour that is all the more dishonourable because it has come to them from their own folly rather than their misfortune. You, if you take the right view, will be careful to avoid this. You will see that there is nothing disgraceful in giving way to the greatest city in Hellas when she is offering you such reasonable terms—alliance on a tribute-paying basis and liberty to enjoy your own property. And, when you are allowed to choose between war and safety, you will not be so insensitively arrogant as to make the wrong choice. This is the safe rule—to stand up to one's equals, to behave with deference towards one's superiors, and to treat one's inferiors with moderation. Think it over again, then, when we have withdrawn from the meeting, and let this be a point that constantly recurs to your minds—that you are discussing the fate of your country, that you have only one country, and that its future for good or ill depends on this one single decision which you are going to make.

The Athenians then withdrew from the discussion. The Melians, left to themselves, reached a conclusion which was much the same as they had indicated in their previous replies. Their answer was as follows:

'Our decision, Athenians, is just the same as it was at first. We are not prepared to give up in a short moment the liberty which our city has enjoyed from its foundation for 700 years. We put our trust in the fortune that the gods will send and which has saved us up to now, and in the help of men— that is, of the Spartans; and so we shall try to save ourselves. But we invite you to allow us to be friends of yours and enemies to neither side, to make a treaty which shall be agreeable to both you and us, and so to leave our country.'

The Melians made this reply, and the Athenians, just as they were breaking off the discussion, said:

'Well, at any rate, judging from this decision of yours, you seem to us quite unique in your ability to consider the future as something more certain than what is before your eyes, and to see uncertainties as realities, simply because you would like them to be so. As you have staked most on and trusted most in Spartans, luck, and hopes, so in all these you will find yourselves most completely deluded.'

The Athenian representatives then went back to the army, and the Athenian generals, finding that the Melians would not submit, immediately commenced hostilities and built a wall completely round the city of Melos, dividing the work out among the various states. Later they left behind a garrison of some of their own and some allied troops to blockade the place by land and sea, and with the greater part of their army returned home. The force left behind stayed on and continued with the siege.

About the same time the Argives invaded Phliasia and were ambushed by the Phliasians and the exiles from Argos, losing about eighty men.

Then, too, the Athenians at Pylos captured a great quantity of plunder from Spartan territory. Not even after this did the Spartans renounce the treaty and make war, but they issued a proclamation saying that any of their people who wished to do so were free to make raids on the Athenians. The Corinthians also made some attacks on the Athenians because of private quarrels of their own, but the rest of the Pelopponnesians stayed quiet.

Meanwhile the Melians made a night attack and captured the part of the Athenian lines opposite the market-place. They killed some of the troops, and then, after bringing in corn and everything else useful that they could lay their hands on, retired again and made no further move, while the Athenians took measures to make their blockade more efficient in future. So the summer came to an end.

In the following winter the Spartans planned to invade the territory of Argos, but when the sacrifices for crossing the frontier turned out unfavourably, they gave up the expedition. The fact that they had intended to invade made the Argives suspect certain people in their city, some of whom they arrested, though others succeeded in escaping.

About this same time the Melians again captured another part of the Athenian lines where there were only a few of the garrison on guard. As a result of this, another force came out afterwards from Athens under the command of Philocrates, the son of Demeas. Siege operations were now carried on vigorously and, as there was also some treachery from inside, the Melians surrendered unconditionally to the Athenians, who put to death all the men of military age whom they took, and sold the women and children as slaves. Melos itself they took over for themselves, sending out later a colony of 500 men.[1]

Note

[1] That there were Melian survivors, who were restored by Lysander at the end of the war, is stated by Xenophon (*Hellenica*, II, 2, 9).

Melvin in the Sixth Grade

Dana Johnson

Maybe it was around the time that the Crips sliced up my brother's arm for refusing to join their gang. Or it could have been around the time that the Crips *and* the Bloods shot up the neighborhood one Halloween so we couldn't go trick-or-treating. It could have even been the time that my brother's friend, Anthony, got shot for being at the wrong place at the wrong time. But my father decided it was time to take advantage of a veteran's loan, get out of L.A., and move to the suburbs. Even if I can't quite nail the events that spurred the move, I know that one and a half months after I climbed into my father's rusted-out Buick Wildcat and said good-bye to 80th Street and hello to Verdugo Street with its lawns and streets without sidewalks, I fell for my first man.

From the day Mrs. Campbell introduced him to the class, reprimanded us for laughing at his name, and sat him down next to me, I was struck by Melvin Bukeford with his stiff jeans, white creases ironed down the middle, huge bell-bottoms that rang, the kids claimed, every time the bells knocked against each other. Shiny jeans because he *starched* them. Melvin sporting a crew cut in 1981 when everybody else had long scraggly hair like the guys in Judas Priest or Journey. Pointed ears that stuck out like Halloween fake ones. The way he dragged out every single last word on account of being from Oklahoma. The long pointed nose and the freckles splattered all over his permanently pink face. Taller than everybody else because he was thirteen.

All that and a new kid is why nobody liked him. Plus he had to be named Melvin. All us kids, we'd never seen anything like him before, not in school, not for real, not in California. And for me he was even more of a wonder because I was just getting used to the white folks in West Covina, the way they spoke, the clothes they wore. Melvin was even weirder to me than the rest of them. It was almost like he wasn't white. He was an alien of some kind. My beautiful alien from Planet Cowboy.

I was writing *Melvin Melvin Melvin Melvin, Mrs. Avery Arlington Bukeford* on my Pee Chee folder by Melvin's second week of school. We walked the same way home every single school day. I fell in love with the drawl of his voice, the way he forgot the "e" in Avery; "Av'ry," he said it soft, or "AV'ry" when he thought I'd said the funniest thing, squinting at me sideways and giving me that dimple in his left cheek. All that made me feel like, well, just like I wanted to kiss my pillow at night and call it Melvin. So I did. "Ohhh, Mellllvin," I said, making out with my pillow every night. "Ohhh yeahh, Melvin."

I was keeping all that a secret until my eighteen-year-old brother saw my folder one day and asked me who Melvin was. "None ya," I said, and he said he knew it had to be some crazy-looking white boy—or a Mexican, because that's all West Covina had.

"Avery's done gone white boy crazy!" he called out. "I'ma tell Daddy!"

I ran into my room and slammed the door to stare at my four bare walls because Daddy had made me take down the posters I'd had up, all centerfolds from *Teen Beat* and *Tiger Beat* magazines. For one glamorous week I had Andy Gibb, Shaun Cassidy, and Leif Garret looking down on me while I slept. But one day Daddy passed my door, took one look at Leif Garret all blonde and golden tan in his tight white jeans that showed off a *very* big bulge, and asked me, "Avery, who in the *hell* are all these white boys?"

"Oh, Daddy, that's just Andy—"

"Get that shit down off those walls right now," Daddy said. He glared at Leif Garret.

I couldn't figure out why he was yelling at me. "But why—"

"What did I say?" he demanded.

"Take the posters down," I mumbled. And that's why I was staring at four blank walls.

But that was OK, because Melvin was my world. I didn't need him up on the wall. I had him in my head. I turned on the radio to listen to Ozzy Osbourne, who'd just bitten the head off a dove a few days before, singing about going off the rails on a crazy train.

Two months since being the new girl myself, Melvin was the only one who called me by my name; otherwise the other kids usually named me after my hairstyle. Like Minnie Mouse or Cocoa Puffs if I wore my hair in Afro puffs. Or Afro Sheen if my mother had greased my hair and pressed it into submission the night before. Or Electric Socket if I was wearing a plain old Afro. Avery. To hear that coming out of someone else's mouth at school was like hearing "Hey, Superstar."

They were warming up to me, though. Lisa White, who always smelled like pee, had invited me to her Disneyland party. Why, I don't know, but I was going, grateful to be going. For no reason, one day, she said, "Hey, you," when she saw me standing by the monkey bars watching her and a bunch of friends jumping rope. "Come to my party if you want to." What I heard was something like, "Hey you, you just won a trillion, bizillion, cabillion dollars."

But everything had become even more tricky than usual. Lisa didn't like Melvin. Nobody did.

One day when the smog wasn't so bad in the San Gabriel Valley (the air was only orange, not brown, and you could sort of see the mountains if you squeezed your eyes some), Melvin and I stopped at the same place we did every day after school: by the ivy in front of Loretta Morales's house on the corner, fat Loretta with feathered hair and green eyes, in high school now, even though we used to play Barbies together, who got down with boys now, who had a mother in a wheelchair for no reason I could figure out. She could walk, Mrs. Morales.

Melvin stuck his hand in the ivy, pulling at this and that, not finding what he was looking for. "Hmm," he said. "Av'ry girl, I b'lieve you done took my cigarettes for yourself, ain't you?"

"Nuh uh!" I grinned at him and hugged my folders and books to my chest. "You just ain't looking good."

"Well, then, help me out some." He brushed his hands through the ivy like he was running them through bathwater to test it.

"There's rats in there." I wasn't going to put my hands in the ivy because it was dark and I couldn't see. If I couldn't see, there was no need to just stick my hands into all that dark space like a crazy person, I didn't think.

Melvin took off his jean jacket and handed it to me. It had MEL spelled out on the back with silver studs you pressed into the fabric. He was getting serious about looking for those Winstons. I put my face in his jacket and smelled it, since he wasn't watching me. It smelled like smoke and sweat and general boy. From then on forever, I decided, I would love the smell of boy.

"Here we go," he said in a minute. He stood up, tapped the package on his palm, pulled out the cigarette, popped it in his mouth, took the match that always seemed to be tucked behind his ear, struck it on his boot, and cupped the match while he lit his smoke, so the fire wouldn't go out. He drew a deep suck on his cigarette and then threw his head back and blew the smoke up toward the sky. Then he rolled the packet of cigarettes in the sleeve of his white T-shirt. I watched all this like a miracle.

"I been dying for that cigarette all day long. You don't know," he said, letting it dangle between his lips. He winked at me. "Whoo weee!" he hollered.

But I did know. How it felt to want something so bad. Whoo weee, Melvin. How could *you* not know?

Melvin tried to take his jacket back. "I got it," I said.

He shrugged. "If you wont to."

But five steps later we were at my street. Verdugo. So I had to give the jacket back anyway.

"Hey, Melvin," I started, trying to kill time and keep him with me a little longer, "you going to Lisa White's Disneyland party?" But the second the words were out of my mouth, I knew it was the dumbest question I could have asked. Like Lisa would have asked Melvin to her party, like Lisa even *thought* about Melvin. That was just stupid to even think. How dumb *are* you? I asked myself.

Melvin took his cigarette out of his mouth and offered me a puff, he knew I wouldn't. We had that little joke going on between us. He got a kick out of me being a Goody Two-shoes and not taking a puff, even though I nearly died at the thought of my lips touching something that Melvin's lips touched. He grinned. "There's your brother," he said, trying to scare me about the cigarette, but I knew Owen was already at work.

"You ain't funny, Melvin Bukeford," I said, and punched him in the shoulder.

He rubbed it like it hurt. I guess I punched him harder than I thought. "Dang, Killer, you tough when you wont to be, ain't you?" He took another puff before he said, "Lisa ast me to go to her party, but I said I didn't b'lieve I could cause of the money, but shoot, I can steal me enough money to go to Disneyland, I just ain't too impressed with her or no Disneyland neither."

I could not believe what I was hearing. Lisa asked Melvin *and* he said no? I thought I was asked because I was liked—or on my way to be liked.

Melvin said, "She just askin everybody to say that everybody came to her little party. So what about her little pissy party." He stubbed out his cigarette. "Later, Miss Av'ry," he said, pulling on his jacket. "And don't be reaching into my stash of cigs else a big rat'll chew off your fingers."

"Nuh uh, Melvin!" I sang. I still stung from Lisa not really warming up to me that much after all, but Melvin's teasing and winking and dimples and smoke drifting hazy over his watery blue eyes made me happier. I would never need anything else in a man as long as I walked the planet earth. I watched him walk downhill in that odd slopey way he did, knees bending a little too deep at every step, like a flamingo. A flamingo smoking a cigarette wearing a studded denim jacket.

By the time I was walking through the door, home from school, Mama was running out the door to catch the bus to her first job at the sprinkler factory and later, her room-cleaning job, like always. I was only eleven but already taller than she was—and bigger all the way around. She was a little woman with a tiny neat Afro, but you didn't mess around and confuse the little and the tiny with the way she ran things. And with Daddy, when you saw big and tall, you didn't mess around with that either.

She didn't wait for me to speak before she started telling me what all I had to do. ". . . And the dishes, and put that pot of beans on. I already seasoned them. Don't put no more salt in them beans and mess em up, do and you know what you gone be in for. And your Aunt Rochelle sent you some more clothes. They in the living room. Be sweet." She patted me on the shoulders, hard, heavy so you could hear it even. Then she was out the door.

I was afraid to even look in the living room to see what kind of clothes were waiting for me. Aunt Rochelle's hand-me-downs from somebody's friend's cousin's daughter, used to be cool, but now that I was living in this new house in this new city far enough from L.A. that we were grateful when we saw other black people around town, I didn't like the hand-me-downs so much anymore because they were one more thing the kids could pick on me about. The fancy pants were Dittos or Chemin de Fers or Sergio Valentes or jackets that were Members Only. When they weren't calling me Afro Sheen they were calling me Polyester or Kmart, where I got my good clothes. Or they called me Welfare for getting in the "county" line when I lined up for my lunch from the free lunch program for people who needed it.

When I told my mother and father that I wanted different clothes, my mother said, "Chemin de Who for how much? You must be out your mind."

And of course I was. All eleven-year-olds were. I was out of my mind, especially for Melvin. Couldn't anybody understand that if I had just one cool outfit, like Melvin, I'd be on my way to the kids liking me for reals? Cool outfits may not have worked for Melvin, but he was an alien. I wasn't. If I tried hard enough, I'd be *in.* I found these lime-green polyester slacks that I really liked and put the rest of the clothes in the bottom of my bedroom closet. I imagined him saying, "Whoo wee, Ay'ry! Check you out!"

Melvin was going to get his ass kicked after school. I heard it from Terri Stovendorf, the tomboy with the protruding forehead and sharp teeth on the side like a dog. She got drunk behind the portables, cheap mobile add-ons to the rest of the elementary school. She was always pushing me around, making fun of the way I spoke. I didn't know there was anything wrong with the way I spoke. I said "prolly" when it was "probably." I said "fort" when they said "fart." I said I was "finna" go home and not "getting ready" to go home. That's how we'd always spoken and it was good enough until the suburbs. I started studying the kids and editing myself. *Mama*, I practiced in the mirror at home. *I'm go-eng to do my homework. Go-eng. Who farted? Somebody farted?*

"Groovy Jan and Cindy and Bobby and Marcia," Owen said, whenever he heard me. "Grue-vee."

When Terri told me the news, I was at the water fountain at recess taking a break from tetherball, trying to get some water from the warm trickle coming out. I had to put my lips right up against the spout and tried not to look at the gum somebody had stuck down by the drain. When I picked my head up and wiped the water from my mouth, Terri called me. "Hey, Burnt Toast."

I turned around.

"Nice pants."

"Really? Thanks." I smiled at her shyly.

"I was kidding, dumb-ass."

I scratched my scalp because I didn't know what else to do. I had eight neat cornrows that ran from my hairline to the base of my neck.

"Listen," Terri said, suddenly doing business. "You and that country cowboy guy are always going around." We said "going around" to mean dating. I smiled at the thought that people thought Melvin and I were together, even though I was still trying to keep my distance from him in front of other people. I was scared of having more wrath heaped on me.

"What are you smiling at, stupid?"

"We're not going together," I mumbled. I started kicking around a rock with my imitation Vans, which were cooler than cool sneakers. Mine were knockoffs from Kmart.

"No duh," Terri said. "Like Country Cowboy would even go around with a nigger. I meant, like, walking around and stuff."

I had been called so many names that even "nigger" didn't faze me anymore. Not so much anymore. There were Mexicans and Philippinos and Chinese kids sprinkled throughout the class, but they blended better than me. There was more than one of each of them, and when they were called "taco" when they were from Portugal or "chink," even when they happened to be Philippino or Korean, that was the best kids like Terri could do with them. With me, there seemed to be endless creativity. So all I said to Terri was "Melvin and me don't go around, walk around together. His house is on *my* way home."

"Whatever. He's going to get his ass kicked after school today, and you better not tell him."

"Why?"

"Because I'll kick your ass, too."

"No, I mean . . ." I started cracking my knuckles. A bad habit I still have. I finally left the rock alone. "I mean, why are y'all going to beat up Melvin?"

Terri looked at me with disgust and wonder, like I was eating my own boogers, like Casey McLaughlin did. He modeled kid underwear because he was good looking; long eyelashes like a deer, and lips that always looked like there was lipstick on them. You could see him in those color junk ads that were always shoved in every mailbox in the neighborhoods, and he was as stupid as a stick.

"Are you a total moron?" Terri ran her hands through her stringy brown hair and left before I could answer.

I went looking for Melvin to tell, but I couldn't be *seen* telling him. I saw him sitting on a swing, all alone. Spinning in one direction real fast to tighten the swing chains and then spinning the other way as fast as he could to get that dizzy rush. The playground was full: a bunch of kids were playing touch football in the field, all the tetherballs were taken, two dodgeball games were going on, and both of the handball courts were taken. I couldn't see Terri, or cross-eyed Eddie Chambers, or nasty Hector Hernandez, who was always grabbing himself and lapping his tongue in and out like a snake at the girls. They would all be the ringleaders after school. The coast seemed clear enough to warn Melvin, but before I could make my way over to him, somebody called me.

"Hey, Turd Head," Harry Collins called out to me, my name whenever I wore cornrows. "We need one more person for butt ball." He walked over toward me with the red rubber ball while I tried to figure out how to say no. Butt ball hurt. You and one other person had to volunteer to get on your hands and knees facing the handball wall while two people threw the ball at you and tried to nail you in the behind. It hurt, for one, and for another, I never seemed to get my chance to try to nail somebody in the behind. Plus, that day there were my lime-green pants to think about. I didn't want to get dirt smudges on them. "Well?" Harry bounced the ball as though each bounce was a second ticking away. I stared at his stomach, which was always, no matter what, poking out from a shirt that was too small for him.

"I don't want to, Harry."

"Tough titty. We need another person."

"Well, I don't want to get my pants dirty." I kept looking over at Melvin to make sure he was still on the swings across the playground. If recess ended before I got a chance to tell him, he wouldn't have a warning.

"C'mon, man," Harry said. "Quit wasting time." He grabbed the front of my 94.7 KMET T-shirt that I'd gotten from somewhere and wore in hopes I'd have at least one cool piece of clothing. It was one of the radio stations that played Def Leppard and AC/DC, though in secret I still liked my Chi Lites 45, "Have You Seen Her?" better. Harry started pulling me toward the handball court, and when I resisted, he pulled so hard I fell down. I looked over at the swings. Melvin wasn't there. My slacks had a tear where I fell on my knees.

I got mad because I told him to leave me alone and he didn't. I started to cry because I was mad and couldn't kick Harry's ass, couldn't do anything.

"You all right, Av'ry?" Melvin drawled, and suddenly he was standing beside me. I was happy he was there and scared to talk to him, to be caught with Melvin, be a combo with Melvin, permanently paired so nobody would ever accept me because of my connection to Country Cowboy. But I was still in love with his pointy costume ears, and when he spoke my name, it was the first time I'd heard it all day. Not even our teacher, old powdery Mrs. Campbell, had called on me that day. So I mumbled a thanks, I'm OK, and Harry sneered at the both of us just when the freeze bell rang.

It was the bell that told us recess was over and we were to stop whatever it was we were doing, whatever games we were playing, and come back inside. We always took the bell literally. Until the bell stopped ringing, we froze right on the spot, like statues, like mannequins. There were me, Harry, and Melvin, frozen, along with everybody else on the playground, while tetherballs kept twirling and balls kept bouncing.

This is how kids start fights: "Hey, so and so. I'ma kick your ass." For no reason, out of the blue. So when Melvin was trying to leave school with his jean jacket slung over his shoulder, that's what cross-eyed Eddie said to him. Everybody else just agreed. I had warned Melvin, but all he did was frown and offer me half his piece of Juicy Fruit.

There was, then, the usually core group of fighters and the spectators when Eddie shoved Melvin. "C'mon, Country Cowboy. Fuckin Elvis." Eddie wasn't as tall as Melvin, but he was big and sloppy. Melvin didn't seem concerned, though. He ran his right hand over his crew cut and took his jacket off his shoulder. Melvin didn't want it to get dirty. He handed it to the person closest to him without thinking, gapped-tooth John Thompson, who said, "I'm not holding your stupid jacket, Country Ass," and dropped it on the ground. Just for that instant, Melvin looked dumb and awkward, as though he honestly didn't expect such rudeness from anybody. He picked up his jacket and dusted it off. I was behind him and panicked when I thought he might know this, turn around, and ask me to hold his jacket while he fought. What would I do? It had taken me weeks to get to where I was, which wasn't very far, but I was grateful for that slight break in the torture. The tiny thaw in the frost. I was going to Disneyland with Lisa White, and even if she didn't like me so much now, maybe at the party she would see who I really was and then like me.

"Av'ry, hold my jacket, will you?" Melvin held it out and his nostrils flared a little bit when I hesitated. I glanced at Terri, who was looking straight at me with a psychotic grin on her face. Melvin thrust the jacket at me. I took it. And then, well, it slipped from my fingers and fell to the ground. Melvin looked at his jacket and then at me, those pale blue eyes looking at me brand new and different from any time before. We both left the jacket there, and then he beat the shit out of Harry, then Hector, then Eddie. Not Terri, because she was a girl, but she chased me home for two weeks straight, even though I didn't hold the jacket, and even though Melvin didn't care when I told him that they were going to kick his ass after school.

Walking home after the fight, Melvin didn't say more than five words to me. I can't even say that he walked home *with* me, because he was walking fast and I couldn't keep up. His legs were so long, and for every stride he took I had to take two. I was looking forward to him searching for his cigarettes in the ivy, but he said he wasn't going to go the way we usually went. He was going home another way. I couldn't blame him for being disappointed in me, I'd let him down after he'd come to my rescue during recess. But couldn't he understand that, really and truly, it wasn't a personal thing. Couldn't he understand that I could be completely in love with him, but just not want to make waves? And anyway, it wasn't like I *threw* the jacket down or anything. It slipped.

"But, Melvin," I said, trying to get him to go my way. "This is the quickest way to get home. Your house is straight ahead. Plus, what about your cigarettes? Aren't you dying for a cigarette?"

"Darlin . . ." He pulled a cigarette from his jacket pocket and put it behind his ear. "I can get by with what I got right here until later."

Darlin. I'd never heard that from him, calling me that before. I didn't like the way it felt, like a pat on the head. Not like when he said my name, which felt like a kiss.

"See ya round," Melvin said and turned, walking uphill. I watched him for as long as I could see him, and I still didn't know that he was never going to walk my way again, but I was thinking, *You probably should have picked up his jacket. Pro-ba-bly.*

Too late. Melvin got farther and farther away, MEL on the back of his jacket, shimmering like diamonds, like he was some superstar. And me, I was feeling as though I wished somebody fighting had slugged me, too.

I walked up the hill to my house and replayed Melvin's fight. Only in my mind, it wasn't Melvin's fight. It became my fight. I imagined I had on a bad outfit, windowpane pants and a leather jacket, new—not used—and a large, perfectly round Afro like the one Foxy Brown had when she pulled a gun from it and blew away some white man who was messing with her. Owen was obsessed with Pam Grier and her big breasts, and I was awed by her ability to whup ass. People who messed with Foxy were sorry, all right. Just when they though she was all brown sugar in a halter top, she had a gun or a karate kick to set them straight.

Listen, I said. I was talking to myself. *All y'all mothafuckas better leave Melvin alone. That's right, I cussed. And I did say, muthafucka, not mo-ther fuck-er. It's the way I speak, dumb-asses, and unless you want your butt kicked, you best to leave me and my man alone. Who you calling a nigga?* I swung around and pointed a gun at the nearest palm tree. *That's what I thought.*

I kept replaying my and Melvin's fight. When I got in the house, I was surprised to see Owen at the refrigerator, home from work early, drinking milk from a carton.

"You not supposed to be doing that. Mama said."

"Mama said," he mimicked me. "You always got to do everything everybody say, goody-goody. Who were you talking to, anyway?"

I put my books down on the dining room table, round and glass. I didn't want to stop my daydream. Melvin was holding my hand. *Darlin, I guess you told them what side of the sidewalk they can spit on, didn't you?*

I went to the cabinet for a glass and poured myself a glass of milk dramatically, to show Owen how it was supposed to be done. He thumped me on the head.

"You still ain't told me who you was talking to all loud."

I drank my milk down in two gulps, washed my glass out then and there because Mama liked her kitchen kept neat, and then I picked up my books so I could go to my room and get out of my torn green pants. "Nobody. OK? I wasn't saying anything to anybody. I was just talking to myself."

"Trippin," he said, making his way to his room. He hardly seemed fazed by anything, not even moving to the suburbs.

"Hey," I said. "Owen."

"What?"

"Isn't it weird going to school with all these white people sometime? Don't it make you feel . . ." My voice trailed off. I was looking for the word. "Bad? *Doesn't* it make you feel bad?"

"What?" Owen rolled his eyes. "I'm graduating this year, Ave, I ain't stuttin these white folks." He went into his room and closed the door and soon I could hear Peabo Bryson blaring from his stereo, *I'm so into you, I don't know what I'm going to do.*

Stuttin, Owen said. Stuttin meant "studying." I repealed the word in my head. I'd heard that word my whole life from my grandmamas, Mama, Daddy, everybody. But when Owen said it then, "stuttin" sounded like a word he'd just made up. For the first time I really heard what the kids in school heard when I spoke. Owen sounded strange to me, from someplace else, using that word. Part of a language I knew but was already beginning to forget.

Identity

from *Silent Spring*

Rachel Carson

2. The Obligation to Endure

The history of life on earth has been a history of interaction between living things and their surroundings. To a large extent, the physical form and the habits of the earth's vegetation and its animal life have been molded by the environment. Considering the whole span of earthly time, the opposite effect, in which life actually modifies its surroundings, has been relatively slight. Only within the moment of time represented by the present century has one species—man—acquired significant power to alter the nature of his world.

During the past quarter century this power has not only increased to one of disturbing magnitude but it has changed in character. The most alarming of all man's assaults upon the environment is the contamination of air, earth, rivers, and sea with dangerous and even lethal materials. This pollution is for the most part irrecoverable; the chain of evil it initiates not only in the world that must support life but in living tissues is for the most part irreversible. In this now universal contamination of the environment, chemicals are the sinister and little recognized partners of radiation in changing the very nature of the world—the very nature of its life. Strontium 90, released through nuclear explosions into the air, comes to earth in rain or drifts down as fallout, lodges in soil, enters the grass or corn or wheat grown there, and in time takes up its abode in the bones of a human being, there to remain until his death. Similarly, chemicals sprayed on croplands or forests or garden lie long in soil, entering into living organisms, passing from one to another in a chain of poisoning and death. Or they pass mysteriously by underground streams until they emerge and through the alchemy of air and sunlight, combine into new forms that kill vegetation, sicken cattle, and work unknown harm on those who drink from once pure wells. As Albert Schweitzer has said, "Man can hardly even recognize the devils of his own creation."

It took hundreds of millions of years to produce the life that now inhabits the earth—eons of time in which that developing and evolving and diversifying life reached a state of adjustment and balance with its surroundings. The environment, rigorously shaping and directing the life it supported, contained elements that were hostile as well as supporting. Certain rocks gave out dangerous radiation; even within the light of the sun, from which all life draws its energy, there were short-wave radiations with power to injure. Given time—time not in years but in millennia—life adjusts, and a balance has been reached. For time is the essential ingredient; but in the modern world there is no time.

The rapidity of change and the speed with which new situations are created follow the impetuous and heedless pace of man rather than the deliberate pace of nature. Radiation is no longer merely the background radiation of rocks, the bombardment of cosmic rays, the ultraviolet of the sun that have existed before there was any life on earth; radiation is now the unnatural creation of man's tampering with the atom. The chemicals to which life is asked to make its adjustment are no longer merely the calcium and silica and copper and all the rest of the minerals washed out of the rocks and carried in rivers to the sea; they are the synthetic creations of man's inventive mind, brewed in his laboratories, and having no counterparts in nature.

To adjust to these chemicals would require time on the scale that is nature's; it would require not merely the years of a man's life but the life of generations. And even this, were it by some miracle possible, would be futile, for the new chemicals come from our laboratories in an endless stream; almost five hundred annually find their way into actual use in the United States alone. The figure is staggering and its implications are not easily grasped—500 new chemicals to which the bodies of men and animals are required somehow to adapt each year, chemicals totally outside the limits of biologic experience.

Among them are many that are used in man's war against nature. Since the mid-1940s over 200 basic chemicals have been created for use in killing insects, weeds, rodents, and other organisms described in the modern vernacular as "pests"; and they are sold under several thousand different brand names.

These sprays, dusts, and aerosols are now applied almost universally to farms, gardens, forests, and homes—nonselective chemicals that have the power to kill every insect, the "good" and the "bad," to still the song of birds and the leaping of fish in the streams, to coat the leaves with a deadly film, and to linger on in soil—all this though the intended target may be only a few weeds or insects. Can anyone believe it is possible to lay down such a barrage of poisons on the surface of the earth without making it unfit for all life? They should not be called "insecticides," but "biocides."

The whole process of spraying seems caught up in an endless spiral. Since DDT was released for civilian use, a process of escalation has been going on in which ever more toxic materials must be found. This has happened because insects, in a triumphant vindication of Darwin's principle of the survival of the fittest, have evolved super races immune to the particular insecticide used, hence a deadlier one has always to be developed—and then a deadlier one than that. It has happened also because destructive insects often undergo a "flare-back," or resurgence, after spraying, in numbers greater than before. Thus the chemical war is never won, and all life is caught in its violent crossfire.

Along with the possibility of the extinction of mankind by nuclear war, the central problem of our age has therefore become the contamination of man's total environment with such substances of incredible potential for harm—substances that accumulate in the tissues of plants and animals and even penetrate the germ cells to shatter or alter the very material of heredity upon which the shape of the future depends.

Some would-be architects of our future look toward a time when it will be possible to alter the human germ plasm by design. But we may easily be doing so now by inadvertence, for many chemicals, like radiation, bring about gene mutations. It is ironic to think that man might determine his own future by something so seemingly trivial as the choice of an insect spray.

All this has been risked—for what? Future historians may well be amazed by our distorted sense of proportion. How could intelligent beings seek to control a few unwanted species by a method that contaminated the entire environment and brought the threat of disease and death even to their own kind? Yet this is precisely what we have done. We have done it, moreover, for reasons that collapse the moment we examine them. We are told that the enormous and expanding use of pesticides is necessary to maintain farm production. Yet is our real problem not one of *overproduction?* Our farms, despite measures to remove acreages from production and to pay farmers *not* to produce, have yielded such a staggering excess of crops that the American taxpayer in 1962 is paying out more than one billion dollars a year as the total carrying cost of the surplus-food storage program. And is the situation helped when one branch of the Agriculture Department tries to reduce production while another states, as it did in 1958, "It is believed generally that reduction of crop acreages under provisions of the Soil Bank will stimulate interest in use of chemicals to obtain maximum production on the land retained in crops."

All this is not to say there is no insect problem and no need of control. I am saying, rather, that control must be geared to realities, not to mythical situations, and that the methods employed must be such that they do not destroy us along with the insects.

The problem whose attempted solution has brought such a train of disaster in its wake is an accompaniment of our modern way of life. Long before the age of man, insects inhabited the earth—a group of extraordinarily varied and adaptable beings. Over the course of time since man's advent, a small percentage of the more than half a million species of insects have come into conflict with human welfare in two principal ways: as competitors for the food supply and as carriers of human disease.

Disease-carrying insects become important where human beings are crowded together, especially under conditions where sanitation is poor, as in time of natural disaster or war or in situations of extreme poverty and deprivation. Then control of some sort becomes necessary. It is a sobering fact, however, that the method of massive chemical control has had only limited success, and also threatens to worsen the very conditions it is intended to curb.

Under primitive agricultural conditions the farmer had few insect problems. These arose with the intensification of agriculture—the devotion of immense acreages to a single crop. Such a system set the stage for explosive increases in specific insect populations. Single-crop farming does not take advantage of the principles by which nature works; it is agriculture as an engineer might conceive it to be. Nature has introduced great variety into the landscape, but man has displayed a passion for simplifying it. Thus he undoes the built-in checks and balances by which nature holds the species within bounds. One important natural check is a limit on the amount of suitable habitat for each species. Obviously then, an insect that lives on wheat can build up its population to much higher levels on a farm devoted to wheat than on one in which wheat is intermingled with other crops to which the insect is not adapted.

The same thing happens in other situations. A generation or more ago, the towns of large areas of the United States lined their streets with the noble elm tree. Now the beauty they hopefully created is threatened with complete destruction as disease sweeps through the elms, carried by a beetle that would have only limited chance to build up large populations and to spread from tree to tree if the elms were only occasional trees in a richly diversified planting.

Another factor in the modern insect problem is one that must be viewed against a background of geologic and human history: the spreading of thousands of different kinds of organisms from their native homes to invade new territories. This worldwide migration has been studied and graphically described by the British ecologist Charles Elton in his recent book _The Ecology of Invasions_. During the Cretaceous Period, some hundred million years ago, flooding seas cut many land bridges between continents and living things found themselves confined in what Elton calls "colossal separate nature reserves." There, isolated from others of their kind, they developed many new species. When some of the land masses were joined again, about 15 million years ago, these species began to move out into new territories—a movement that is not only still in progress but is now receiving considerable assistance from man.

The importation of plants is the primary agent in the modern spread of species, for animals have almost invariably gone along with the plants, quarantine being a comparatively recent and not completely effective innovation. The United States Office of Plant Introduction alone has introduced almost 200,000 species and varieties of plants from all over the world. Nearly half of the 180 or so major insect enemies of plants in the United States are accidental imports from abroad, and most of them have come as hitchhikers on plants.

In new territory, out of reach of the restraining hand of the natural enemies that kept down its numbers in its native land, an invading plant or animal is able to become enormously abundant. Thus it is no accident that our most troublesome insects are introduced species.

These invasions, both the naturally occurring and those dependent on human assistance, are likely to continue indefinitely. Quarantine and massive chemical campaigns are only extremely expensive ways of buying time. We are faced, according to Dr. Elton, "with a life-and-death need not just to find new technological means of suppressing this plant or that animal"; instead we need the basic knowledge of animal populations and their relations to their surroundings that will "promote an even balance and damp down the explosive power of outbreaks and new invasions."

Much of the necessary knowledge is now available but we do not use it. We train ecologists in our universities and even employ them in our government agencies but we seldom take their advice. We allow the chemical death rain to fall as though there were no alternative, whereas in fact there are many, and our ingenuity could soon discover many more if given opportunity.

Have we fallen into a mesmerized state that makes us accept as inevitable that which is inferior or detrimental, as though having lost the will or the vision to demand that which is good? Such thinking, in the words of the ecologist Paul Shepard, "idealizes life with only its head out of the water, inches above the limits of toleration of the corruption of its own environment. . . . Why should we tolerate a diet of weak poisons, a home in insipid surroundings, a circle of acquaintances who are not quite our enemies, the noise of motors with just enough relief to prevent insanity? Who would want to live in a world which is just not quite fatal?"

Yet such a world is pressed upon us. The crusade to create a chemically sterile, insect-free world seems to have engendered a fanatic zeal on the part of many specialists and most of the so-called control agencies. On every hand there is evidence that those engaged in spraying operations exercise a ruthless power. "The regulatory entomologist . . . function as prosecutor, judge and jury, tax assessor and collector and sheriff to enforce their own orders," said Connecticut entomologist Neely Turner. The most flagrant abuses go unchecked in both state and federal agencies.

It is not my contention that chemical insecticides must never be used. I do contend that we have put poisonous and biologically potent chemicals indiscriminately into the hands of persons largely or wholly ignorant of their potentials for harm. We have subjected enormous numbers of people to contact with these poisons, without their consent and often without their knowledge. If the Bill of Rights contains no guarantee that a citizen shall be secure against lethal poisons distributed either by private individuals or by public officials, it is surely only because our forefathers, despite their considerable wisdom and foresight, could conceive of no such problem.

I contend, furthermore, that we have allowed these chemicals to be used with little or no advance investigation of their effect on soil, water, wildlife, and man himself. Future generations are unlikely to condone our lack of prudent concern for the integrity of the natural world that supports all life.

There is still very limited awareness of the nature of the threat. This is an era of specialists, each of whom sees his own problem and is unaware of or intolerant of the larger frame into which it fits. It is also an era dominated by industry, in which the right to make a dollar at whatever cost is seldom challenged. When the public protests, confronted with some obvious evidence of damaging results of pesticide applications, it is fed little tranquilizing pills of half truth. We urgently need an end to these false assurances, to the sugar coating of unpalatable facts. It is the public that is being asked to assume the risks that the insect controllers calculate. The public must decide whether it wishes to continue on the present road, and it can do so only when in full possession of the facts. In the words of Jean Rostand, "The obligation to endure gives us the right to know."

Who will fund agencies to oversee control?

Do we n...

12. The Human Price

As the tide of chemicals born of the Industrial Age has arisen to engulf our environment, a drastic change has come about in the nature of the most serious public health problems. Only yesterday mankind lived in fear of the scourges of smallpox, cholera, and plague that once swept nations before them. Now our major concern is no longer with the disease organisms that once were omnipresent; sanitation, better living conditions, and new drugs have given us a high degree of control over infectious disease. Today we are concerned with a different kind of hazard that lurks in our environment—a hazard we ourselves have introduced into our world as our modern way of life has evolved.

The new environmental health problems are multiple—created by radiation in all its forms, born of the never-ending stream of chemicals of which pesticides are a part, chemicals now pervading the world in which we live, acting upon us directly and indirectly, separately and collectively. Their presence casts a shadow that is no less ominous because it is formless and obscure, no less frightening because it is simply impossible to predict the effects of lifetime exposure to chemical and physical agents that are not part of the biological experience of man.

"We all live under the haunting fear that something may corrupt the environment to the point where man joins the dinosaurs as an obsolete form of life," says Dr. David Price of the United States Public Health Service. "And what makes these thoughts all the more disturbing is the knowledge that our fate could perhaps be sealed twenty or more years before the development of symptoms."

Where do pesticides fit into the picture of environmental disease? We have seen that they now contaminate soil, water, and food, that they have the power to make our streams fishless and our gardens and woodlands silent and birdless. Man, however much he may like to pretend the contrary, is part of nature. Can he escape a pollution that is now so thoroughly distributed throughout our world?

We know that even single exposures to these chemicals, if the amount is large enough, can precipitate acute poisoning. But this is not the major problem. The sudden illness or death of farmers, spraymen, pilots, and others exposed to appreciable quantities of pesticides are tragic and should not occur. For the population as a whole, we must be more concerned with the delayed effects of absorbing small amounts of the pesticides that invisibly contaminate our world.

Responsible public health officials have pointed out that the biological effects of chemicals are cumulative over long periods of time, and that the hazard to the individual may depend on the sum of the exposures received throughout his lifetime. For these very reasons the danger is easily ignored. It is human nature to shrug off what may seem to us a vague threat of future disaster. "Men are naturally most impressed by diseases which have obvious manifestations," says a wise physician, Dr. Rene Dubos, "yet some of their worst enemies creep on them unobtrusively."

For each of us, as for the robin in Michigan or the salmon in the Miramichi, this is a problem of ecology, of interrelationships, of interdependence. We poison the caddis flies in a stream and the salmon runs dwindle and die. We poison the gnats in a lake and the poison travels from link to link of the food chain and soon the birds of the lake margins become its victims. We spray our elms and the following springs are silent of robin song, not because we sprayed the robins directly but because the poison traveled, step by step, through the now familiar elm leaf-earthworm-robin cycle. These are matters of record, observable, part of the visible world around us. They reflect the web of life—or death—that scientists know as ecology.

But there is also an ecology of the world within our bodies. In this unseen world minute causes produce mighty effects; the effect, moreover, is often seemingly unrelated to the cause, appearing in a part of the body remote from the area where the original injury was sustained. "A change at one point, in one molecule even, may reverberate throughout the entire system to initiate changes in seemingly unrelated organs and tissues," says a recent summary of the present status of medical research. When one is concerned with the mysterious and wonderful functioning of the human body, cause and effect are seldom simple and easily demonstrated relationships. They may be widely separated both in space and time. To discover the agent of disease and death depends on a patient piecing together of many seemingly distinct and unrelated facts developed through a vast amount of research in widely separated fields.

We are accustomed to look for the gross and immediate effect and to ignore all else. Unless this appears promptly and in such obvious form that it cannot be ignored, we deny the existence of hazard. Even research men suffer from the handicap of inadequate methods of detecting the beginnings of injury. The lack of sufficiently delicate methods to detect injury before symptoms appear is one of the great unsolved problems in medicine.

"But," someone will object, "I have used dieldrin sprays on the lawn many times but I have never had convulsions like the World Health Organization spraymen—so it hasn't harmed me." It is not that simple. Despite the absence of sudden and dramatic symptoms, one who handles such materials is unquestionably storing up toxic materials in his body. Storage of the chlorinated hydrocarbons, as we have seen, is cumulative, beginning with the smallest intake. The toxic materials become lodged in all the fatty tissues of the body. When these reserves of fat are drawn upon the poison may then strike quickly. A New Zealand medical journal recently provided an example. A man under treatment for obesity suddenly developed symptoms of poisoning. On examination his fat was found to contain stored dieldrin, which had been metabolized as he lost weight. The same thing could happen with loss of weight in illness.

The results of storage, on the other hand, could be even less obvious. Several years ago the *Journal* of the American Medical Association warned strongly of the hazards of insecticide storage in adipose tissue, pointing out that drugs or chemicals that are cumulative require greater caution than those having no tendency to be stored in the tissues. The adipose tissue, we are warned, is not merely a place for the deposition of fat (which makes up about 18 per cent of the body weight), but has many important functions with which the stored poisons may interfere. Furthermore, fats are very widely distributed in the organs and tissues of the whole body, even being constituents of cell membranes. It is important to remember, therefore, that the fat-soluble insecticides become stored in individual cells, where they are in position to interfere with the most vital and necessary functions of oxidation and energy production. . . .

One of the most significant facts about the chlorinated hydrocarbon insecticides is their effect on the liver. Of all organs in the body the liver is most extraordinary. In its versatility and in the indispensable nature of its functions it has no equal. It presides over so many vital activities that even the slightest damage to it is fraught with serious consequences. Not only does it provide bile for the digestion of fats, but because of its location and the special circulatory pathways that converge upon it the liver receives blood directly from the digestive tract and is deeply involved in the metabolism of all the principal foodstuffs. It stores sugar in the form of glycogen and releases it as glucose in carefully measured quantities to keep the blood sugar at a normal level. It builds body proteins, including some essential elements of blood plasma concerned with blood-clotting. It maintains cholesterol at its proper level in the blood plasma, and inactivates the male and female hormones when they reach excessive levels. It is a storehouse of many vitamins, some of which in turn contribute to its own proper functioning.

Without a normally functioning liver the body would be disarmed—defenseless against the great variety of poisons that continually invade it. Some of these are normal by-products of metabolism, which the liver swiftly and efficiently makes harmless by withdrawing their nitrogen. But poisons that have no normal place in the body may also be detoxified. The "harmless" insecticides malathion and methoxychlor are less poisonous than their relatives only because a liver enzyme deals with them, altering their molecules in such a way that their capacity for harm is lessened. In similar ways the liver deals with the majority of the toxic materials to which we are exposed.

Our line of defense against invading poisons or poisons from within is now weakened and crumbling. A liver damaged by pesticides is not only incapable of protecting us from poisons, the whole wide range of its activities may be interfered with. Not only are the consequences far-reaching, but because of their variety and the fact that they may not immediately appear they may not be attributed to their true cause.

In connection with the nearly universal use of insecticides that are liver poisons, it is interesting to note the sharp rise in hepatitis that began during the 1950's and is continuing a fluctuating climb. Cirrhosis also is said to be increasing. While it is admittedly difficult, in dealing with human beings rather than laboratory animals, to "prove" that cause A produces effect B, plain common sense suggests that the relation between a soaring rate of liver disease and the prevalence of liver poisons in the environment is no coincidence. Whether or not the chlorinated hydrocarbons are the primary cause, it seems hardly sensible under the circumstances to expose ourselves to poisons that have a proven ability to damage the liver and so presumably to make it less resistant to disease.

Both major types of insecticides, the chlorinated hydrocarbons and the organic phosphates, directly affect the nervous system, although in somewhat different ways. This has been made clear by an infinite number of experiments on animals and by observations on human subjects as well. As for DDT, the first of the new organic insecticides to be widely used, its action is primarily on the central nervous system of man; the cerebellum and the higher motor cortex are thought to be the areas chiefly affected. Abnormal sensations as of prickling, burning, or itching, as well as tremors or even convulsions may follow exposure to appreciable amounts, according to a standard textbook of toxicology.

Our first knowledge of the symptoms of acute poisoning by DDT was furnished by several British investigators, who deliberately exposed themselves in order to learn the consequences. Two scientists at the British Royal Navy Physiological Laboratory invited absorption of DDT through the skin by direct contact with walls covered with a water-soluble paint containing 2 percent DDT, overlaid with a thin film of oil. The direct effect on the nervous system is apparent in their eloquent description of their symptoms: "The tiredness, heaviness, and aching of limbs were very real things, and the mental state was also most distressing . . . [there was] extreme irritability . . . great distaste for work of any sort . . . a feeling of mental incompetence in tackling the simplest mental task. The joint pains were quite violent at times."

Another British experimenter who applied DDT in acetone solution to his skin reported heaviness and aching of limbs, muscular weakness, and "spasms of extreme nervous tension." He took a holiday and improved, but on return to work his condition deteriorated. He then spent three weeks in bed, made miserable by constant aching in limbs, insomnia, nervous tension, and feelings of acute anxiety. On occasion tremors shook his whole body—tremors of the sort now made all too familiar by the sight of birds poisoned by DDT. The experimenter lost 10 weeks from his work, and at the end of a year, when his case was reported in a British medical journal, recovery was not complete.

(Despite this evidence, several American investigators conducting an experiment with DDT on volunteer subjects dismissed the complaint of headache and "pain in every bone" as "obviously of psychoneurotic origin.")

There are now many cases on record in which both the symptoms and the whole course of the illness point to insecticides as the cause. Typically, such a victim has had a known exposure to one of the insecticides, his symptoms have subsided under treatment which included the exclusion of all insecticides from his environment, and most significantly *have returned with each renewed contact* with the offending chemicals. This sort of evidence—and no more—forms the basis of a vast amount of medical therapy in many other disorders. There is no reason why it should not serve as a warning that it is no longer sensible to take the "calculated risk" of saturating our environment with pesticides.

Why does not everyone handling and using insecticides develop the same symptoms? Here the matter of individual sensitivity enters in. There is some evidence that women are more susceptible than men, the very young more than adults, those who lead sedentary, indoor lives more than those leading a rugged life of work or exercise in the open. Beyond these differences are others that are no less real because they are intangible. What makes one person allergic to dust or pollen, sensitive to a poison, or susceptible to an infection whereas another is not is a medical mystery for which there is at present no explanation. The problem nevertheless exists and it affects significant numbers of the population. Some physicians estimate that a third or more of their patients show signs of some form of sensitivity, and that the number is growing. And unfortunately, sensitivity may suddenly develop in a person previously insensitive. In fact, some medical men believe that intermittent exposures to chemicals may produce just such sensitivity. If this is true, it may

Cholinesterase = enzyme which hydrolyses esters of choline and which is concerned with the transmission of neural impulse

hydrolyses, subject to hydrolysis, hydrolysis.

phosphate = a salt or ester, an ester = a derivative of an acid.

from *Silent Spring* ◆ 179

explain why some studies on men subjected to continuous occupational exposure find little evidence of toxic effects. By their constant contact with the chemicals these men keep themselves desensitized—as an allergist keeps his patients desensitized by repeated small injections of the allergen.

The whole problem of pesticide poisoning is enormously complicated by the fact that a human being, unlike a laboratory animal living under rigidly controlled conditions, is never exposed to one chemical alone. Between the major groups of insecticides, and between them and other chemicals, there are interactions that have serious potentials. Whether released into soil or water or a man's blood, these unrelated chemicals do not remain segregated; there are mysterious and unseen changes by which one alters the power of another for harm.

There is interaction even between the two major groups of insecticides usually thought to be completely distinct in their action. The power of the organic phosphates, those poisoners of the nerve-protective enzyme cholinesterase, may become greater if the body has first been exposed to a chlorinated hydrocarbon which injures the liver. This is because, when liver function is disturbed, the cholinesterase level drops below normal. The added depressive effect of the organic phosphate may then be enough to precipitate acute symptoms. And as we have seen, pairs of the organic phosphates themselves may interact in such a way as to increase their toxicity a hundredfold. Or the organic phosphates may interact with various drugs, or with synthetic materials, food additives—who can say what else of the infinite number of man-made substances that now pervade our world?

The effect of a chemical of supposedly innocuous nature can be drastically changed by the action of another; one of the best examples is a close relative of DDT called methoxychlor. (Actually, methoxychlor may not be as free from dangerous qualities as it is generally said to be, for recent work on experimental animals shows a direct action on the uterus and a blocking effect on some of the powerful pituitary hormones—reminding us again that these are chemicals with enormous biologic effect. Other work shows that methoxychlor has a potential ability to damage the kidneys.) Because it is not stored to any great extent when given alone, we are told that methoxychlor is a safe chemical. But this is not necessarily true. If the liver has been damaged by another agent, methoxychlor is stored in the body at *100 times* its normal rate, and will then imitate the effects of DDT with long-lasting effects on the nervous system. Yet the liver damage that brings this about might be so slight as to pass unnoticed. It might have been the result of any of a number of commonplace situations—using another insecticide, using a cleaning fluid containing carbon tetrachloride, or taking one of the so-called tranquilizing drugs,

methoxychlor

a number (but not all) of which are chlorinated hydrocarbons and possess power to damage the liver.

Damage to the nervous system is not confined to acute poisoning; there may also be delayed effects from exposure. Long-lasting damage to brain or nerves has been reported for methoxychlor and others. Dieldrin, besides its immediate consequences, can have long delayed effects ranging from "loss of memory, insomnia, and nightmares to mania." Lindane, according to medical findings, is stored in significant amounts in the brain and functioning liver tissue and may induce "profound and long lasting effects on the central nervous system." Yet this chemical, a form of benzene hexachloride, is much used in vaporizers, devices that pour a stream of volatilized insecticide vapor into homes, offices, restaurants.

The organic phosphates, usually considered only in relation to their more violent manifestations in acute poisoning, also have the power to produce lasting physical damage to nerve tissues and, according to recent findings, to induce mental disorders. Various cases of delayed paralysis have followed use of one or another of these insecticides. A bizarre happening in the United States during the prohibition era about 1930 was an omen of things to come. It was caused not by an insecticide but by a substance belonging chemically to the same group as the organic phosphate insecticides. During that period some medicinal substances were being pressed into service as substitutes for liquor, being exempt from the prohibition law. One of these was Jamaica ginger. But the *United States Pharmacopeia* product was expensive, and bootleggers conceived the idea of making a substitute Jamaica ginger. They succeeded so well that their spurious product responded to the appropriate chemical tests and deceived the government chemists. To give their false ginger the necessary tang they had introduced a chemical known as triorthocresyl phosphate. This chemical, like parathion and its relatives, destroys the protective enzyme cholinesterase. As a consequence of drinking the bootleggers' product some 15,000 people developed a permanently crippling type of paralysis of the leg muscles, a condition now called "ginger paralysis." The paralysis was accompanied by destruction of the nerve sheaths and by degeneration of the cells of the anterior horns of the spinal cord.

About two decades later various other organic phosphates came into use as insecticides, as we have seen, and soon cases reminiscent of the ginger paralysis episode began to occur. One was a greenhouse worker in Germany who became paralyzed several months after experiencing mild symptoms of poisoning on a few occasions after using parathion. Then a group of three chemical plant workers developed acute poisoning from exposure to other insecticides of

enzyme
phosphate

this group. They recovered under treatment, but ten days later two of them developed muscular weakness in the legs. This persisted for 10 months in one; the other, a young woman chemist, was more severely affected, with paralysis in both legs and some involvement of the hands and arms. Two years later when her case was reported in a medical journal she was still unable to walk.

The insecticide responsible for these cases has been withdrawn from the market, but some of those now in use may be capable of like harm. Malathion (beloved of gardeners) has induced severe muscular weakness in experiments on chickens. This was attended (as in ginger paralysis) by destruction of the sheaths of the sciatic and spinal nerves.

All these consequences of organic phosphate poisoning, if survived, may be a prelude to worse. In view of the severe damage they inflict upon the nervous system, it was perhaps inevitable that these insecticides would eventually be linked with mental disease. That link has recently been supplied by investigators at the University of Melbourne and Prince Henry's Hospital in Melbourne, who reported on 16 cases of mental disease. All had a history of prolonged exposure to organic phosphorus insecticides. Three were scientists checking the efficacy of sprays; 8 worked in greenhouses; 5 were farm workers. Their symptoms ranged from impairment of memory to schizophrenic and depressive reactions. All had normal medical histories before the chemicals they were using boomeranged and struck them down.

Echoes of this sort of thing are to be found, as we have seen, widely scattered throughout medical literature, sometimes involving the chlorinated hydrocarbons, sometimes the organic phosphates. Confusion, delusions, loss of memory, mania—a heavy price to pay for the temporary destruction of a few insects, but a price that will continue to be exacted as long as we insist upon using chemicals that strike directly at the nervous system.

from *Almagest*

Ptolemy — AD 90 – 168
Egyptian under Rome rule

Book I

1. {*Preface*}[4]

The true philosophers, Syrus,[5] were, I think, quite right to distinguish the theoretical part of philosophy from the practical. For even if practical philosophy,
before it is practical, turns out to be theoretical,[6] nevertheless one can see that
there is a great difference between the two: in the first place, it is possible for
many people to possess some of the moral virtues even without being taught,
whereas it is impossible to achieve theoretical understanding of the universe
without instruction; furthermore, one derives most benefit in the first case
[practical philosophy] from continuous practice in actual affairs, but in the
other [theoretical philosophy] from making progress in the theory. Hence we
thought it fitting to guide our actions (under the impulse of our actual ideas
[of what is to be done]) in such a way as never to forget, even in ordinary
affairs, to strive for a noble and disciplined disposition, but to devote most of
our time to intellectual matters, in order to teach theories, which are so many
and beautiful, and especially those to which the epithet 'mathematical' is particularly applied. For Aristotle divides theoretical philosophy too, very fittingly,
into three primary categories, physics, mathematics and theology.[7] For everything that exists is composed of matter, form and motion; none of these [three]
can be observed in its substratum by itself, without the others: they can only
be imagined. Now the first cause of the first motion of the universe, if one considers it simply, can be thought of as an invisible and motionless deity; the division [of theoretical philosophy] concerned with investigating this [can be
called] 'theology', since this kind of activity, somewhere up in the highest
reaches of the universe, can only be imagined, and is completely separated
from perceptible reality. The division [of theoretical philosophy] which investigates material and ever-moving nature, and which concerns itself with
'white', 'hot', 'sweet', 'soft' and suchlike qualities one may call 'physics'; such
an order of being is situated (for the most part) amongst corruptible bodies

and below the lunar sphere. That division [of theoretical philosophy] which determines the nature involved in forms and motion from place to place, and which serves to investigate shape, number, size, and place, time and suchlike, one may define as 'mathematics'. Its subject-matter falls as it were in the middle between the other two, since, firstly, it can be conceived of both with and without the aid of the senses, and, secondly, it is an attribute of all existing things without exception, both mortal and immortal: for those things which are perpetually changing in their inseparable form, it changes with them, while for eternal things which have an aethereal[8] nature, it keeps their unchanging form unchanged.

From all this we concluded:[9] that the first two divisions of theoretical philosophy should rather be called guesswork than knowledge, theology because of its completely invisible and ungraspable nature, physics because of the unstable and unclear nature of matter; hence there is no hope that philosophers will ever be agreed about them; and that only mathematics can provide sure and unshakeable knowledge to its devotees, provided one approaches it rigorously. For its kind of proof proceeds by indisputable methods, namely arithmetic and geometry. Hence we were drawn to the investigation of that part of theoretical philosophy, as far as we were able to the whole of it, but especially to the theory concerning divine and heavenly things. For that alone is devoted to the investigation of the eternally unchanging. For that reason it too can be eternal and unchanging (which is a proper attribute of knowledge) in its own domain, which is neither unclear nor disorderly. Furthermore it can work in the domains of the other [two divisions of theoretical philosophy] no less than they do. For this is the best science to help theology along its way, since it is the only one which can make a good guess at [the nature of] that activity which is unmoved and separated; [it can do this because] it is familiar with the attributes of those beings[10] which are on the one hand perceptible, moving and being moved, but on the other hand eternal and unchanging, [I mean the attributes] having to do with motions and the arrangements of motions. As for physics, mathematics can make a significant contribution. For almost every peculiar attribute of material nature becomes apparent from the peculiarities of its motion from place to place. [Thus one can distinguish] the corruptible from the incorruptible by [whether it undergoes] motion in a straight line or in a circle, and heavy from light, and passive from active, by [whether it moves] towards the centre or away from the centre. With regard to virtuous conduct in practical actions and character, this science, above all things, could make men see clearly; from the constancy, order, symmetry and calm which are associated with the divine, it makes its followers lovers of this divine beauty, accustoming them and reforming their natures, as it were, to a similar spiritual state. ' It is this love of the contemplation of the eternal and unchanging which we constantly strive to increase, by studying those parts of these sciences which have already been mastered by those who approached them in a genuine spirit of enquiry, and by ourselves attempting to contribute as much advancement as has been made possible by the additional time between those people and ourselves.[11] We shall try to note down[12] everything which we think we have discovered up to the present time; we shall do this as concisely as possible and in a manner which can be followed by those who have already made some progress in the field.[13] For the sake of completeness in our treatment we shall set out everything useful for the theory of the heavens in the proper order, but to avoid undue length we shall merely recount what has been adequately established by the ancients. However, those topics which have not been dealt with [by our predecessors] at all, or not as usefully as they might have been, will be discussed at length, to the best of our ability.

2. {*On the order of the theorems*}

In the treatise which we propose, then, the first order of business is to grasp the relationship of the earth taken as a whole to the heavens taken as a whole.[14] In the treatment of the individual aspects which follows, we must first discuss the position of the ecliptic[15] and the regions of our part of the inhabited world and also the features differentiating each from the others due to the [varying] latitude at each horizon taken in order.[16] For if the theory of these matters is treated first it will make examination of the rest easier. Secondly, we have to go through the motion of the sun and of the moon, and the phenomena accompanying these [motions];[17] for it would be impossible to examine the theory of the stars[18] thoroughly without first having a grasp of these matters. Our final task in this way of approach is the theory of the stars. Here too it would be appropriate to deal first with the sphere of the so-called 'fixed stars',[19] and follow that by treating the five 'planets', as they are called.[20] We shall try to provide proofs in all of these topics by using as starting-points and foundations, as it were, for our search the obvious phenomena, and those observations made by the ancients and in our own times which are reliable. We shall attach the subsequent structure of ideas to this [foundation] by means of proofs using geometrical methods.

The general preliminary discussion covers the following topics: the heaven is spherical in shape, and moves as a sphere; the earth too is sensibly spherical in shape, when taken as a whole; in position it lies in the middle of the heavens very much like its centre; in size and distance it has the ratio of a point to the sphere of the fixed stars; and it has no motion from place to place. We shall briefly discuss each of these points for the sake of reminder.

3. {*That the heavens move like a sphere*}[21]

It is plausible to suppose that the ancients got their first notions on these topics from the following kind of observations. They saw that the sun, moon and other stars were carried from east to west along circles which were always parallel to each other, that they began to rise up from below the earth itself, as it were, gradually got up high, then kept on going round in similar fashion and getting lower, until, falling to earth, so to speak, they vanished completely, then, after remaining invisible for some time, again rose afresh and set; and [they saw] that the periods of these [motions], and also the places of rising and setting, were, on the whole, fixed and the same.

What chiefly led them to the concept of a sphere was the revolution of the ever-visible stars, which was observed to be circular, and always taking place about one centre, the same [for all]. For by necessity that point became [for them] the pole of the heavenly sphere: those stars which were closer to it revolved on smaller circles, those that were farther away described circles ever greater in proportion to their distance, until one reaches the distance of the stars which become invisible. In the case of these, too, they saw that those near the ever-visible stars remained invisible for a short time, while those farther away remained invisible for a long time, again in proportion [to their distance]. The result was that in the beginning they got to the aforementioned notion solely from such considerations; but from then on, in their subsequent investigation, they found that everything else accorded with it, since absolutely all phenomena are in contradiction to the alternative notions which have been propounded.

For if one were to suppose that the stars' motion takes place in a straight line towards infinity, as some people have thought,[22] what device could one conceive of which would cause each of them to appear to begin their motion from the same starting-point every day? How could the stars turn back if their motion is towards infinity? Or, if they did turn back, how could this not be obvious? [On such a hypothesis], they must gradually diminish in size until they disappear, whereas, on the contrary, they are seen to be greater at the very moment of their disappearance, at which time they are gradually obstructed and cut off, as it were, by the earth's surface.

But to suppose that they are kindled as they rise out of the earth and are extinguished again as they fall to earth is a completely absurd hypothesis.[23] For even if we were to concede that the strict order in their size and number, their intervals, positions and periods could be restored by such a random and chance process; that one whole area of the earth has a kindling nature, and another an extinguishing one, or rather that the same part [of the earth] kindles for one set of observers and extinguishes for another set; and that the same stars are already kindled or extinguished for some observers while they are not yet for others: even if, I say, we were to concede all these ridiculous consequences, what could we say about the ever-visible stars, which neither rise nor set? Those stars which are kindled and extinguished ought to rise and set for observers everywhere, while those which are not kindled and extinguished ought always to be visible for observers everywhere. What cause could we assign for the fact that this is not so? We will surely not say that stars which are kindled and extinguished for some observers never undergo this process for other observers. Yet it is utterly obvious that the same stars rise and set in certain regions [of the earth] and do neither at others.

To sum up, if one assumes any motion whatever, except spherical, for the heavenly bodies, it necessarily follows that their distances, measured from the earth upwards, must vary, wherever and however one supposes the earth itself to be situated. Hence the sizes and mutual distances of the stars must appear to vary for the same observers during the course of each revolution, since at one time they must be at a greater distance, at another at a lesser. Yet we see that no such variation occurs. For the apparent increase in their sizes at the horizons[24] is caused, not by a decrease in their distances, but by the exhalations of moisture surrounding the earth being interposed between the place from which we observe and the heavenly bodies, just as objects placed in water appear bigger than they are, and the lower they sink, the bigger they appear.

The following considerations also lead us to the concept of the sphericity of the heavens. No other hypothesis but this can explain how sundial constructions produce correct results; furthermore, the motion of the heavenly bodies is the most unhampered and free of all motions, and freest motion belongs among plane figures to the circle and among solid shapes to the sphere; similarly, since of different shapes having an equal boundary those with more angles are greater [in area or volume], the circle is greater than [all other] surfaces, and the sphere greater than [all other] solids;[25] [likewise] the heavens are greater than all other bodies.

Furthermore, one can reach this kind of notion from certain physical considerations. E.g., the aether is, of all bodies, the one with constituent parts which are finest and most like each other; now bodies with parts like each other have surfaces with parts like each other; but the only surfaces with parts like each other are the circular, among planes, and the spherical, among three-dimensional surfaces. And since the aether is not plane, but three-dimensional, here the greek is expostomology when al has As you know ? how are we today like or fallen back into Ptolemy's Mason What he says is what is real..

from *Almagest* ◆ 187

it follows that it is spherical in shape. Similarly, nature formed all earthly and corruptible bodies out of shapes which are round but of unlike parts, but all aethereal and divine bodies out of shapes which are of like parts and spherical. For if they were flat or shaped like a discus[26] they would not always display a circular shape to all those observing them simultaneously from different places on earth. For this reason it is plausible that the aether surrounding them, too, being of the same nature, is spherical, and because of the likeness of its parts moves in a circular and uniform fashion.

4. {*That the earth too, taken as a whole, is sensibly spherical*}[27] Why was it flat then ?

That the earth, too, taken as a whole,[28] is sensibly spherical can best be grasped from the following considerations. We can see, again, that the sun, moon and other stars do not rise and set simultaneously for everyone on earth, but do so earlier for those more towards the east, later for those towards the west. For we find that the phenomena at eclipses, especially lunar eclipses,[29] which take place at the same time [for all observers], are nevertheless not recorded as occurring at the same hour (that is at an equal distance from noon) by all observers. Rather, the hour recorded by the more easterly observers is always later than that recorded by the more westerly. We find that the differences in the hour are proportional to the distances between the places [of observation]. Hence one can reasonably conclude that the earth's surface is spherical, because its evenly curving surface (for so it is when considered as a whole) cuts off [the heavenly bodies] for each set of observers in turn in a regular fashion. If the earth's shape were any other, this would not happen, as one can see from the following arguments. If it were concave, the stars would be seen rising; first by those more towards the west; if it were plane, they would rise and set simultaneously for everyone on earth; if it were triangular or square or any other polygonal shape, by a similar argument, they would rise and set simultaneously for all those living on the same plane surface. Yet it is apparent that nothing like this takes place. Nor could it be cylindrical, with the curved surface in the east-west direction, and the flat sides towards the poles of the universe, which some might suppose more plausible. This is clear from the following: for those living on the curved surface none of the stars would be ever-visible, but either all stars would rise and set for all observers, or the same stars, for an equal [celestial] distance from each of the poles, would always be invisible for all observers. In fact, the further we travel toward the north, the more[30] of the southern stars disappear and the more of the northern stars appear. Hence it is clear that here too the curvature of the earth cuts off [the heavenly bodies] in a regular fashion in a north-south direction, and proves the sphericity [of the earth] in all directions.

earth
curvature
known
from
Ptolemy.

There is the further consideration that if we sail towards mountains or elevated places from and to any direction whatever, they are observed to increase gradually in size as if rising up from the sea itself in which they had previously been submerged: this is due to the curvature of the surface of the water.

5. {That the earth is in the middle of the heavens}[31]

Once one has grasped this, if one next considers the position of the earth, one will find that the phenomena associated with it could take place only if we assume that it is in the middle of the heavens, like the centre of a sphere. For if this were not the case, the earth would have to be either

[a] not on the axis [of the universe] but equidistant from both poles, or

[b] on the axis but removed towards one of the poles, or

[c] neither on the axis nor equidistant from both poles.

Against the first of these three positions militate the following arguments. If we imagined [the earth] removed towards the zenith or the nadir of some observer, then, if he were at *sphaera recta*, he would never experience equinox, since the horizon would always divide the heavens into two unequal parts, one above and one below the earth; if he were at *sphaera obliqua*, either, again, equinox would never occur at all, or, [if it did occur,] it would not be at a position halfway between summer and winter solstices, since these intervals would necessarily be unequal, because the equator, which is the greatest of all parallel circles drawn about the poles of the [daily] motion, would no longer be bisected by the horizon; instead [the horizon would bisect] one of the circles parallel to the equator, either to the north or to the south of it. Yet absolutely everyone agrees that these intervals are equal everywhere on earth, since [everywhere] the increment of the longest day over the equinoctial day at the summer solstice is equal to the decrement of the shortest day from the equinoctial day at the winter solstice. But if, on the other hand, we imagined the displacement to be towards the east or west of some observer, he would find that the sizes and distances of the stars would not remain constant and unchanged at eastern and western horizons, and that the time-interval from rising to culmination would not be equal to the interval from culmination to setting. This is obviously completely in disaccord with the phenomena.

Against the second position, in which the earth is imagined to lie on the axis removed towards one of the poles, one can make the following objections. If this were so, the plane of the horizon would divide the heavens into a part above the earth and a part below the earth which are unequal and always different for different latitudes,[32] whether one considers the relationship of the same part at two different latitudes or the two parts at the same latitude. Only at *sphaera recta* could the horizon bisect the sphere; at a *sphaera obliqua* situation such that the nearer pole were the ever-visible one, the horizon would always make the part above the earth lesser and the part below the earth greater; hence another phenomenon would be that the great circle of the ecliptic would be divided into unequal parts by the plane of the horizon. Yet it is apparent that this is by no means so. Instead, six zodiacal signs are visible above the earth at all times and places, while the remaining six are invisible; then again [at a later time] the latter are visible in their entirety above the earth, while at the same time the others are not visible. Hence it is obvious that the horizon bisects the zodiac, since the same semi-circles are cut off by it, so as to appear at one time completely above the earth, and at another [completely] below it.

And in general, if the earth were not situated exactly below the [celestial] equator, but were removed towards the north or south in the direction of one of the poles, the result would be that at the equinoxes the shadow of the gnomon at sunrise would no longer form a straight line with its shadow at sunset in a plane parallel to the horizon, not even sensibly.[33] Yet this is a phenomenon which is plainly observed everywhere.

It is immediately clear that the third position enumerated is likewise impossible, since the sorts of objection which we made to the first [two] will both arise in that case.

To sum up, if the earth did not lie in the middle [of the universe], the whole order of things which we observe in the increase and decrease of the length of daylight would be fundamentally upset. Furthermore, eclipses of the moon would not be restricted to situations where the moon is diametrically opposite the sun (whatever part of the heaven [the luminaries are in]), since the earth would often come between them when they were not diametrically opposite, but at intervals of less than a semi-circle.

6. {*That the earth has the ratio of a point to the heavens*}[34]

Moreover, the earth has, to the senses, the ratio of a point to the distance of the sphere of the so-called fixed stars.[35] A strong indication of this is the fact that the sizes and distances of the stars, at any given time, appear equal and the same from all parts of the earth everywhere, as observations of the same [celestial] objects from different latitudes are found to have not the least discrepancy from each other. One must also consider the fact that gnomons set up in any part of the earth whatever, and likewise the centres of armillary spheres,[36] operate like the real centre of the earth; that is, the lines of sight [to heavenly bodies] and the paths of shadows caused by them agree as closely with the [mathematical] hypotheses explaining the phenomena as if they actually passed through the real centre-point of the earth.

Another clear indication that this is so is that the planes drawn through the observer's lines of sight at any point [on earth], which we call 'horizons', always bisect the whole heavenly sphere. This would not happen if the earth were of perceptible size in relation to the distance of the heavenly bodies; in that case only the plane drawn through the centre of the earth could bisect the sphere, while a plane through any point on the surface of the earth would always make the section [of the heavens] below the earth greater than the section above it.

7. {*That the earth does not have any motion from place to place, either*}[37]

One can show by the same arguments as the preceding that the earth cannot have any motion in the aforementioned directions, or indeed ever move at all from its position at the centre. For the same phenomena would result as would if it had any position other than the central one. Hence I think it is idle to seek for causes for the motion of objects towards the centre, once it has been so clearly established from the actual phenomena that the earth occupies the middle place in the universe, and that all heavy objects are carried towards the earth. The following fact alone would most readily lead one to this notion [that all objects fall towards the centre]. In absolutely all parts of the earth, which, as we said, has been shown to be spherical and in the middle of the universe, the direction[38] and path of the motion (I mean the proper, [natural] motion) of all bodies possessing weight is always and everywhere at right angles to the rigid plane drawn tangent to the point of impact. It is clear from this fact that, if [these falling objects] were not arrested by the surface of the earth, they would certainly reach the centre of the earth itself, since the straight line to the centre is also always at right, angles to the plane tangent to the sphere at the point of intersection [of that radius] and the tangent.

Those who think it paradoxical that the earth, having such a great weight, is not supported by anything and yet does not move, seem to me to be making the mistake of judging on the basis of their own experience instead of taking into account the peculiar nature of the universe. They would not, I think, consider such a thing strange once they realised that this great bulk of the earth, when compared with the whole surrounding mass [of the universe], has the ratio of a point to it. For when one looks at it in that way, it will seem quite possible that that which is relatively smallest should be overpowered and pressed in equally from all directions to a position of equilibrium by that which is the greatest of all and of uniform nature. For there is no up and down in the universe with respect to itself,[39] any more than one could imagine such a thing in a sphere: instead the proper and natural motion of the compound bodies in it is as follows: light and rarefied bodies drift outwards towards the circumference, but seem to move in the direction which is 'up' for each observer, since the overhead direction for all of us, which is also called 'up', points towards the surrounding surface;[40] heavy and dense bodies, on the other hand, are carried towards the middle and the centre, but seem to fall downwards, because, again, the direction which is for all us towards our feet, called 'down', also points towards the centre of the earth. These heavy bodies, as one would expect, settle about the centre because of their mutual pressure and resistance, which is equal and uniform from all directions. Hence, too, one can see that it is plausible that the earth, since its total mass is so great compared with the bodies which fall towards it, can remain motionless under the impact of these very small weights (for they strike it from all sides), and receive, as it were, the objects falling on it. If the earth had a single motion in common with other heavy objects, it is obvious that it would be carried down faster than all of them because of its much greater size: living things and individual heavy objects would be left behind, riding on the air, and the earth itself would very soon have fallen completely out of the heavens. But such things are utterly ridiculous merely to think of.

But certain people,[41] [propounding] what they consider a more persuasive view, agree with the above, since they have no argument to bring against it, but think that there could be no evidence to oppose their view if, for instance, they supposed the heavens to remain motionless, and the earth to revolve from west to east about the same axis [as the heavens], making approximately one revolution each day;[42] or if they made both heaven and earth move by any amount whatever, provided, as we said, it is about the same axis, and in such a way as to preserve the overtaking of one by the other. However, they do not realise that, although there is perhaps nothing in the celestial phenomena which would count against that hypothesis, at least from simpler considerations, nevertheless from what would occur here on earth and in the air, one can see that such a notion is quite ridiculous. Let us concede to them [for the sake of argument] that such an unnatural thing could happen as that the most rare and light of matter should either not move at all or should move in a way no different from that of matter with the opposite nature (although things in the air, which are less rare [than the heavens] so obviously move with a more rapid motion than any earthy object); [let us concede that] the densest and heaviest objects have a proper motion of the quick and uniform kind which they suppose (although, again, as all agree, earthy objects are sometimes not readily moved even by an external force). Nevertheless, they would have to admit that the revolving motion of the earth must be the most violent of all motions associated with it, seeing that it makes one revolution in such a short time; the result would be that all objects not actually standing on the earth would appear to have the same motion, opposite to that of the earth: neither clouds nor other flying or thrown objects would ever be seen moving towards the east, since the earth's motion towards the east would always outrun and overtake them, so that all other objects would seem to move in the direction of the west and the rear. But if they said that the air is carried around in the same direction and with the same speed as the earth, the compound objects in the air would none the less always seem to be left behind by the motion of both [earth and air]; or if those objects too were carried around, fused, as it were, to the air, then they would never appear to have any motion either in advance or rearwards: they would always appear still, neither wandering about nor changing position, whether they were flying or thrown objects. Yet we quite plainly see that they do undergo all these kinds of motion, in such a way that they are not even slowed down or speeded up at all by any motion of the earth.

Notes

^{4} This 'philosophical' preface and its relationship to Ptolemy's attitude to philosophy is discussed by Boll, *Studien* 68–76, to which the reader is referred for the relevant passages in ancient literature. The general standpoint is Aristotelian.

^{5} Syrus is also the addressee of a number of other works by Ptolemy (see Toomer[5] 187). Nothing is known about him. The name is very common in (but not confined to) Greco-Roman Egypt. The statement in a scholion to the Tetrabiblos (quoted by Boll, *Studien* 67, n. 2) that some say he was a fictitious person, others that he was a doctor, merely reveals that he was equally unknown in late antiquity.

^{6} Theon in his commentary (Rome II 320, 13–14) gives φησὶ . . . συμβεβηκέναι τῷ πρακτικῷ τό πρότερον αὐτοῦ τοῦ θεωρητικοῦ τυγχάνειν. This is a paraphrase rather than a different reading, but shows that he understood the text as I have translated it. By this obscure expression I take Ptolemy to mean that before actually practising virtues one must have some concept of them (even though this is innate rather than taught).

^{7} E. g. Metaphysics E I, 1026a 18 ff., ὥστε τρεῖς ἄν εἶεν φιλοσοφίαι θεωρητικαί, μαθηματική, φυσική, θεολογική.

^{8} 'aethereal' (αἰθερώδης) has a precise meaning in Aristotelian physics: everything above the sphere of the moon is composed of an 'incorruptible' substance, unlike anything known on earth in its consistency (very thin) and in its natural motion (circular). See I 3 p. 40. One of the names for this substance is 'aether', another 'fifth essence'. See Campanus IV n. 56, pp. 394–5.

^{9} In this exaltation of mathematics above the other two divisions of philosophy Ptolemy parts company with Aristotle, for whom theology was the most noble pursuit for the human mind.

^{10} The heavenly bodies.

^{11} This notion of the advancement of science, and particularly astronomy, by the additional time available is one to which Ptolemy recurs in the epilogue (XIII 11 p. 647), and also, in a specifically astronomical context, at VII 1 p. 321 and VII 3 p. 329.

^{12} ὑπομνηματίσασθαι. A ὑπόμνημα is a 'memoir', usually implying summary brevity. Ptolemy recurs to this too in the epilogue (XIII 11 p. 647).

^{13} Ptolemy assumes that his readers will have a certain competence. See Introduction p. 6.

^{14} I 3–8. On the logic of Ptolemy's order see Introduction pp. 5–6.

^{15} I 12–16. The mathematical section I 10–11 is not specifically mentioned here.

^{16} Book II.

^{17} Books III–VI.

^{18} 'Stars' here and throughout chs. 3–8 includes both fixed stars and planets (see Introduction p. 21) and also, sometimes, sun and moon.

^{19} Books VII–VIII.

[20] Books IX–XIII.

[21] See Pedersen 36–7.

[22] According to Theon's commentary (Rome II 338) this belief was Epicurean, but I know of no other evidence. The only other relevant passage appears to be Xenophanes, Diels-Kranz A41a (the sun really moves towards infinity).

[23] Theon (Rome II 340) ascribes this to Heraclitus. Otherwise it is attested for Xenophanes (Diels-Kranz A38), and was admitted as one possible explanation by Epicurus (e.g. *Letter to Pythocles* 92) and his followers.

[24] Ptolemy refers to the well-known phenomenon that the sun and moon appear larger when close to the horizon. He gives an incorrect physical and optical explanation here. In a later work (*Optics* III 60, ed. Lejeune p. 116) he correctly explains it as a purely psychological phenomenon. No doubt instrumental measurement of the apparent diameters had convinced him that the enlargement is entirely illusory.

[25] These propositions were proved in a work by Zenodorus (early second century B.C., see Toomer[1]) from which extensive excerpts are given by (among others) Theon (Rome II 355–79). There is a good summary in Heath *HGM* II 207–13.

[26] The only relevant passage I know is Empedocles, Diels-Kranz A60, who maintained that the moon is disk-shaped.

[27] See Pedersen 37–9.

[28] 'taken as a whole': ignoring local irregularities such as mountains, which are negligible in comparison to the total mass.

[29] The timings for solar eclipses are complicated by parallax.

[30] Reading πλείονα (with D) for τὰ πλείονα at H16,9. Corrected by Manitius.

[31] See Pedersen 39–42.

[32] The word translated here and elsewhere as '[terrestrial] latitude' is κλίμα, for the meaning of which see Introduction p. 19.

[33] The *caveat* 'sensibly' is inserted because the equinox is not a date but an instant of time. Therefore on the day of equinox the sun does not rise due east and set due west (as is implied by the rising and setting shadows lying on the same straight line). However, the difference would be 'imperceptible to the senses'.

[34] See Pedersen 42–3.

[35] Ptolemy qualifies the traditional terminology for the fixed stars as 'so-called' (καλουμένων) because they do in fact, according to him, have a motion (the modern 'precession'). He develops the point further at VII 1 p. 321, q.v. In general, however, he uses the traditional terminology without qualification.

[36] An example of an armillary sphere (κρικωτὴ σφαῖρα) is the 'astrolabe' described in V 1. For references to the term in other works see LSJ s.v. κρικωτός.

[37] See Pedersen 43–4.

[38] πρόσνευσις, which I have translated 'the direction of motion' here, means basically 'direction in which something points' (for astronomical usages see V 5 p. 227 n. 19 and VI 11 p. 313 n. 77). Thus it would also include here the direction of a plumb-line (cf. I 12 p. 62).

[39] Reading αὐτόν (with D, Is) for αὐτήν at H23,1.

[40] It is not clear to me whether Ptolemy means the outmost boundary of the *universe* or merely the surface (of the 'aether') surrounding the *earth*.

[41] Heraclides of Pontos (late fourth century B.C.) is the earliest certain authority for the view that the earth rotates on its axis. See *HAMA* II 694–6. It was also adopted by Aristarchus as part of his more radical heliocentric hypothesis.

[42] 'approximately' because one revolution takes place in a sidereal, not a solar day.

Discoveries and Opinions of Galileo:
The Starry Messenger

sidereal = of a with
respect to the
distant stars

Translated by Stillman Drake

AN ASTRONOMICAL MESSAGE
Which contains and explains recent observations
made with the aid of a new spyglass[1]
concerning the surface of the moon,
the Milky Way, nebulous stars, and
innumerable fixed stars,
as well as four planets never before seen, and
now named
THE MEDICEAN STARS

Great indeed are the things which in this brief treatise I propose for observation and consideration by all students of nature. I say great, because of the excellence of the subject itself, the entirely unexpected and novel character of these things, and finally because of the instrument by means of which they have been revealed to our senses.

Surely it is a great thing to increase the numerous host of fixed stars previously visible to the unaided vision, adding countless more which have never before been seen, exposing these plainly to the eye in numbers ten times exceeding the old and familiar stars.

It is a very beautiful thing, and most gratifying to the sight, to behold the body of the moon, distant from us almost sixty earthly radii,[2] as if it were no farther away than two such measures—so that its diameter appears almost thirty times larger, its surface nearly nine hundred times, and its volume twenty-seven thousand times as large as when viewed with the naked eye. In this way one may learn with all the certainty of sense evidence that the moon is not robed in a smooth and polished surface but is in fact rough and uneven, covered everywhere, just like the earth's surface, with huge prominences, deep valleys, and chasms.

Again, it seems to me a matter of no small importance to have ended the dispute about the Milky Way by making its nature manifest to the very

194

senses as well as to the intellect. Similarly it will be a pleasant and elegant thing to demonstrate that the nature of those stars which astronomers have previously called "nebulous" is far different from what has been believed hitherto. But what surpasses all wonders by far, and what particularly moves us to seek the attention of all astronomers and philosophers, is the discovery of four wandering stars not known or observed by any man before us. Like Venus and Mercury, which have their own periods about the sun, these have theirs about a certain star that is conspicuous among those already known, which they sometimes precede and sometimes follow, without ever departing from it beyond certain limits. All these facts were discovered and observed by me not many days ago with the aid of a spyglass which I devised, after first being illuminated by divine grace. Perhaps other things, still more remarkable, will in time be discovered by me or by other observers with the aid of such an instrument, the form and construction of which I shall first briefly explain, as well as the occasion of its having been devised. Afterwards I shall relate the story of the observations I have made.

About ten months ago a report reached my ears that a certain Fleming[3] had constructed a spyglass by means of which visible objects, though very distant from the eye of the observer, were distinctly seen as if nearby. Of this truly remarkable effect several experiences were related, to which some persons gave credence while others denied them. A few days later the report was confirmed to me in a letter from a noble Frenchman at Paris, Jacques Badovere,[4] which caused me to apply myself wholeheartedly to inquire into the means by which I might arrive at the invention of a similar instrument. This I did shortly afterwards, my basis being the theory of refraction. First I prepared a tube of lead, at the ends of which I fitted two glass lenses, both plane on one side while on the other side one was spherically convex and the other concave. Then placing my eye near the concave lens I perceived objects satisfactorily large and near, for they appeared three times closer and nine times larger than when seen with the naked eye alone. Next I constructed another one, more accurate, which represented objects as enlarged more than sixty times. Finally, sparing neither labor nor expense, I succeeded in constructing for myself so excellent an instrument that objects seen by means of it appeared nearly one thousand times larger and over thirty times closer than when regarded with our natural vision.

It would be superfluous to enumerate the number and importance of the advantages of such an instrument at sea as well as on land. But forsaking terrestrial observations, I turned to celestial ones, and first I saw the moon from as near at hand as if it were scarcely two terrestrial radii away. After that I observed often with wondering delight both the planets and the fixed stars, and since I saw these latter to be very crowded, I began to seek (and eventually found) a method by which I might measure their distances apart.

Here it is appropriate to convey certain cautions to all who intend to undertake observations of this sort, for in the first place it is necessary to prepare quite a perfect telescope, which will show all objects bright, distinct, and free from any haziness, while magnifying them at least four hundred times and thus showing them twenty times closer. Unless the instrument is of this kind it will be vain to attempt to observe all the things which I have seen in the heavens, and which will presently be set forth. Now in order to determine without much trouble the magnifying power of an instrument, trace on paper the contour of two circles or two squares of which one is four hundred times as large as the other, as it will be when the diameter of one is twenty times that of the other. Then with both these figures attached to the same wall, observe them simultaneously from a distance, looking at the smaller one through the telescope and at the larger one with the other eye unaided. This may be done without inconvenience while holding both eyes open at the same time; the two figures will appear to be of the same size if the instrument magnifies objects in the desired proportion.

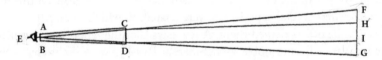

Such an instrument having been prepared, we seek a method of measuring distances apart. This we shall accomplish by the following contrivance.

Let ABCD be the tube and E be the eye of the observer. Then if there were no lenses in the tube, the rays would reach the object FG along the straight lines ECF and EDG. But when the lenses have been inserted, the rays go along the refracted lines ECH and EDI; thus they are brought closer together, and those which were previously directed freely to the object FG now include only the portion of it HI. The ratio of the distance EH to the line HI then being found, one may by means of a table of sines determine the size of the angle formed at the eye by the object HI, which we shall find to be but a few minutes of arc. Now, if to the lens CD we fit thin plates, some pierced with larger and some with smaller apertures, putting now one plate and now another over the lens as required, we may form at pleasure different angles subtending more or fewer minutes of arc, and by this means we may easily measure the intervals between stars which are but a few minutes apart, with no greater error than one or two minutes. And for the present let it suffice that we have

[handwritten left margin:] sine [L bend] the *per—* *pendicular* *dropped* *from one end* *of a circular* *are upon* *the radius* *of the other* *end; the* *ratio of this* *perpendicular* *to the ratio*

[handwritten bottom:] refract [L re + frango break] to bend from a direct course; turn aside
refraction : the change of direction of a ray, as of light or heat
refractory : not amenable to control; disobedient; unmanageable; obstinate

touched lightly on these matters and scarcely more than mentioned them, as on some other occasion we shall explain the entire theory of this instrument.

Now let us review the observations made during the past two months, once more inviting the attention of all who are eager for true philosophy to the first steps of such important contemplations. Let us speak first of that surface of the moon which faces us. For greater clarity I distinguish two parts of this surface, a lighter and a darker; the lighter part seems to surround and to pervade the whole hemisphere, while the darker part discolors the moon's surface like a kind of cloud, and makes it appear covered with spots. Now those spots which are fairly dark and rather large are plain to everyone and have been seen throughout the ages; these I shall call the "large" or "ancient" spots, distinguishing them from others that are smaller in size but so numerous as to occur all over the lunar surface, and especially the lighter part. The latter spots had never been seen by anyone before me. From observations of these spots repeated many times I have been led to the opinion and conviction that the surface of the moon is not smooth, uniform, and precisely spherical as a great number of philosophers believe it (and the other heavenly bodies) to be, but is uneven, rough, and full of cavities and prominences, being not unlike the face of the earth, relieved by chains of mountains and deep valleys. The things I have seen by which I was enabled to draw this conclusion are as follows.

On the fourth or fifth day after new moon, when the moon is seen with brilliant horns, the boundary which divides the dark part from the light does not extend uniformly in an oval line as would happen on a perfectly spherical solid, but traces out an uneven, rough, and very wavy line as shown in the figure below. Indeed, many luminous excrescences extend beyond the boundary into the darker portion, while on the other hand some dark patches invade the illuminated part. Moreover a great quantity of small blackish spots, entirely separated from the dark region, are scattered almost all over the area illuminated by the sun with the exception only of that part which is occupied by the large and ancient spots. Let us note, however, that the said small spots always agree in having their blackened parts directed toward the sun, while on the side opposite the sun they are crowned with bright contours, like shining summits. There is a similar sight on earth about sunrise, when we behold the valleys not yet flooded with light though the mountains surrounding them are already ablaze with glowing splendor on the side opposite the sun. And just as the shadows in the hollows on earth diminish in size as the sun rises higher, so these spots on the moon lose their blackness as the illuminated region grows larger and larger.

excrescense : [to excresere to grow out] any abnormal n disfiguring outgrowth or addition as a barnion

Again, not only are the boundaries of shadow and light in the moon seen to be uneven and wavy, but still more astonishingly many bright points appear within the darkened portion of the moon, completely divided and separated from the illuminated part and at a considerable distance from it. After a time these gradually increase in size and brightness, and an hour or two later they become joined with the rest of the lighted part which has now increased in size. Meanwhile more and more peaks shoot up as if sprouting now here, now there, lighting up within the shadowed portion; these become larger, and finally they too are united with that same luminous surface which extends even further. An illustration of this is to be seen in the figure above. And on the earth, before the rising of the sun, are not the highest peaks of the mountains illuminated by the sun's rays while the plains remain in shadow? Does not the light go on spreading while the larger central parts of those mountains are becoming illuminated? And when the sun has finally risen, does not the illumination of plains and hills finally become one? But on the moon the variety of elevations and depressions appears to surpass in every way the roughness of the terrestrial surface, as we shall demonstrate further on.

At present I cannot pass over in silence something worthy of consideration which I observed when the moon was approaching first quarter, as shown in the previous figure. Into the luminous part there extended a great dark gulf in the neighborhood of the lower cusp. When I had observed it for a long time and had seen it completely dark, a bright peak began to emerge, a little below its center, after about two hours. Gradually growing, this presented itself in a triangular shape, remaining completely detached and separated from the lighted surface. Around it three other small points soon began to shine, and finally, when the moon was about to set, this triangular shape (which had meanwhile become more widely extended) joined with the rest of the illuminated region

cusp: – [L *cuspis*. point] one of the points of the crescent moon, or
   something resembling it; a prominence or point, as on the
   crown of a tooth

Discoveries and Opinions of Galileo: **The Starry Messenger** ◆ 199

and suddenly burst into the gulf of shadow like a vast promontory of light, surrounded still by the three bright peaks already mentioned. Beyond the ends of
the cusps, both above and below, certain bright points emerged which were
quite detached from the remaining lighted part, as may be seen depicted in the
same figure. There were also a great number of dark spots in both the horns,
especially in the lower one; those nearest the boundary of light and shadow
appeared larger and darker, while those more distant from the boundary were
not so dark and distinct. But in all cases, as we have mentioned earlier, the
blackish portion of each spot is turned toward the source of the sun's radiance,
while a bright rim surrounds the spot on the side away from the sun in the
direction of the shadowy region of the moon. This part of the moon's surface,
where it is spotted as the tail of a peacock is sprinkled with azure eyes, resem-
bles those glass vases which have been plunged while still hot into cold water
and have thus acquired a crackled and wavy surface from which they receive
their common name of "ice-cups."

   As to the large lunar spots, these are not seen to be broken in the above
manner and full of cavities and prominences; rather, they are even and uniform,
and brighter patches crop up only here and there. Hence if anyone wished to
revive the old Pythagorean[5] opinion that the moon is like another earth, its
brighter part might very fitly represent the surface of the land and its darker
region that of the water. I have never doubted that if our globe were seen from
afar when flooded with sunlight, the land regions would appear brighter and
the watery regions darker.[6] The large spots in the moon are also seen to be less
elevated than the brighter tracts, for whether the moon is waxing or waning
there are always seen, here and there along its boundary of light and shadow,
certain ridges of brighter hue around the large spots (and we have attended to
this in preparing the diagrams); the edges of these spots are not only lower, but
also more uniform, being uninterrupted by peaks or ruggedness.

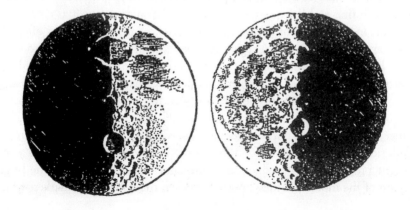

Near the large spots the brighter part stands out particularly in such a way that before first quarter and toward last quarter, in the vicinity of a certain spot in the upper (or northern) region of the moon, some vast prominences arise both above and below as shown in the figure reproduced below. Before last quarter this same spot is seen to be walled about with certain blacker contours which, like the loftiest mountaintops, appear darker on the side away from the sun and brighter on that which faces the sun. (This is the opposite of what happens in the cavities, for there the part away from the sun appears brilliant, while that which is turned toward the sun is dark and in shadow.) After a time, when the lighted portion of the moon's surface has diminished in size and when all (or nearly all) the said spot is covered with shadow, the brighter ridges of the mountains gradually emerge from the shade. This double aspect of the spot is illustrated in the ensuing figure.

There is another thing which I must not omit, for I beheld it not without a certain wonder; this is that almost in the center of the moon there is a cavity larger than all the rest, and perfectly round in shape. I have observed it near both first and last quarters, and have tried to represent it as correctly as possible in the second of the above figures. As to light and shade, it offers the same appearance as would a region like Bohemia if that were enclosed on all sides by very lofty mountains arranged exactly in a circle. Indeed, this area on the moon is surrounded by such enormous peaks that the bounding edge adjacent to the dark portion of the moon is seen to be bathed in sunlight before the boundary of light and shadow reaches halfway across the same space. As in other spots, its shaded portion faces the sun while its lighted part is toward the dark side of the moon; and for a third time I draw attention to this as a very cogent proof of the ruggedness and unevenness that pervades all the bright region of the moon. Of these spots, moreover, those are always darkest which touch the boundary line between light and shadow, while those farther off appear both smaller and less dark, so that when the moon ultimately becomes full (at opposition[8] to the sun), the shade of the cavities is distinguished from the light of the places in relief by a subdued and very tenuous separation.

The things we have reviewed are to be seen in the brighter region of the moon. In the large spots, no such contrast of depressions and prominences is perceived as that which we are compelled to recognize in the brighter parts by the changes of aspect that occur under varying illumination by the sun's rays throughout the multiplicity of positions from which the latter reach the moon. In the large spots there exist some holes rather darker than the rest, as we have shown in the illustrations. Yet these present always the same appearance, and their darkness is neither intensified nor diminished, although with some minute difference they appear sometimes a little more shaded and sometimes a little lighter according as the rays of the sun fall on them more or less obliquely. Moreover, they join with the neighboring regions of the spots in a gentle linkage, the boundaries mixing and mingling. It is quite different with the spots which occupy the brighter surface of the moon; these, like precipitous crags having rough and jagged peaks, stand out starkly in sharp contrasts of light and shade. And inside the large spots there are observed certain other zones that are brighter, some of them very bright indeed. Still, both these and the darker parts present always the same appearance; there is no change either of shape or of light and shadow; hence one may affirm beyond any doubt that they owe their appearance to some real dissimilarity of parts. They cannot be attributed merely to irregularity of shape, wherein shadows move in consequence of varied illuminations from the sun, as indeed is the case with the other, smaller, spots which occupy the brighter part of the moon and which change, grow, shrink, or disappear from one day to the next, as owing their origin only to shadows of prominences.

But here I foresee that many persons will be assailed by uncertainty and drawn into a grave difficulty, feeling constrained to doubt a conclusion already explained and confirmed by many phenomena. If that part of the lunar surface which reflects sunlight more brightly is full of chasms (that is, of countless prominences and hollows), why is it that the western edge of the waxing moon, the eastern edge of the waning moon, and the entire periphery of the full moon are not seen to be uneven, rough, and wavy? On the contrary they look as precisely round as if they were drawn with a compass; and yet the whole periphery consists of that brighter lunar substance which we have declared to be filled with heights and chasms. In fact not a single one of the great spots extends to the extreme periphery of the moon, but all are grouped together at a distance from the edge.

Now let me explain the twofold reason for this troublesome fact, and in turn give a double solution to the difficulty. In the first place, if the protuberances and cavities in the lunar body existed only along the extreme edge of the circular periphery bounding the visible hemisphere, the moon might (indeed, would necessarily) look to us almost like a toothed wheel, terminated by a warty or wavy edge. Imagine, however, that there is not a single series of prominences arranged only along the very circumference, but a great many ranges of mountains together with their valleys and canyons disposed in ranks near the edge of the moon, and not only in the hemisphere visible to us but everywhere near the boundary line of the two hemispheres. Then an eye viewing them from afar will not be able to detect the separation of prominences by cavities, because the intervals between the mountains located in a given circle or a given chain will be hidden by the interposition of other heights situated in yet other ranges. This will be especially true if the eye of the observer is placed in the same straight line with the summits of these elevations. Thus on earth the summits of several mountains close together appear to be situated in one plane if the spectator is a long way off and is placed at an equal elevation. Similarly in a rough sea the tops of the waves seem to lie in one plane, though between one high crest and another there are many gulfs and chasms of such depth as not only to hide the hulls but even the bulwarks, masts, and rigging of stately ships. Now since there are many chains of mountains and chasms on the moon in addition to those around its periphery, and since the eye, regarding these from a great distance, lies nearly in the plane of their summits, no one need wonder that they appear as arranged in a regular and unbroken line.

To the above explanation another may he added; namely, that there exists around the body of the moon, just as around the earth, a globe of some substance denser than the rest of the aether.[9] This may serve to receive and reflect the sun's radiations without being sufficiently opaque to prevent our seeing through it, especially when it is not illuminated. Such a globe, lighted by the sun's rays, makes the body of the moon appear larger than it really is, and if it were thicker it would be able to prevent our seeing the actual body of the moon. And it actually is thicker near the circumference of the moon; I do not mean in an absolute sense, but relatively to the rays of our vision, which cut it obliquely there. Thus it may obstruct our vision, especially when it is lighted, and cloak the lunar periphery that is exposed to the sun. This may be more clearly understood from the figure below, in which the body of the moon, ABC, is surrounded by the vaporous globe DEG.

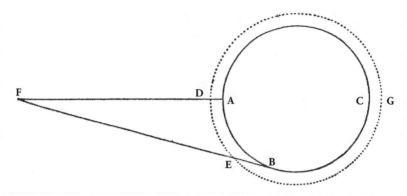

The eyesight from F reaches the moon in the central region, at A for example, through a lesser thickness of the vapors DA, while toward the extreme edges a deeper stratum of vapors, EB, limits and shuts out our sight. One indication of this is that the illuminated portion of the moon appears to be larger in circumference than the rest of the orb, which lies in shadow. And perhaps this same cause will appeal to some as reasonably explaining why the larger spots on the moon are nowhere seen to reach the very edge, probable though it is that some should occur there. Possibly they are invisible by being hidden under a thicker and more luminous mass of vapors.

That the lighter surface of the moon is everywhere dotted with protuberances and gaps has, I think, been made sufficiently clear from the appearances already explained. It remains for me to speak of their dimensions, and to show that the earth's irregularities are far less than those of the moon. I mean that they are absolutely less, and not merely in relation to the sizes of the respective globes. This is plainly demonstrated as follows.

I had often observed, in various situations of the moon with respect to the sun, that some summits within the shadowy portion appeared lighted, though lying some distance from the boundary of the light. By comparing this separation of the whole diameter of the moon, I found that it sometimes exceeded one-twentieth of the diameter. Accordingly, let CAF be a great circle of the lunar body, E its center, and CF a diameter, which is to the diameter of the earth as two is to seven.

Since according to very precise observations the diameter of the earth is seven thousand miles, CF will be two thousand, CE one thousand, and one-twentieth of CF will be one hundred miles. Now let CF be the diameter of the great circle which divides the light part of the moon from the dark part (for because of the very great distance of the sun from the moon, this does not differ appreciably from a great circle), and let A be distant from C by one-twentieth of

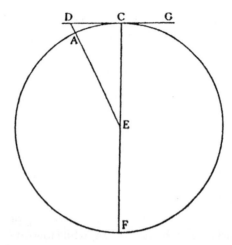

this. Draw the radius EA, which, when produced, cuts the tangent line GCD (representing the illuminating ray) in the point D. Then the arc CA, or rather the straight line CD, will consist of one hundred units whereof CE contains one thousand, and the sum of the squares of DC and CE will be 1,010,000. This is equal to the square of DE; hence ED will exceed 1,004, and AD will be more than four of those units of which CE contains one thousand. Therefore the altitude AD on the moon, which represents a summit reaching up to the solar ray GCD and standing at the distance CD from C, exceeds four miles. But on the earth we have no mountains which reach to a perpendicular height of even one mile.[10] Hence it is quite clear that the prominences on the moon are loftier than those on the earth.

Here I wish to assign the cause of another lunar phenomenon well worthy of notice. I observed this not just recently, but many years ago, and pointed it out to some of my friends and pupils, explaining it to them and giving its true cause. Yet since it is rendered more evident and easier to observe with the aid of the telescope, I think it not unsuitable for introduction in this place, especially as it shows more clearly the connection between the moon and the earth.

When the moon is not far from the sun, just before or after new moon, its globe offers itself to view not only on the side where it is adorned with shining horns, but a certain faint light is also seen to mark out the periphery of the dark part which faces away from the sun, separating this from the darker background of the aether. Now if we examine the matter more closely, we shall see that not only does the extreme limb of the shaded side glow with this uncertain light, but the entire face of the moon (including the side which does not receive the glare of the sun) is whitened by a not inconsiderable gleam. At first glance only a thin luminous circumference appears, contrasting with the darker sky coterminous with it; the rest of the surface appears darker from its contact with the shining horns which distract our vision. But if we place ourselves so as to interpose a roof or chimney or some other object at a considerable distance from the eye, the shining horns may be hidden while the rest of the lunar globe remains exposed to view. It is then found that this region of the moon, though deprived of sunlight, also shines not a little. The effect is heightened if the gloom of night has already deepened through departure of the sun, for in a darker field a given light appears brighter.

Moreover, it is found that this secondary light of the moon (so to speak) is greater according as the moon is closer to the sun. It diminishes more and more as the moon recedes from that body until, after the first quarter and before the last, it is seen very weakly and uncertainly even when observed in the darkest sky. But when the moon is within sixty degrees of the sun it shines remarkably, even in twilight; so brightly indeed that with the aid of a good telescope one may distinguish the large spots. This remarkable gleam has afforded no small perplexity to philosophers, and in order to assign a cause for it some have offered one idea and some another. Some would say it is an inherent and natural light of the moon's own; others, that it is imparted by Venus; others yet, by all the stars together; and still others derive it from the sun, whose rays they would have permeate the thick solidity of the moon. But statements of this sort are refuted and their falsity evinced with little difficulty. For if this kind of light were the moon's own, or were contributed by the stars, the moon would retain it and would display it particularly during eclipses, when it is left in an unusually dark sky. This is contradicted by experience, for the brightness which is seen on the moon during eclipses is much fainter and is ruddy, almost copper-colored, while this is brighter and whitish. Moreover the other light is variable and movable, for it covers the face of the moon in such a way that the place near the edge of the earth's shadow is always seen to be brighter than the rest of the moon; this undoubtedly results from contact of the tangent solar rays with some denser zone which girds the moon about.[11] By this contact a sort of twilight is diffused over the neighboring regions of the moon, just as on earth a sort of crepuscular light is spread both morning and evening; but with this I shall deal more fully in my book on the system of the world.[12]

To assert that the moon's secondary light is imparted by Venus is so childish as to deserve no reply. Who is so ignorant as not to understand that from new moon to a separation of sixty degrees between moon and sun, no part of the moon which is averted from the sun can possibly be seen from Venus? And it is likewise unthinkable that this light should depend upon the sun's rays penetrating the thick solid mass of the moon, for then this light would never dwindle, inasmuch as one hemisphere of the moon is always illuminated except during lunar eclipses. And the light does diminish as the moon approaches first quarter, becoming completely obscured after that is passed.

Now since the secondary light does not inherently belong to the moon, and is not received from any star or from the sun, and since in the whole universe there is no other body left but the earth, what must we conclude? What is to be proposed? Surely we must assert that the lunar body (or any other dark and sunless orb) is illuminated by the earth. Yet what is there so remarkable about this? The earth, in fair and grateful exchange, pays back to the moon an illumination similar to that which it receives from her throughout nearly all the darkest gloom of night.

Let us explain this matter more fully. At conjunction the moon occupies a position between the sun and the earth; it is then illuminated by the sun's rays on the side which is turned away from the earth. The other hemisphere, which faces the earth, is covered with darkness; hence the moon does not illuminate the surface of the earth at all. Next, departing gradually from the sun, the moon comes to be lighted partly upon the side it turns toward us, and its whitish horns, still very thin, illuminate the earth with a faint light. The sun's illumination of the moon increasing now as the moon approaches first quarter, a reflection of that light to the earth also increases. Soon the splendor on the moon extends into a semicircle, and our nights grow brighter; at length the entire visible face of the moon is irradiated by the sun's resplendent rays, and at full moon the whole surface of the earth shines in a flood of moonlight. Now the moon, waning, sends us her beams more weakly, and the earth is less strongly lighted; at length the moon returns to conjunction with the sun, and black night covers the earth.

In this monthly period, then, the moonlight gives us alternations of brighter and fainter illumination; and the benefit is repaid by the earth in equal measure. For while the moon is between us and the sun (at new moon), there lies before it the entire surface of that hemisphere of the earth which is exposed to the sun and illuminated by vivid rays. The moon receives the light which this reflects, and thus the nearer hemisphere of the moon—that is, the one deprived of sunlight—appears by virtue of this illumination to be not a little luminous. When the moon is ninety degrees away from the sun it sees but half the earth illuminated (the western half), for the other (the eastern half) is enveloped in night. Hence the moon itself is illuminated less brightly from the earth, and as a result its secondary light appears fainter to us. When the moon is in opposition to the sun, it faces a hemisphere of the earth that is steeped in the gloom of night, and if this position occurs in the plane of the ecliptic the moon will receive no light at all, being deprived of both the solar and the terrestrial rays. In its various other positions with respect to the earth and sun, the moon receives more or less light according as it faces a greater or smaller portion of the illuminated hemisphere of the earth. And between these two globes a relation is maintained such that whenever the earth is most brightly lighted by the moon, the moon is least lighted by the earth, and vice versa.

Let these few remarks suffice us here concerning this matter, which will be more fully treated in our *System of the World.* In that book, by a multitude of arguments and experiences, the solar reflection from the earth will be shown to be quite real—against those who argue that the earth must be excluded from the dancing whirl of stars for the specific reason that it is devoid of motion and of light. We shall prove the earth to be a wandering body surpassing the moon in splendor, and not the sink of all dull refuse of the universe; this we shall support by an infinitude of arguments drawn from nature.

Thus far we have spoken of our observations concerning the body of the moon. Let us now set forth briefly what has thus far been observed regarding the fixed stars. And first of all, the following fact deserves consideration: The stars, whether fixed or wandering,[13] appear not to be enlarged by the telescope in the same proportion as that in which it magnifies other objects, and even the moon itself. In the stars this enlargement seems to be so much less that a telescope which is sufficiently powerful to magnify other objects a hundredfold is scarcely able to enlarge the stars four or five times. The reason for this is as follows.

When stars are viewed by means of unaided natural vision, they present themselves to us not as of their simple (and, so to speak, their physical) size, but as irradiated by a certain fulgor and as fringed with sparkling rays, especially when the night is far advanced. From this they appear larger than they would if stripped of those adventitious hairs of light, for the angle at the eye is determined not by the primary body of the star but by the brightness which extends so widely about it. This appears quite clearly from the fact that when the stars first emerge from twilight at sunset they look very small, even if they are of the first magnitude; Venus itself, when visible in broad daylight, is so small as scarcely to appear equal to a star of the sixth magnitude. Things fall out differently with other objects, and even with the moon itself; these, whether seen in daylight or the deepest night, appear always of the same bulk. Therefore the stars are seen crowned among shadows, while daylight is able to remove their headgear; and not daylight alone, but any thin cloud that interposes itself between a star and the eye of the observer. The same effect is produced by black veils or colored glasses, through the interposition of which obstacles the stars are abandoned by their surrounding brilliance. A telescope similarly accomplishes the same result. It removes from the stars their adventitious and accidental rays, and then it enlarges their simple globes (if indeed the stars are naturally globular) so that they seem to be magnified in a lesser ratio than other objects. In fact a star of the fifth or sixth magnitude when seen through a telescope presents itself as one of the first magnitude.

Deserving of notice also is the difference between the appearances of the planets and of the fixed stars.[14] The planets show their globes perfectly round and definitely bounded, looking like little moons, spherical and flooded all over with light; the fixed stars are never seen to be bounded by a circular periphery, but have rather the aspect of blazes whose rays vibrate about them and scintillate a great deal. Viewed with a telescope they appear of a shape similar to that which they present to the naked eye, but sufficiently enlarged so that a star of the fifth or sixth magnitude seems to equal the Dog Star, largest of all the fixed stars. Now, in addition to stars of the sixth magnitude, a host of other stars are perceived through the telescope which escape the naked eye; these are so numerous as almost to surpass belief. One may, in fact, see more of them than all the stars included among the first six magnitudes. The largest of these, which we may call stars of the seventh magnitude, or the first magnitude of invisible stars, appear through the telescope as larger and brighter than stars of the second magnitude when the latter are viewed with the naked eye. In order to give one or two proofs of their almost inconceivable number, I have adjoined pictures of two constellations. With these as samples, you may judge of all the others.

In the first I had intended to depict the entire constellation of Orion, but I was overwhelmed by the vast quantity of stars and by limitations of time, so I have deferred this to another occasion. There are more than five hundred new stars distributed among the old ones within limits of one or two degrees of arc. Hence to the three stars in the Belt of Orion and the six in the Sword which were previously known, I have added eighty adjacent stars discovered recently, preserving the intervals between them as exactly as I could. To distinguish the known or ancient stars, I have depicted them larger and have outlined them doubly; the other (invisible) stars I have drawn smaller and without the extra line. I have also preserved differences of magnitude as well as possible.

The Belt and Sword of Orion

In the second example I have depicted the six stars of Taurus known as the Pleiades (I say six, inasmuch as the seventh is hardly ever visible) which lie within very narrow limits in the sky. Near them are more than forty others, invisible, no one of which is much more than half a degree away from the original six. I have shown thirty-six of these in the diagram; as in the case of Orion I have preserved their intervals and magnitudes, as well as the distinction between old stars and new.

1st discov = moon like earth
2nd [...] scope planets resolve to hard edged discs but not stars so S = farther away as Copernicus said
3rd discovery [...] = 4 largest moons of Jupiter = moon of J revolved around Jupiter

210 ◆ **Critical Strategies and Great Questions**

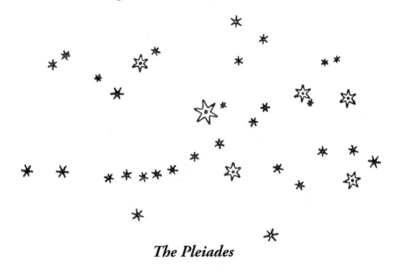

The Pleiades

Third, I have observed the nature and the material of the Milky Way. With the aid of the telescope this has been scrutinized so directly and with such ocular certainty that all the disputes which have vexed philosophers through so many ages have been resolved, and we are at last freed from wordy debates about it. The galaxy is, in fact, nothing but a congeries of innumerable stars grouped together in clusters. Upon whatever part of it the telescope is directed, a vast crowd of stars is immediately presented to view. Many of them are rather large and quite bright, while the number of smaller ones is quite beyond calculation.

But it is not only in the Milky Way that whitish clouds are seen; several patches of similar aspect shine with faint light here and there throughout the aether, and if the telescope is turned upon any of these it confronts us with a tight mass of stars. And what is even more remarkable, the stars which have been called "nebulous" by every astronomer up to this time turn out to be groups of very small stars arranged in a wonderful manner. Although each star separately escapes our sight on account of its smallness or the immense distance from us, the mingling of their rays gives rise to that gleam which was formerly believed to be some denser part of the aether that was capable of reflecting rays from stars or from the sun. I have observed some of these constellations and have decided to depict two of them.

In the first you have the nebula called the Head of Orion, in which I have counted twenty-one stars. The second contains the nebula called Praesepe,[15] which is not a single star but a mass of more than forty starlets. Of these I have shown thirty-six, in addition to the Aselli, arranged in the order shown.

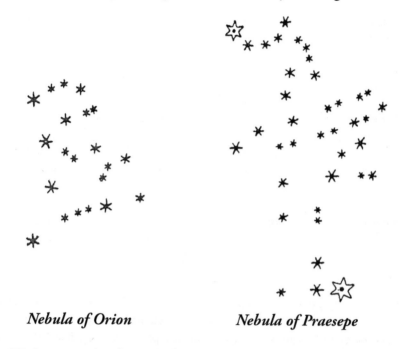

Nebula of Orion   **Nebula of Praesepe**

We have now briefly recounted the observations made thus far with regard to the moon, the fixed stars, and the Milky Way. There remains the matter which in my opinion deserves to be considered the most important of all—the disclosure of four Planets never seen from the creation of the world up to our own time, together with the occasion of my having discovered and studied them, their arrangements, and the observations made of their movements and alterations during the past two months. I invite all astronomers to apply themselves to examine them and determine their periodic times, something which has so far been quite impossible to complete, owing to the shortness of the time. Once more, however, warning is given that it will be necessary to have a very accurate telescope such as we have described at the beginning of this discourse.

On the seventh day of January in this present year 1610, at the first hour of night, when I was viewing the heavenly bodies with a telescope, Jupiter presented itself to me; and because I had prepared a very excellent instrument for myself, I perceived (as I had not before, on account of the weakness of my previous instrument) that beside the planet there were three starlets, small indeed, but very bright. Though I believed them to be among the host of fixed stars, they aroused my curiosity somewhat by appearing to lie in an exact straight line parallel to the ecliptic, and by their being more splendid than others of their size. Their arrangement with respect to Jupiter and each other was the following:

East   ✳ ✳ ◯ ✳   **West**

that is, there were two stars on the eastern side and one to the west. The most easterly star and the western one appeared larger than the other. I paid no attention to the distances between them and Jupiter, for at the outset I thought them to be fixed stars, as I have said.[16] But returning to the same investigation on January eighth—led by what, I do not know—I found a very different arrangement. The three starlets were now all to the west of Jupiter, closer together, and at equal intervals from one another as shown in the following sketch:

East   ◯ ✳ ✳ ✳   **West**

At this time, though I did not yet turn my attention to the way the stars had come together, I began to concern myself with the question how Jupiter could be east of all these stars when on the previous day it had been west of two of them. I commenced to wonder whether Jupiter was not moving eastward at that time, contrary to the computations of the astronomers, and had got in front of them by that motion.[17] Hence it was with great interest that I awaited the next night. But I was disappointed in my hopes, for the sky was then covered with clouds everywhere.

On the tenth of January, however, the stars appeared in this position with respect to Jupiter:

East   ✳ ✳ ◯   **West**

that is, there were but two of them, both easterly, the third (as I supposed) being hidden behind Jupiter. As at first, they were in the same straight line with Jupiter and were arranged precisely in the line of the zodiac. Noticing this, and knowing that there was no way in which such alterations could be attributed to Jupiter's motion, yet being certain that these were still the same stars I had observed (in fact no other was to be found along the line of the zodiac for a long way on either side of Jupiter), my perplexity was now transformed into amazement. I was sure that the apparent changes belonged not to Jupiter but to the observed stars, and I resolved to pursue this investigation with greater care and attention.

And thus, on the eleventh of January, I saw the following disposition:

East   ✳   ✳   ◯   *West*

There were two stars, both to the east, the central one being three times as far from Jupiter as from the one farther east. The latter star was nearly double the size of the former, whereas on the night before they had appeared approximately equal.

I had now decided beyond all question that there existed in the heavens three stars wandering about Jupiter as do Venus and Mercury about the sun, and this became plainer than daylight from observations on similar occasions which followed. Nor were there just three such stars; four wanderers complete their revolutions about Jupiter, and of their alterations as observed more precisely later on we shall give a description here. Also I measured the distances between them by means of the telescope, using the method explained before. Moreover I recorded the times of the observations, especially when more than one was made during the same night—for the revolutions of these planets are so speedily completed that it is usually possible to take even their hourly variations.

Thus on the twelfth of January at the first hour of night I saw the stars arranged in this way:

East   ✳ ✳◯   ✳   *West*

The most easterly star was larger than the western one, though both were easily visible and quite bright. Each was about two minutes of arc distant from Jupiter. The third star was invisible at first, but commenced to appear after two hours; it almost touched Jupiter on the east, and was quite small. All were on the same straight line directed along the ecliptic.

On the thirteenth of January four stars were seen by me for the first time, in this situation relative to Jupiter:

East   ✳   ◯ ✳ ✳ ✳   *West*

Three were westerly and one was to the east; they formed a straight line except that the middle western star departed slightly toward the north. The eastern star was two minutes of arc away from Jupiter, and the intervals of the rest from one another and from Jupiter were about one minute. All the stars appeared to be of the same magnitude, and though small were very bright, much brighter than fixed stars of the same size.[18]

• • •

On the twenty-sixth of February, midway in the first hour of night, there were only two stars:

East   ✳   ◯   ✳   *West*

One was to the east, ten minutes from Jupiter; the other to the west, six minutes away. The eastern one was somewhat smaller than the western. But at the fifth hour three stars were seen:

East   ✳   ◯ ✳   ✳   *West*

In addition to the two already noticed, a third was discovered to the west near Jupiter; it had at first been hidden behind Jupiter and was now one minute away. The eastern one appeared farther away than before, being eleven minutes from Jupiter.

This night for the first time I wanted to observe the progress of Jupiter and its accompanying planets along the line of the zodiac in relation to some fixed star, and such a star was seen to the east, eleven minutes distant from the easterly starlet and a little removed toward the south, in the following manner:

East   ✳   ◯ ✳   ✳   *West*

★

On the twenty-seventh of February, four minutes after the first hour, the stars appeared in this configuration:

East   ✳   ✳◯   ✳ ✳   *West*

The most easterly was ten minutes from Jupiter; the next, thirty seconds; the next to the west was two minutes thirty seconds from Jupiter, and the most westerly was one minute from that. Those nearest Jupiter appeared very small, while the end ones were plainly visible, especially the westernmost. They marked out an exactly straight line along the course of the ecliptic. The progress of these planets toward the east is seen quite clearly by reference to the fixed star mentioned, since Jupiter and its accompanying planets were closer to it, as may be seen in the figure above. At the fifth hour, the eastern star closer to Jupiter was one minute away.

At the first hour on February twenty-eighth, two stars only were seen; one easterly, distant nine minutes from Jupiter, and one to the west, two minutes away. They were easily visible and on the same straight line. The fixed star, perpendicular to this line, now fell under the eastern planet as in this figure:

At the fifth hour a third star, two minutes east of Jupiter, was seen in this position:

East   ✳   ✳ ◯ ✳   West

On the first of March, forty minutes after sunset, four stars all to the east were seen, of which the nearest to Jupiter was two minutes away, the next was one minute from this, the third two seconds from that and brighter than any of the others; from this in turn the most easterly was four minutes distant, and it was smaller than the rest. They marked out almost a straight line, but the third one counting from Jupiter was a little to the north. The fixed star formed an equilateral triangle with Jupiter and the most easterly star, as in this figure:

On March second, half an hour after sunset, there were three planets, two to the east and one to the west, in this configuration:

East   ✳*   ◯   ✳   *West*

The most easterly was seven minutes from Jupiter and thirty seconds from its neighbor; the western one was two minutes away from Jupiter. The end stars were very bright and were larger than that in the middle, which appeared very small. The most easterly star appeared a little elevated toward the north from the straight line through the other planets and Jupiter. The fixed star previously mentioned was eight minutes from the western planet along the line drawn from it perpendicularly to the straight line through all the planets, as shown above.

I have reported these relations of Jupiter and its companions with the fixed star so that anyone may comprehend that the progress of those planets, both in longitude and latitude, agrees exactly with the movements derived from planetary tables.

Such are the observations concerning the four Medicean planets recently first discovered by me, and although from these data their periods have not yet been reconstructed in numerical form, it is legitimate at least to put in evidence some facts worthy of note. Above all, since they sometimes follow and sometimes precede Jupiter by the same intervals, and they remain within very limited distances either to east or west of Jupiter, accompanying that planet in both its retrograde and direct movements in a constant manner, no one can doubt that they complete their revolutions about Jupiter and at the same time effect all together a twelve-year period about the center of the universe. That they also revolve in unequal circles is manifestly deduced from the fact that at the greatest elongation[19] from Jupiter it is never possible to see two of these planets in conjunction, whereas in the vicinity of Jupiter they are found united two, three, and sometimes all four together. It is also observed that the revolutions are swifter in those planets which describe smaller circles about Jupiter, since the stars closest to Jupiter are usually seen to the east when on the previous day they appeared to the west, and vice versa, while the planet which traces the largest orbit appears upon accurate observation of its returns to have a semimonthly period.

Here we have a fine and elegant argument for quieting the doubts of those who, while accepting with tranquil mind the revolutions of the planets about the sun in the Copernican system, are mightily disturbed to have the moon alone revolve about the earth and accompany it in an annual rotation about the sun. Some have believed that this structure of the universe should be rejected as impossible. But now we have not just one planet rotating about another while both run through a great orbit around the sun; our own eyes show us four stars which wander around Jupiter as does the moon around the earth, while all together trace out a grand revolution about the sun in the space of twelve years.

And finally we should not omit the reason for which the Medicean stars appear sometimes to be twice as large as at other times, though their orbits about Jupiter are very restricted. We certainly cannot seek the cause in terrestrial vapors, as Jupiter and its neighboring fixed stars are not seen to change size in the least while this increase and diminution are taking place. It is quite unthinkable that the cause of variation should be their change of distance from the earth at perigee and apogee, since a small circular rotation could by no means produce this effect, and an oval motion (which in this case would have to be nearly straight) seems unthinkable and quite inconsistent with the appearances.[20] But I shall gladly explain what occurs to me on this matter, offering it freely to the judgment and criticism of thoughtful men. It is known that the interposition of terrestrial vapors makes the sun and moon appear large, while the fixed stars and planets are made to appear smaller. Thus the two great luminaries are seen larger when close to the horizon, while the stars appear smaller and for the most part hardly visible. Hence the stars appear very feeble by day and in twilight, though the moon does not, as we have said. Now from what has been said above, and even more from what we shall say at greater length in our *System*, it follows that not only the earth but also the moon is surrounded by an envelope of vapors, and we may apply precisely the same judgment to the rest of the planets. Hence it does not appear entirely impossible to assume that around Jupiter also there exists an envelope denser than the rest of the aether, about which the Medicean planets revolve as does the moon about the elemental sphere. Through the interposition of this envelope they appear larger when they are in perigee by the removal, or at least the attenuation, of this envelope.

Time prevents my proceeding further, but the gentle reader may expect more soon.

Finis

Notes

[1] The word "telescope" was not coined until 1611. A detailed account of its origin is given by Edward Rosen in *The Naming of the Telescope* (New York, 1947). In the present translation the modern term has been introduced for the sake of dignity and ease of reading, but only after the passage in which Galileo describes the circumstances which led him to construct the instrument (pp. 28–29).

[2] The original text reads "diameters" here and in another place. That this error was Galileo's and not the printer's has been convincingly shown by Edward Rosen (*Isis*, 1, 1952, pp. 344ff). The slip was a curious one, as astronomers of all schools had long agreed that the maximum distance of the moon was approximately sixty terrestrial radii. Still more curious is the fact that neither Kepler nor any other correspondent appears to have called Galileo's attention to this error; not even a friend who ventured to criticize the calculations in this very passage.

[3] Credit for the original invention is generally assigned to Hans Lippeshey, a lens grinder in Holland who chanced upon this property of combined lenses and applied for a patent on it in 1608.

[4] Badovere studied in Italy toward the close of the sixteenth century and is said to have been a pupil of Galileo's about 1598. When he wrote concerning the new instrument in 1609 he was in the French diplomatic service at Paris, where he died in 1620.

[5] Pythagoras was a mathematician and philosopher of the sixth century B.C., a semi-legendary figure whose followers were credited at Galileo's time with having anticipated the Copernican system. This tradition was based upon a misunderstanding. The Pythagoreans made the earth revolve about a "central fire" whose light and heat were reflected to the earth by the sun.

[6] Leonardo da Vinci had previously suggested that the dark and light regions of the moon were bodies of land and water, though Galileo probably did not know this. Da Vinci, however, had mistakenly supposed that the water would appear brighter than the land.

[7] This casual comparison between a part of the moon and a specific region on earth was later the basis of much trouble for Galileo. Even in antiquity the idea that the moon (or any other heavenly body) was of the same nature as the earth had been dangerous to hold. The Athenians banished the philosopher Anaxagoras for teaching such notions, and charged Socrates with blasphemy for repeating them.

[8] Opposition of the sun and moon occurs when they are in line with the earth between them (full moon, or lunar eclipse); conjunction, when they are in line on the same side of the earth (new moon, or eclipse of the sun).

[9] The aether, or "ever moving," was as the special substance of which the sky and all the heavenly bodies were supposed to be made, a substance essentially different from

all the earthly "elements." In later years Galileo abandoned his suggestion here that the moon has a vaporous atmosphere.

[10] Galileo's estimate of four miles for the height of some lunar mountains was a very good one. His remark about the maximum height of mountains on the earth was, however, quite mistaken. An English propagandist for his views, John Wilkins, took pains to correct this error in his anonymous *Discovery of a New World . . . in the Moon* (London, 1638), Prop. ix.

[11] Kepler had correctly accounted for the existence of this light and its ruddy color. It is caused by refraction of sunlight in the earth's atmosphere, and does not require a lunar atmosphere as supposed by Galileo.

[12] The book thus promised was destined not to appear for more than two decades. Events which will presently be recounted prevented its publication for many years, and then it had to be modified to present the arguments for both the Ptolemaic and Copernican systems instead of just the latter as Galileo here planned. Even then it was suppressed and the author was condemned to life imprisonment.

[13] That is, planets. Among these bodies Galileo counted his newly discovered satellites of Jupiter. The term "satellites" was introduced somewhat later by Kepler.

[14] Fixed stars are so distant that their light reaches the earth as from dimensionless points. Hence their images are not enlarged by even the best telescopes, which serve only to gather more of their light and in that way increase their visibility. Galileo was never entirely clear about this distinction. Nevertheless, by applying his knowledge of the effects described here, he greatly reduced the prevailing overestimation of visual dimensions of stars and planets.

[15] Praesepe, "the Manger," is a small whitish cluster of stars lying between the two Aselli (ass-colts) which are imagined as feeding from it. It lies in the constellation Cancer.

[16] The reader should remember that the telescope was nightly revealing to Galileo hundreds of fixed stars never previously observed. His unusual gifts for astronomical observation are illustrated by his having noticed and remembered these three merely by reason of their alignment, and recalling them so well that when by chance he happened to see them the following night he was certain that they had changed their positions. No such plausible and candid account of the discovery was given by the rival astronomer Simon Mayr, who four years later claimed priority.

[17] Jupiter was at this time in "retrograde" motion; that is, the earth's motion made the planet appear to be moving westward among the fixed stars.

[18] Galileo's day-by-day journal of observations continued in unbroken sequence until ten days before publication of the book, which he remained in Venice to supervise. The observations omitted here contained nothing of a novel character.

[19] By this is meant the greatest angular separation from Jupiter attained by any of the satellites.

[20] The marked variation in brightness of the satellites which Galileo observed may be attributed mainly to markings upon their surfaces, though this was not determined until two centuries later. The mention here of a possible oval shape of the orbits is the closest Galileo ever came to accepting Kepler's great discovery of the previous year. Even here, however, he was probably not thinking of Kepler's work but of an idea proposed by earlier astronomers for the moon and the planet Venus.

Matthew 5–7

New American Standard Version

The Sermon on the Mount; The Beatitudes

1 **5** When Jesus saw the crowds, He went up on the ªmountain; and after He
2 sat down, His disciples came to Him. •He opened His mouth and *began* to
teach them, saying,

3   "ᵇBlessed are the ᶜpoor in spirit, for theirs is the kingdom of heaven.
4   "Blessed are those who mourn, for they shall be comforted.
5   "Blessed are the ᵈgentle, for they shall inherit the earth.
6   "Blessed are those who hunger and thirst for righteousness, for they shall
be satisfied.
7   "Blessed are the merciful, for they shall receive mercy.
8   "Blessed are the pure in heart, for they shall see God.
9   "Blessed are the peacemakers, for they shall be called sons of God.
10   "Blessed are those who have been persecuted for the sake of righteousness, for theirs is the kingdom of heaven.
11   "Blessed are you when *people* insult you and persecute you, and falsely say
12 all kinds of evil against you because of Me. •Rejoice and be glad, for your
reward in heaven is great; for in the same way they persecuted the prophets
who were before you.

Disciples and the World

13   "You are the salt of the earth; but if the salt has become tasteless, how ᵉcan
it be made salty *again*? It is no longer good for anything, except to be thrown
out and trampled under foot by men.
14, 15   "You are the light of the world. A city set on a ᶠhill cannot be hidden; •nor
does *anyone* light a lamp and put it under a ᵍbasket, but on the lampstand, and
16 it gives light to all who are in the house. •Let your light shine before men in
such a way that they may see your good works, and glorify your Father who is
in heaven.

17 "Do not think that I came to abolish the Law or the Prophets; I did not
18 come to abolish but to fulfill. •For truly I say to you, until heaven and earth
pass away, not [h]the smallest letter or stroke shall pass from the Law until all is
19 accomplished. •Whoever then annuls one of the least of these command-
ments, and teaches [i]others *to do* the same, shall be called least in the kingdom
of heaven; but whoever [j]keeps and teaches *them*, he shall be called great in the
kingdom of heaven.
20 "For I say to you that unless your righteousness surpasses *that* of the
scribes and Pharisees, you will not enter the kingdom of heaven.

Personal Relationships

21 "You have heard that [k]the ancients were told, 'YOU SHALL NOT COMMIT
22 MURDER' and 'Whoever commits murder shall be [l]liable to the court.' •But I
say to you that everyone who is angry with his brother shall be [m]guilty before
the court; and whoever says to his brother, '[n]You good-for-nothing,' shall be
[o]guilty before [p]the supreme court; and whoever says, 'You fool,' shall be [q]guilty
23 *enough to go* into the [r]fiery hell. •Therefore if you are presenting your [s]offering
24 at the altar, and there remember that your brother has something against you,
•leave your [t]offering there before the altar and go; first be reconciled to your
25 brother, and then come and present your [u]offering. •Make friends quickly with
your opponent at law while you are with him on the way, so that your opponent may not hand you over to the judge, and the judge to the officer, and you
26 be thrown into prison. •Truly I say to you, you will not come out of there until
you have paid up the last [v]cent.
27 "You have heard that it was said, 'YOU SHALL NOT COMMIT ADULTERY';
28 •but I say to you that everyone who looks at a woman with lust for her has
29 already committed adultery with her in his heart. •If your right eye makes
you [w]stumble, tear it out and throw it from you; for it is better for you [x]to lose
one of the parts of your body, [y]than for your whole body to be thrown into
30 [z]hell. •If your right hand makes you [aa]stumble, cut it off and throw it from
you; for it is better for you [ab]to lose one of the parts of your body, [ac]than for
your whole body to go into [ad]hell.
31 "It was said, 'WHOEVER SENDS HIS WIFE AWAY, LET HIM GIVE HER A CER-
32 TIFICATE OF DIVORCE'; •but I say to you that everyone who [ae]divorces his wife,
except for *the* reason of unchastity, makes her commit adultery; and whoever
marries a [af]divorced woman commits adultery.
33 "Again, you have heard that [ag]the ancients were told, '[ah]YOU SHALL NOT
34 [ai]MAKE FALSE VOWS, BUT SHALL FULFILL YOUR [aj]VOWS TO THE LORD.' •But I say

35 to you, make no oath at all, either by heaven, for it is the throne of God, •or
by the earth, for it is the footstool of His feet, or ^{ak}by Jerusalem, for it is THE
36 CITY OF THE GREAT KING. •Nor shall you make an oath by your head, for you
37 cannot make one hair white or black. •But let your statement be, 'Yes, yes' *or*
'No, no'; anything beyond these is ^{al}of evil.

38   "You have heard that it was said, 'AN EYE FOR AN EYE, AND A TOOTH FOR
39 A TOOTH.' •But I say to you, do not resist an evil person; but whoever slaps you
40 on your right cheek, turn the other to him also. •If anyone wants to sue you
41 and take your ^{am}shirt, let him have your ^{an}coat also. •Whoever ^{ao}forces you to
42 go one mile, go with him two. •Give to him who asks of you, and do not turn
away from him who wants to borrow from you.

43   "You have heard that it was said, 'YOU SHALL LOVE YOUR NEIGHBOR
44 AND HATE YOUR ENEMY.' •But I say to you, love your enemies and pray for
45 those who persecute you, •so that you may ^{ap}be sons of your Father who is
in heaven; for He causes His sun to rise on *the* evil and *the* good, and sends
46 rain on *the* righteous and *the* unrighteous. •For if you love those who love
you, what reward do you have? Do not even the tax collectors do the same?
47 If you greet only your brothers, what more are you doing *than others*? Do not
48 even the Gentiles do the same? •Therefore ^{aq}you are to be perfect, as your
heavenly Father is perfect.

Giving to the Poor and Prayer

1 **6**"Beware of practicing your righteousness before men to be noticed by
them; otherwise you have no reward with your Father who is in heaven.
2   "So when you ^{ar}give to the poor, do not sound a trumpet before you, as
the hypocrites do in the synagogues and in the streets, so that they may be
3 honored by men. Truly I say to you, they have their reward in full. •But when
you ^{as}give to the poor, do not let your left hand know what your right hand is
4 doing, •so that your ^{at}giving will be in secret; and your Father *who sees what is
done* in secret will reward you.

5   "When you pray, you are not to be like the hypocrites; for they love to
stand and pray in the synagogues and on the street corners ^{au}so that they may
6 be seen by men. Truly I say to you, they have their reward in full. •But you,
when you pray, go into your inner room, close your door and pray to your
Father who is in secret, and your Father who sees *what is done* in secret will
reward you.

7   "And when you are praying, do not use meaningless repetition as the
8 Gentiles do, for they suppose that they will be heard for their many words. •So
do not be like them; for your Father knows what you need before you ask Him.

9   "Pray, then, in this way:
'Our Father who is in heaven,
Hallowed be Your name.

10   'Your kingdom come.
Your will be done,
On earth as it is in heaven.

11   'Give us this day ᵃᵛour daily bread.

12   'And forgive us our debts, as we also have forgiven our debtors.

13   'And do not lead us into temptation, but deliver us from ᵃʷevil.
ᵃˣ[For Yours is the kingdom and the power and the glory forever. Amen.']

14   For if you forgive ᵃʸothers for their transgressions, your heavenly Father
15 will also forgive you. •But if you do not forgive ᵃᶻothers, then your Father will not forgive your transgressions.

Fasting; The True Treasure; Wealth (Mammon)

16   "Whenever you fast, do not put on a gloomy face as the hypocrites do, for they ᵇᵃneglect their appearance so that they will be noticed by men when
17 they are fasting. Truly I say to you, they have their reward in full. •But you,
18 when you fast, anoint your head and wash your face •so that your fasting will not be noticed by men, but by your Father who is in secret; and your Father who sees *what is done* in secret will reward you.

19   19 "Do not store up for yourselves treasures on earth, where moth and rust
20 destroy, and where thieves break in and steal. •But store up for yourselves treasures in heaven, where neither moth nor rust destroys, and where thieves do not
21 break in or steal; •for where your treasure is, there your heart will be also.

22   "The eye is the lamp of the body; so then if your eye is ᵇᵇclear, your
23 whole body will be full of light. •But if your eye is ᵇᶜbad, your whole body will be full of darkness. If then the light that is in you is darkness, how great is the darkness!

24   "No one can serve two masters; for either he will hate the one and love the other, or he will be devoted to one and despise the other. You cannot serve God and ᵇᵈwealth.

The Cure for Anxiety

25   "For this reason I say to you, ᵇᵉdo not be worried about your ᵇᶠlife, *as to*
26 what you will eat or what you will drink; nor for your body, *as to* what you will put on. Is not life more than food, and the body more than clothing? •Look at the birds of the ᵇᵍair, that they do not sow, nor reap nor gather into barns,

and *yet* your heavenly Father feeds them. Are you not worth much more than
27 they? •And who of you by being worried can add a *single* ᵇʰhour to his ᵇⁱ life?
28 •And why are you worried about clothing? Observe how the lilies of the field
29 grow; they do not toil nor do they spin, •yet I say to you that not even
30 Solomon in all his glory clothed himself like one of these. •But if God so
clothes the grass of the field, which is *alive* today and tomorrow is thrown into
31 the furnace, *will He* not much more *clothe* you? You of little faith! •Do not
worry then, saying, 'What will we eat?' or 'What will we drink?' or 'What will
32 we wear for clothing?' •For the Gentiles eagerly seek all these things; for your
33 heavenly Father knows that you need all these things. •But ᵇʲseek first ᵇᵏHis
kingdom and His righteousness, and all these things will be ᵇˡadded to you.
34   "So do not worry about tomorrow; for tomorrow will ᵇᵐcare for itself.
ᵇⁿEach day has enough trouble of its own.

Judging Others

1, 2 7"Do not judge so that you will not be judged. •For in the way you judge,
you will be judged; and ᵇᵒby your standard of measure, it will be measured
3 to you. •Why do you look at the speck that is in your brother's eye, but do not
4 notice the log that is in your own eye? •Or how ᵇᵖcan you say to your brother,
'Let me take the speck out of your eye,' and behold, the log is in your own eye?
5 •You hypocrite, first take the log out of your own eye, and then you will see
clearly to take the speck out of your brother's eye.
6   "Do not give what is holy to dogs, and do not throw your pearls before
swine, or they will trample them under their feet, and turn and tear you to
pieces.

Prayer and the Golden Rule

7   "ᵇᑫAsk, and it will be given to you; ᵇʳseek, and you will find; ᵇˢknock, and
8 it will be opened to you. •For everyone who asks receives, and he who seeks
9 finds, and to him who knocks it will be opened. •Or what man is there among
10 you ᵇᵗwho, when his son asks for a loaf, ᵇᵘwill give him a stone? •Or ᵇᵛif he asks
11 for a fish, he will not give him a snake, will he? •If you then, being evil, know
how to give good gifts to your children, how much more will your Father who
is in heaven give what is good to those who ask Him!
12   "In everything, therefore, ᵇʷtreat people the same way you want ᵇˣthem
to treat you, for this is the Law and the Prophets.

The Narrow and Wide Gates

Self not gm [handwritten]

13 "Enter through the narrow gate; for the gate is wide and the way is broad
14 that leads to destruction, and there are many who enter through it. •For the gate
is small and the way is narrow that leads to life, and there are few who find it.

A Tree and Its Fruit

wtr [handwritten]

15 "Beware of the false prophets, who come to you in sheep's clothing, but
16 inwardly are ravenous wolves. •You will ^by^know them by their fruits. ^bz^Grapes
17 are not gathered from thorn *bushes* nor figs from thistles, are they? •So every
18 good tree bears good fruit, but the bad tree bears bad fruit. •A good tree can-
19 not produce bad fruit, nor can a bad tree produce good fruit. •Every tree that
20 does not bear good fruit is cut down and thrown into the fire. •So then, you
will ^ca^know them by their fruits.

21 "Not everyone who says to Me, 'Lord, Lord,' will enter the kingdom of
heaven, but he who does the will of My Father who is in heaven *will enter.*
22 Many will say to Me on that day, 'Lord, Lord, did we not prophesy in Your
name, and in Your name cast out demons, and in Your name perform many
23 ^cb^miracles?' •And then I will declare to them, 'I never knew you; DEPART FROM
ME, YOU WHO PRACTICE LAWLESSNESS.' *) evildoers [handwritten]*

The Two Foundations

24 "Therefore everyone who hears these words of Mine and ^cc^acts on them,
25 ^cd^may be compared to a wise man who built his house on the rock. •And the
rain fell, and the ^ce^floods came, and the winds blew and slammed against that
26 house; and yet it did not fall, for it had been founded on the rock. •Everyone
who hears these words of Mine and does not ^cf^act on them, will be like a fool-
27 ish man who built his house on the sand. •The rain fell, and the ^cg^floods came,
and the winds blew and slammed against that house; and it fell—and great was
its fall."

28 ^ch^When Jesus had finished these words, the crowds were amazed at
29 His teaching; •for He was teaching them as *one* having authority, and not
as their scribes.

Have we built on sand? [handwritten]

Notes

^a 5:1 Or *hill*

^b 5:3 I.e. fortunate or prosperous, and so through v 11

^c 5:3 I.e. those who are not spiritually arrogant

^d 5:5 Or *humble, meek*

^e 5:13 Lit *will*

^f 5:14 Or *mountain*

^g 5:15 Or *peck-measure*

^h 5:18 Lit *one iota* (Heb yodh) or *one projection of a letter* (serif)

ⁱ 5:19 Gr *anthropoi*

^j 5:19 Lit *does*

^k 5:21 Lit *it was said to the ancients*

^l 5:21 Or *guilty before*

^m 5:22 Or *liable to*

ⁿ 5:22 Or *empty-head*; Gr *Raka (Raca)* fr Aram *reqa*

^o 5:22 Or *liable* to

^p 5:22 Lit *the Sanhedrin*

^q 5:22 Or *liable to*

^r 5:22 Lit *Gehenna of fire*

^s 5:23 Or *gift*

^t 5:24 Or *gift*

^u 5:24 Or *gift*

^v 5:26 Lit *quadrans* (equaling two mites); i.e. 1/64 of a daily wage

^w 5:29 I.e. sin

^x 5:29 Lit *that one . . . be lost*

^y 5:29 Lit *not your whole body*

^z 5:29 Gr *Gehenna*

^{aa} 5:30 I.e. sin

^{ab} 5:30 Lit *that one . . . be lost*

^{ac} 5:30 Lit *not your whole body*

^{ad} 5:30 Gr *Gehenna*

^{ae} 5:32 Or *sends away*

^{af} 5:32 Or *sent away*

^{ag} 5:33 Lit *it was said to the ancients*

ah 5:33 *you* and *your* are singular here

ai 5:33 Or *break your vows*

aj 5:33 Lit *oaths*

ak 5:35 Or *toward*

al 5:37 Or *from the evil one*

am 5:40 Lit *tunic;* i.e. a garment worn next to the body

an 5:40 Lit *cloak;* i.e. an outer garment

ao 5:41 Lit *will force*

ap 5:45 Or *show yourselves to be*

aq 5:48 Lit *you shall be*

ar 6:2 Or *give alms*

as 6:3 Or *give alms*

at 6:4 Or *alms*

au 6:5 Lit *to be apparent to men*

av 6:11 Or *our bread for tomorrow*

aw 6:13 Or *the evil one*

ay 6:14 Gr anthropoi

az 6:15 Gr *anthropoi*

ba 6:16 Lit *distort their faces,* i.e. discolor their faces with makeup

bb 6:22 Or *healthy;* or *sincere*

bc 6:23 Or *evil*

bd 6:24 Gr *mamonas,* for Aram *mamon* (mammon); i.e. wealth, etc., personified as an object of worship

be 6:25 Or *stop being worried*

bf 6:25 Lit *soul*

bg 6:26 Lit *heaven*

bh 6:27 Lit *cubit* (approx 18 in.)

bi 6:27 Or *height*

bj 6:33 Or *continually seek*

bk 6:33 Or *the kingdom*

bl 6:33 Or *provided*

bm 6:34 Lit *worry about itself*

bn 6:34 Lit *Sufficient for the day is its evils*

bo 7:2 Lit *by what measure you measure*

bp 7:4 Lit *will*

bq 7:7 Or *Keep asking*

br 7:7 Or *keep seeking*

bs 7:7 Or *keep knocking*

bt 7:9 Lit *whom his son will ask*

bu 7:9 Lit *he will not give him a stone, will he?*

bv 7:10 Lit *also will ask*

bw 7:12 Lit *you, too, do so for them*

bx 7:12 Lit *people*; Gr *anthropoi*

by 7:16 Or *recognize*

bz 7:16 Lit *They do not gather*

ca 7:20 Or *recognize*

cb 7:22 Or *works of power*

cc 7:24 Lit *does*

cd 7:24 Lit *will*

ce 7:25 Lit *rivers*

cf 7:26 Lit *do*

cg 7:27 Lit *rivers*

ch 7:28 Lit *And it happened when*

from *Universal Love*

Mo Tzu

[handwritten note: Chinese Philosophy 470 BC – 391 BC]

PART III (section 16)

Mo Tzu said: It is the business of the benevolent man to try to promote what is beneficial to the world and to eliminate what is harmful. Now at the present time, what brings the greatest harm to the world? Great states attacking small ones, great families overthrowing small ones, the strong oppressing the weak, the many harrying the few, the cunning deceiving the stupid, the eminent lording it over the humble—these are harmful to the world. So too are rulers who are not generous, ministers who are not loyal, fathers who are without kindness, and sons who are unfilial, as well as those mean men who, with weapons, knives, poison, fire, and water, seek to injure and undo each other.

When we inquire into the cause of these various harms, what do we find has produced them? Do they come about from loving others and trying to benefit them? Surely not! They come rather from hating others and trying to injure them. And when we set out to classify and describe those men who hate and injure others, shall we say that their actions are motivated by universality or partiality? Surely we must answer, by partiality, and it is this partiality in their dealings with one another that gives rise to all the great harms in the world. Therefore we know that partiality is wrong.

Mo Tzu said: Whoever criticizes others must have some alternative to offer them. To criticize and yet offer no alternative is like trying to stop flood with flood or put out fire with fire. It will surely have no effect. Therefore Mo Tzu said: Partiality should be replaced by universality.

But how can partiality be replaced by universality? If men were to regard the states of others as they regard their own, then who would raise up his state to attack the state of another? It would be like attacking his own. If men were to regard the cities of others as they regard their own, then who would raise up his city to attack the city of another? It would be like attacking his own. If men were to regard the families of others as they regard their own, then who would

230

raise up his family to overthrow that of another? It would be like overthrowing his own. Now when states and cities do not attack and make war on each other and families and individuals do not overthrow or injure one another, is this a harm or a benefit to the world? Surely it is a benefit.

When we inquire into the cause of such benefits, what do we find has produced them? Do they come about from hating others and trying to injure them? Surely not! They come rather from loving others and trying to benefit them. And when we set out to classify and describe those men who love and benefit others, shall we say that their actions are motivated by partiality or by universality? Surely we must answer, by universality, and it is this universality in their dealings with one another that gives rise to all the great benefits in the world. Therefore Mo Tzu has said that universality is right. I have said previously that it is the business of the benevolent man to try to promote what is beneficial to the world and to eliminate what is harmful. Now I have demonstrated that universality is the source of all the great benefits in the world and partiality is the source of all the great harm. It is for this reason that Mo Tzu has said that partiality is wrong and universality is right.

Now if we seek to benefit the world by taking universality as our standard, those with sharp ears and clear eyes will see and hear for others, those with sturdy limbs will work for others, and those with a knowledge of the Way will endeavor to teach others. Those who are old and without wives or children will find means of support and be able to live out their days; the young and orphaned who have no parents will find someone to care for them and look after their needs. When all these benefits may be secured merely by taking universality as our standard, I cannot understand how the men of the world can hear about this doctrine of universality and still criticize it!

And yet the men of the world continue to criticize it, saying, "It may be a good thing, but how can it be put to use?" Mo Tzu said: If it cannot be put to use, even I would criticize it. But how can there be a good thing that still cannot be put to use? Let us try considering both sides of the question. Suppose there are two men, one of them holding to partiality, the other to universality. The believer in partiality says, "How could I possibly regard my friend the same as myself, or my friend's father the same as my own?" Because he views his friend in this way, he will not feed him when he is hungry, clothe him when he is cold, nourish him when he is sick, or bury him when he dies. Such are the words of the partial man, and such his actions. But the words and actions of the universal-minded man are not like these. He will say, "I have heard that the truly superior man of the world regards his friend the same as himself, and his friend's father the same as his own. Only if he does this can he be considered a truly superior man." Because he views his friend in this way, he will feed him when he is hungry, clothe him when he is cold, nourish him when he is sick, and bury him when he dies. Such are the words and actions of the universal-minded man.

So the words of these two men disagree and their actions are diametrically opposed. Yet let us suppose that both of them are determined to carry out their words in action, so that word and deed agree like the two parts of a tally and nothing they say is not put into action. Then let us venture to inquire further. Suppose that here is a broad plain, a vast wilderness, and a man is buckling on his armor and donning his helmet to set out for the field of battle, where the fortunes of life and death are unknown; or he is setting out in his lord's name upon a distant mission to Pa or Yüeh, Ch'i or Ching, and his return is uncertain. Now let us ask,[1] to whom would he entrust the support of his parents and the care of his wife and children? Would it be to the universal-minded man, or to the partial man? It seems to me that, on occasions like these, there are no fools in the world. Though one may disapprove of universality himself, he would surely think it best to entrust his family to the universal-minded man. Thus people condemn universality in words but adopt it in practice, and word and deed belie each other. I cannot understand how the men of the world can hear about this doctrine of universality and still criticize it!

And yet the men of the world continue to criticize, saying, "Such a principle may be all right as a basis in choosing among ordinary men, but it cannot be used in selecting a ruler."

Let us try considering both sides of the question. Suppose there are two rulers, one of them holding to universality, the other to partiality. The partial ruler says, "How could I possibly regard my countless subjects the same as I regard myself? That would be completely at variance with human nature! Man's life on earth is as brief as the passing of a team of horses glimpsed through a crack in the wall." Because he views his subjects in this way, he will not feed them when they are hungry, clothe them when they are cold, nourish them when they are sick, or bury them when they die. Such are the words of the partial ruler, and such his actions. But the words and actions of the universal-minded ruler are not like these. He will say, "I have heard that the truly enlightened ruler must think of his subjects first, and of himself last. Only then can he be considered a truly enlightened ruler." Because he views his subjects in this way, he will feed them when they are hungry, clothe them when they are cold, nourish them when they are sick, and bury them when they die. Such are the words and actions of the universal-minded ruler. So the words of these two rulers disagree and their actions are diametrically opposed. Yet let us suppose that both of them speak in good faith and are determined to carry out their words in action, so that word and deed agree like the two parts of a tally and nothing they say is not put into action. Then let us venture to inquire further. Suppose this year there is plague and disease, many of the people are suffering from hardship and hunger, and the corpses of countless victims lie tumbled in the ditches. If the people could choose between, these two types of ruler, which would they follow? It seems to me that on occasions like this, there are no fools in the world. Though one may disapprove of universality himself, he would surely think it best to follow the universal-minded ruler. Thus people condemn universality in words but adopt it in practice, and word and deed belie each other. I cannot understand how the men of the world can hear about this doctrine of universality and still criticize it!

And yet the men of the world continue to criticize, saying, "This doctrine of universality is benevolent and righteous. And yet how can it be carried out? As we see it, one can no more put it into practice than one can pick up Mount T'ai and leap over a river with it! Thus universality is only something to be longed for, not something that can he put into practice."

Mo Tzu said: As for picking up Mount T'ai and leaping over rivers with it, no one from ancient times to the present, from the beginning of mankind to now, has ever succeeded in doing that! But universal love and mutual aid were actually practiced by four sage kings of antiquity. How do we know that they practiced these?

Mo Tzu said: I did not live at the same time as they did, nor have I in person heard their voices or seen their faces. Yet I know it because of what is written on the bamboo and silk that has been handed down to posterity, what is engraved on metal and stone, and what is inscribed on bowls and basins.

The "Great Oath" says: "King Wen was like the sun or moon, shedding his bright light in the four quarters and over the western land."[2] That is to say, the universal love of King Wen was so broad that it embraced the whole world, as the universal light of the sun and the moon shines upon the whole world without partiality. Such was the universality of King Wen, and the universality which Mo Tzu has been telling you about is patterned after that of King Wen.

Not only the "Great Oath" but the "Oath of Yu"[3] also expresses this idea. Yü said: "All you teeming multitudes, listen to my words! It is not that I, the little child, would dare to act in a disorderly way. But this ruler of the Miao, with his unyielding ways, deserves Heaven's punishment. So I shall lead you, the lords of the various states, to conquer the ruler of the Miao." When Yü went to conquer the ruler of the Miao, it was not that he sought to increase his wealth or eminence, to win fortune or Blessing, or to delight his ears and eyes. It was only that he sought to promote what was beneficial to the world and to eliminate what was harmful. Such was the universality of Yü, and the universality which Mo Tzu has been telling you about is patterned after that of Yü.

And not only the "Oath of Yu" But the "Speech of Tang"[4] also expresses this idea. T'ang said: "I, the little child, Lü, dare to sacrifice a dark beast and make this announcement to the Heavenly Lord above, saying, 'Now Heaven has sent a great drought and it has fallen upon me, Lü. But I do not know what fault I have committed against high or low. If there is good, I dare not conceal it; if there is evil, I dare not pardon it. Judgment resides with the mind of God. If the myriad regions have any fault, may it rest upon my person; but if I have any fault, may it not extend to the myriad regions.'" This shows that, though T'ang was honored as the Son of Heaven and possessed all the riches of the world, he did not hesitate to offer himself as a sacrifice in his prayers and entreaties to the Lord on High and the spirits. Such was the universality of T'ang, and the universality which Mo Tzu has been telling you about is patterned after that of T'ang. This idea is expressed not only in the "Speech of T'ang" but in the odes of Chou as well. In the odes of Chou it says:

> Broad, broad is the way of the king,
> Neither partial nor partisan.
> Fair, fair is the way of the king,
> Neither partisan nor partial.

> It is straight like an arrow,
> Smooth like a whetstone.
> The superior man treads it;
> The small man looks upon it.[5]

So what I have been speaking about is no mere theory of action. In ancient times, when Kings Wen and Wu administered the government and assigned each person his just share, they rewarded the worthy and punished the wicked without showing any favoritism toward their own kin or brothers. Such was the universality of Kings Wen and Wu, and the universality which Mo Tzu has been telling you about is patterned after that of Wen and Wu. I cannot understand how the men of the world can hear about this doctrine of universality and still criticize it!

And yet the men of the world continue to criticize, saying, "If one takes no thought for what is beneficial or harmful to one's parents, how can one be called filial?"

Mo Tzu said: Let us examine for a moment the way in which a filial son plans for the welfare of his parents. When a filial son plans for his parents, does he wish others to love and benefit them, or does he wish others to hate and injure them? It stands to reason that he wishes others to love and benefit his parents. Now if I am a filial son, how do I go about accomplishing this? Do I first make it a point to love and benefit other men's parents, so that they in return will love and benefit my parents? Or do I first make it a point to hate and injure other men's parents, so that they in return will love and benefit my parents? Obviously, I must first make it a point to love and benefit other men's parents, so that they in return will love and benefit my parents. So if all of us are to be filial sons, can we set about it any other way than by first making a point of loving and benefiting other men's parents? And are we to suppose that the filial sons of the world are all too stupid to be capable of doing what is right?

Let us examine further. Among the books of the former kings, in the "Greater Odes" of the *Book of Odes*, it says:

> There are no words that are not answered,
> No kindness that is not requited.
> Throw me a peach,
> I'll requite you a plum.[6]

The meaning is that one who loves will be loved by others, and one who hates will be hated by others. So I cannot understand how the men of the world can hear about this doctrine of universality and still criticize it!

Do they believe that it is too difficult to carry out? Yet there are much more difficult things that have been carried out. In the past King Ling of the state of Ching loved slender waists. During his reign, the people of Ching ate no more than one meal a day, until they were too weak to stand up without a cane, or to walk without leaning against the wall. Now reducing one's diet is a difficult thing to do, and yet people did it because it pleased King Ling. So within the space of a single generation the ways of the people can be changed, for they will strive to ingratiate themselves with their superiors.

Again in the past King Kou-chien of Yüeh admired bravery and for three years trained his soldiers and subjects to be brave. But he was not sure whether they had understood the true meaning of bravery, and so he set fire to his war-ships and then sounded the drum to advance. The soldiers trampled each other down in their haste to go forward, and countless numbers of them perished in the fire and water. At that time, even though he ceased to drum them forward, they did not retreat. The soldiers of Yüeh were truly astonishing. Now consigning one's body to the flames is a difficult thing to do, and yet they did it because it pleased the king of Yüeh. So within the space of a single generation the ways of the people can be changed, for they will strive to ingratiate themselves with their superiors.

Duke Wen of Chin liked coarse clothing, and so during his reign the men of the state of Chin wore robes of coarse cloth, wraps of sheepskin, hats of plain silk, and big rough shoes, whether they were appearing before the duke in the inner chamber or walking about in the outer halls of the court. Now bringing oneself to wear coarse clothing is a difficult thing to do, and yet people did it because it pleased Duke Wen. So within the space of a single generation the ways of the people can be changed, for they will strive to ingratiate themselves with their superiors.

To reduce one's diet, consign one's body to the flames, or wear coarse clothing are among the most difficult things in the world to do. And yet people will do them because they know their superiors will he pleased. So within the space of a single generation the ways of the people can be changed. Why? Because they will strive to ingratiate themselves with their superiors.

Now universal love and mutual benefit are both profitable and easy beyond all measure. The only trouble, as I see it, is that no ruler takes any delight in them. If the rulers really delighted in them, promoted them with rewards and praise, and prevented neglect of them by punishments, then I believe that people would turn to universal love and mutual benefit as naturally as fire turns upward or water turns downward, and nothing in the world could stop them.

The principle of universality is the way of the sage kings, the means of bringing safety to the rulers and officials and of assuring ample food and clothing to the people. Therefore the superior man can do no better than to examine it carefully and strive to put it into practice. If he does, then as a ruler he will be generous, as a subject loyal, as a father kind, as a son filial, as an older brother comradely, and as a younger brother respectful. So if the superior man wishes to be a generous ruler, a loyal subject, a kind father, a filial son, a comradely older brother, and a respectful younger brother, he must put into practice this principle of universality. It is the way of the sage kings and a great benefit to the people.

Notes

[1] The text at this point appears to be corrupt and a few words have been omitted in translation.

[2] The "Great Oath," supposedly a speech by King Wu, the son of King Wen, was a section of the *Book of Documents*. It was lost long ago, and the text by that name included in the present *Book of Documents* is a forgery of the 3d century A.D., though it includes a passage much like the one quoted here by Mo Tzu.

[3] A section of the *Book of Documents*, now lost.

[4] A section of the *Book of Documents*, now lost. Almost the same quotation is found at the Beginning of Book XX of the Confucian *Analects*.

[5] The first four lines are now found, not in the *Book of Odes*, but in the *Hung fan* section of the *Book of Documents*. The last four lines are from the *Book of Odes*, *Hsiao ya* section, "Ta tung" (Mao text no. 203).

[6] The first two lines are from the poem "Yi" (Mao text no. 256), in the "Greater Odes" or *Ta ya* section of the *Book of Odes*. The last two lines, though not found in exactly this form, bear a close resemblance to lines in the poem "Mu-kua" (Mao text no. 64), in the *Kuo feng* or "Airs from the States" section of the *Odes*.